Praise for Dave ...
Welcome t SACRA...

"Dave Zirin is the best you... he's the one who unders... them vividly and show us what they mean in a world spinning out of control."

—Robert Lipsyte, author, *SportsWorld: An American Dreamland*

"Dave Zirin's writing is the opening shot in the battle to reclaim sports."

—Jim Bouton, former NY Yankee; author, *Ball Four*

"Dave Zirin is an incredibly talented and courageous writer, the sort of scribe sorely needed in America in these early days of the twenty-first century. With Zirin no topic is sacred, no argument is ever evaded, no search for truth, real truth, is ever suppressed. That marks, to me, Dave Zirin as a uniquely American writer who understands that freedom of speech, the desire to be free, means nothing if we don't exercise that freedom muscle every single day of our lives."

—Kevin Powell, author, *Someday We'll All Be Free*

"If there was an award for 'Most Valuable Sportswriter,' I would vote for Dave Zirin. His writing combines vivid narrative, good humor, impressive knowledge of the game, and a keen awareness of the connection between sports and the world outside. In our sports saturated society, his is an important voice that demands to be heard. A talented sportswriter with a social conscience—what more can you ask?"

—Howard Zinn, author, *A People's History of the United States*

"In sportswriting, attitude is easy. But Dave Zirin's also got razor smarts, rapier wit, and, most of all, a rebel's large heart. After you read him, you'll never see sports the same way again."

—Jeff Chang, author, *Can't Stop Won't Stop: A History of the Hip-Hop Generation*

"Dave Zirin is one of the few writers in sport who refuses to bend to the increasing power of sport and media. His focus is honest and hard-hitting. This book is invaluable given that we live in a time when professional sports seem to be crossing the line from a neurotic national fantasy to psychotic nightmare."

—Peter Gent, former Dallas Cowboys wide receiver; author, *North Dallas 40*

"Energetic, engaging, passionate, optimistic—and angry at all the right things, Dave Zirin has established himself as perhaps the best young sportswriter in the United States today. There's just no one doing what he does so well: reporting on those many junctures where sports, politics, and the popular culture intersect. He writes with his heart on his sleeve, and his voice is authentic. If you're a sports fan, you'll love this book. If you're politically active, you'll love this book. If you're a politically active sports fan, you've found your bible.

"P.S. Zirin is the only person my 15-year-old, basketball-loving daughter reads on thenation.com."

—Katrina vanden Heuvel, editor and publisher, the *Nation*

"Dave Zirin says things most of the sports media are afraid to. More to the point, he's saying things that most in this business don't have the wisdom or vision to even consider. If your passion for sports reaches beyond the box score—and it should—Zirin is essential."

—Ryan Jones, editor, *SLAM* magazine

"In my opinion, the people who need to read Dave Zirin most are people who don't think sports is important at all. Zirin knows it is and he continually shows how it fits into the rest of our world. For sports fans with brains, Zirin simply offers confirmation of every quaking thought we've ever had. And still loves the games and the players. He's indispensable."

—Dave Marsh, XM Radio

"Dave Zirin is an icon in the world of progressive sports."

—Dave Berkman, Wisconsin Public Radio

"*Welcome to the Terrordome* is both bold and brilliant, funny and fearless, and Dave Zirin may be the most important writer—sports or otherwise—to explode on the scene in many a season."

—Mary Ratliff, editor, *SF Bayview*

"Allen Iverson may be 'the Answer,' but Dave Zirin is 'the TRUTH.' Alarming, compelling, provocative—opinions that will slap the taste out of your mouth, but insights that will make you hark back to Arsenio and say HMMM! Zirin's critical yet out-of-the-box thinking, when mixed together, goes down smooth like Grandma's Kool-Aid. From MLB eating their young, to the intertwining of the souls of the NBA and hip-hop, to grinding with Avery Brundage, to Barry Bonds in pursuit of your Mama! EXPLOSIVE!"

—Bobby Ramos, cohost, *Sportstalk in Black n' White*

"Nobody writes sports like Dave Zirin. He is the sole (and soulful) Bambino of the People's Games. His line-drive analysis cuts left to the basket and tells us what we need to know about the real business and politics of the games we play and watch. Thank you, Dave Zirin, for telling the gut stories buried behind the endless media mega-hype."

—Harvey Wasserman, author, *Harvey Wasserman's History of the United States*

"Dave Zirin is hip, funny, and sharp as a tack. He uses sports—sometimes metaphorically, more often literally, to look at where we've been and where we're headed. His latest book makes you devour every page, savor every word, and crave more, redefining sportswriting and taking it to its quintessential peak."

—Pat Thurston, host, *The Pat Thurston Show*

"Separating sports from the world in which it is a part is like trying to separate Limburger cheese from the smell. Ain't gonna happen. Not that far too many so-called 'serious' sportswriters don't try on a depressingly regular basis. But Dave Zirin ain't going out like that. His essays never shy away from the often troublesome, provocative social context at the heart of this society (or any endeavor, for that matter), but they are also clearly the work of a man who loves his subjects. Forget all those reactionary, noncommittal, beat-down beat writers. Let these sublime, perceptive essays in your life."

—Reuben Jackson, poet laureate of the Jazz Journalist Association; associate curator, Smithsonian Institution

"Dave Zirin is the most provocative observer of the politics of sport in the United States today. *Welcome to the Terrordome* is his best work to date and should be required reading for sports fans and those committed to a more just and humane world."

—Robert W. McChesney, author, *The Problem of the Media*

"As a sports fan I am a big fan of Dave Zirin. He gets into the arenas, dugouts, and bullpens of the mythologies enveloping our modern-day gladiators, the owners who control them, and the media that deify and crucify them. Zirin breaks it all down with insight, humor, and the passion of someone who knows all aspects of the game. He is simply the best sportswriter around."

—David Barsamian, director, Alternative Radio

"Dave Zirin, author of the sizzling *What's My Name, Fool?* has written another book you don't want to miss (*Welcome to the Terrordome*), probing into the hot topics at the intersection of sports and society as no one else could."

—Lester Rodney, sports editor, *The Daily Worker* 1936–1958

"If Chuck D were a sportswriter, he'd be Dave Zirin, intelligent, well researched, and more than willing to give the mainstream sports establishment and our assumptions about race the middle finger. Dave tells the stories that America has purposefully forgotten. His focus is the game within the game. Dave is a real MC."

—Nathan Ive, host, *The Nathan Ive Show*

Welcome to the Terrordome

The Pain, Politics, and Promise of Sports

Dave Zirin

Haymarket
Books

Chicago, Illinois

First published in 2007 by Haymarket Books
PO Box 180165, Chicago, IL 60618
773-583-7884
info@haymarketbooks.org
www.haymarketbooks.org

Trade distribution:
In the U.S. through Consortium Book Sales, www.cbsd.com
In the UK, Turnaround Publisher Services, www.turnaround-psl.com
In Australia, Palgrave MacMillan, www.palgravemacmillan.com.au

This book was published with the generous support of the
Wallace Global Fund.

Cover design by Eric Ruder
Cover image of the Louisiana Superdome after Hurricane Katrina
with a large section of roof blown away.

ISBN-13: 978-931859-41-7

Printed in Canada

Library of Congress CIP Data is available

2 4 6 8 10 9 7 5 3 1

Contents

To Sasha and Amira y las luchas de mañana.
You are both smart and strong and fearless.

Acknowledgments

No one gets thanked before I give all gratitude to Chuck D for teaching a generation of us growing up in the political desert of the 1980s that resistance is righteous.

Eternal thanks to Haymarket Books for continuing to produce "books to change the world" and allowing my work to be in that company. It's an honor, and any writer would be lucky to work with them. For the uninitiated, the Haymarket Dream Team is Anthony Arnove, Julie Fain, Ahmed Shawki, Sarah Macaraeg, Bill Roberts, Eric Ruder, and Rachel Cohen.

Thanks to my editor Elizabeth Terzakis, scourge and slayer of the salacious simile (and foe of alliteration). Elizabeth—when she's not teaching or agitating—happens to be the most talented editor on earth. She deserves all credit for fighting for a vision of what this book could be.

I am very grateful to those who give me the opportunity to write on the regular: the good people at the *Nation*: Katrina vanden Heuvel, Peter Rothberg, and Joan Connell; Gary Spiecker at the *Los Angeles Times*; and the folks at *SLAM*, the only sports magazine that matters: Ryan Jones, Susan Price, and Ben Osborne.

Thanks to the people in the dog-kill-dog SportsWorld who have been generous with their time and encouragement: Robert Lipsyte, Dave Meggyesy, Jeremy Schaap, Dave Krikst,

Greg Sansone, Roy S. Johnson, and the folks at Athletes United for Peace.

Thanks to Dave Maraniss for writing *Clemente: The Passion and Grace of Baseball's Last Hero.*

To the people who explained soccer to me: Nick Chin, Shaun Harkin, and John Cox. Your collective patience is duly appreciated.

Thanks to the unsung work on this book done by Alex Billet, David Thurston, and Jeff Skinner. And to Paul D'Amato, who corrected me when I went astray.

Thank you, Frank Fried for introducing me to Lester Rodney.

Thank you to the people who work at Busboys and Poets and Politics and Prose: two bookstores unafraid of stirring the pot in D.C., particularly Andy Shallal, Don Allen, Pam Pinnock, and of course, Virginia Harabin.

Thank you Harper, Patricia, and Maia Caron for being a breath of fresh air.

And then there is family: my mother, Jane; my father, Jim; my stepmother, Marlene; my sister, Annie; my brother-in-law, Jason; my stepbrother, Peter; my stepsister, Maggie; and my in-laws: Ed, Susan, Bryan, Denise, Matt, Meme, and Pop Pop. I'm damn lucky to know you all.

To my grandfather, Alexander Rubin, who used to sneak me onto a golf course to play baseball. To my grandmother, Sylvia Rubin. I miss you every day.

And lastly to Michele: thank you for making it all matter.

Foreword by Chuck D

My first encounter with Dave Zirin was interviewing him about his book, *What's My Name Fool? Sports and Resistance in the United States* for my radio show *On the Real*, which runs on the Air America radio network. I found this dude to be very much on the cutting edge of where sports journalists need to be today. Be open and aware that history beyond the so-called facts arrives from three sides: pro, con, and neutral. It's wise to back your words with a wide range of perspective, and Mr. Zirin equips himself indeed with a refreshing refrain away from the locker room and neighborhood pub mentality.

When I first wrote the song "Welcome to the Terrordome" in 1989, it was at the edge of the last decade of the millennium, and I just knew—I could just feel—that a period of deep uncertainty was waiting for us. Upon the completion of the song I envisioned a fight announcer in the middle of a boxing ring amidst a rabid crowd. I don't think I recalled anyone of color in that audience, and I felt that boxing ring was a roped-off haven or a petri dish of sorts.

Splattered blood was symbolic in my imagination, and I do remember the flying blood mixed both ways over them ropes, from the aggression of the approaching crowd and the boxers protected in their haven. The song in its literal meaning was introducing a turning point decade for blackfolks in society. I'm quoted in interviews around then saying that the Terrordome was a "test" decade, and based on what I and my group went through in 1989, I felt that it was a litmus test for how well we would do rolling and tumbling through the mainstream and media kaleidoscope.

I also felt that at that time the microscope of society that had been focused on the most high-profile of Black males, the athlete, had veered into the realm of the young Black male entertainer, with even deeper focus—into the social sphere of the masses. Thus the new examination of the Negro via the rap music video and reality shows like *COPS* ushered a previously uninvited type into the American kitchen.

I immediately thought of the Three Mikes who were on top of the American celebrity heap. Jordan, Tyson, and Jackson. More to it than just basketball, boxing, and dance, these areas of performance rank way up high, especially in the appreciation corner of blackfolks. Not that we invented any of them, but in the process of performance, blackfolks had the nerve and audacity to reinvent their focal structure.

The Three Mikes were tested not far into the decade. Tyson lost in Japan to Buster Douglas right at the top and soon thereafter was jailed on rape charges. From there the growing technology of media not only microscoped his visibility but burned him in the process.

Michael Jordan early on was tossed through the T-dome. Winning championships but losing a father to murder, losing the game on accusations of betting, perhaps, but coming back to win and to lose, to time and the media machine, which still strips American idol shine off him to this very minute.

And the world's greatest entertainer, Mike Jax, who ultimately may have been the smartest of them all. After being arraigned, arrested, then acquitted on rape charges and various other accusations in the worlds of the legal and the tabloid, he ended up leaving the stage of the lower forty-eight states for another country entirely. When you're called the world's greatest anything, it's advisable to peep the 191 other countries on the planet to validate that claim, and he did.

I mention these Black cultural "icons" because, on their paths to iconography, something more radioactive than just another piece of shit littered the road. Somehow, the sunsets of John Elway, Jack Nicklaus, and John Havlicek seem less strewn.

In entertainment we just know better. John Wayne and Elvis got another viewpoint directed at their iconoclastic relevance in "Fight the Power"; it was very CNN of me then. Rap music stated its position, thoroughly evaluating many American icons, although in the process seemed to lose itself by connecting to the corporate umbilical cord.

But in Supermedia what giveth is also what taketh away. ESPN, FOX, and their competition in sportsnews, talk, casting, and analysis realized the collision of the collection of athletes and entertainers coming from being "boyz in the same hood" was a convergence of every conversation, contemplation, reservation about race up to that point.

From 1990 to this minute, the Terrordome has completely expanded the stage for all to see, albeit many cannot interpret what is seen. Mike Tyson made me nervous as he entered the ring with the song in every fight from the song's inception in late '89 till the fight before Buster Douglas where he emerged with KRS-ONE's Boogie Down Production's "You Must Learn."

The "hoodology" of the so-called ghetto had seeped through them TV sets and radios entangled with what was soon to be described as a 500-cable knotted matrix. The style of life and the pain of politics were thin-lined and trussed together in one flow. To the point: in judging many of today's athletes born or raised in the era of R&B (Reagan and Bush), it's hard to separate out the influence of the game and its coaches from the influence of the video game and the music video on those same players.

I connect sincerely with Dave Zirin on many points he addresses in his works and writings. It's public knowledge that I grew up longing to be a play-by-play sportscaster, a Knicks fan who wasn't imitating Marv Albert. Being raised in Roosevelt, Long Island, in the 1970s, my hometown was prided by the fact that one Julius "Dr. J" Erving was carrying a whole league just up the block at Nassau Coliseum. Television gave us true images of sport, letting us know that whatever racism was going on in the news of the country, the court, ballpark, arena, stadium, or field wasn't lying about the growing number of participants that looked like they was from around the way.

Wouldn't try if I could to separate sport and politics as a kid. They say a first impression lasts a lifetime. Questions from me as a kid to my dad, where the bond had been welded by sport: "Why did Ali change his name from Clay?" Regarding the '68 Olympics, "Why are those men putting their fists in the air?" And, "What's the fuss about Curt Flood? Why ain't he gonna play for the Senators? Ain't he gonna play for [Senators manager] Ted Williams? How can Lenny Wilkens and Al Attles play *and* coach at the same time?" (I didn't know the great Bill Russell or Dave DeBusschere did it prior to then.) "Why is Hank Aaron getting all this hate mail?" "Why did Jim Brown stop playing at 29?"

Added on to this was having to seriously learn about the meaning of one Jack Roosevelt Robinson for a book report. All this collectively made sport 75 percent of my everyday existence.

Because the radio was a window to sportstalk, mainly on WMCA, with future Yankee announcer John Sterling and Art Rust Jr., a Black man who knew his sports very well, I was exposed indirectly to the venom of racial rhetoric from the callers who seemed to lash out at Black athletes a bit differently from the rest. Sometimes I'd tune my radio deep into the night and listen to the even less liberal opinions from the middle of the country on WWWE in Cleveland, and hear longtime announcer Joe Tait field a batch of Klan-like calls.

All of this sports background fueled me and prepared me to deal with people, this country, and the world. Sport seemingly starts equal and fair: based on one's skill, effort, will, and determination, one can succeed beyond the pack of the masses. Expect this read into the "Pain, Politics, and Promise of Sports" to add some roundedness to the games we consider life, love, and what should be fun. Put your helmet on, though, and welcome to the Terrordome.

The March of Domes

Welcome to the Superdome, home of the historically unsuper New Orleans Saints—a team on the rise that once inspired its own fans to arrive at games with brown paper bags on their heads. The Superdome was built for crowds of 72,000 people, and boasts of "9,000 tons of air-conditioning" and "102 restrooms." It was also the emotional site of the first post–9/11 Super Bowl in 2002, won by the Cinderella New England Patriots. As Steve Serby of the *New York Post* wrote at the time,

> Inside a red, white and blue fortress called the Superdome, they let freedom ring last night, and they let freedom sing, and then they played a football game that stands today as tall as the Twin Towers once did, as a defiant statue of liberty. On the night they wrapped a star-spangled banner around the neck of terror and squeezed tight, they played a football game that will be remembered as Patriots' Day.

But when Hurricane Katrina flattened the Gulf Coast, the "terror" was homegrown. The Superdome morphed into a homeless shelter from hell, inhabited yet uninhabitable for 25,000 of New Orleans' poorest residents. They scraped, suffered, and for the most part survived, in conditions that Jesse Jackson likened to "the hold of a slave ship."

It took Katrina for them to actually see the inside of a stadium whose ticket prices make entry restrictive. At the time of the hurricane, game tickets cost $90, season seats went for $1,300, and luxury boxes for eight home games ran more than $100,000 a year. But the Katrina refugees' tickets were comped, courtesy of the federal and local government's malignant neglect. It was only fitting, since these 25,000 people helped pay for the stadium in the first place. The Superdome was built entirely on the public dime in 1975, a part of efforts to create a "New New Orleans" business district. City officials decided that building the largest domed stadium on the planet was in everyone's best interest. New Orleans leaders have a history of elevating political graft to a finely honed art, and in this case they did not disappoint. Much of Louis Armstrong's historic old neighborhood was ripped up for extra stadium parking, and, in an instance of brutal foreshadowing that would shame Wes Craven, an old, aboveground cemetery was eradicated to make space for the end zones.

In some ways, the makers of the Superdome were ahead of their time. Stadium swindles have since become common, substituting for anything resembling urban policy in the United States. They come gift wrapped as an instant solution to the problems of crumbling schools, urban decay, and suburban flight, SportsWorld shrines to the dogma of trickle-down economics. Over the last ten years, more than $16 billion of the public's money has been spent for stadium construction and upkeep in cities all over the United States. Unfortunately, these costly public projects end up being little more than monuments to corporate greed: $500 million welfare hotels for America's billionaires built with funds that should have been spent on clinics, schools, libraries—and levees.

The "era of big government" may be over, but it has been replaced by the Rise of the Domes. Money for the stadium but not for levees; money for the stadium but not for shelter; money for the stadium but not for evacuation. Post-Katrina

New Orleans showed what these policies reap. And what's good for New Orleans is good for America, right to the top of the political food chain. As journalist Norman Solomon wrote, "The policies are matters of priorities. And the priorities of the Bush White House are clear. For killing in Iraq, they spare no expense. For protecting and sustaining life, the cupboards go bare. The problem is not incompetence. It's inhumanity, cruelty and greed."

The titanic tragedy of Katrina became farce when the Superdome refugees were finally moved: not to government housing, public shelters, or even another location in the area, but to the Houston Astrodome. It was the March of Domes. Here, they were able to encounter a force almost as terrifying as the hurricane: Barbara Bush. The "First Mother" walked among the dispossessed and dazed, coming within touching distance of a poverty she couldn't come close to understanding. "Almost everyone I've talked to," Babs told the press, "says, 'We're going to move to Houston.' What I'm hearing, which is sort of scary, is they all want to stay in Texas. Everyone is so overwhelmed by the hospitality. And so many of the people in the arena here, you know, were underprivileged anyway, so this—this" (she chuckled slightly) "is working very well for them."

Leading this carnival of disgrace was Barbara's spawn, George W. Bush, who demonstrated a touching sympathy...for segregationist Trent Lott: "The good news is—and it's hard for some to see it now—that out of this chaos is going to come a fantastic Gulf Coast, like it was before. Out of the rubble of Trent Lott's house—he's lost his entire house—there's going to be a fantastic house. And I'm looking forward to sitting on the porch."

But as those injured by Katrina and insulted by Barbara attempted to find their footing, something quite remarkable occurred. It made little news, but a wide swath of athletes

In the awful aftermath of Katrina, there were few places for the displaced to find shelter or aid. **Above: Refugees make their way to the Superdome** (AP/Lisa Krantz) **Below: Crowds are turned away from the Superdome** (AP/Dave Martin)

emerged from their cocoons with money, relief, and, more importantly, something to say. Washington Wizards power forward Etan Thomas defended rapper Kanye West when he said "George W. Bush doesn't care about Black people" at an NBC benefit concert. West was called "disgusting" by that arbiter of racial sensitivity, Laura Bush. Thomas came back with conviction, saying, "I definitely agree with Kanye West. Had this been a rich, lily-white suburban area that got hit, you think they would have had to wait five days to get food or water? Then you still don't send help but instead send the National Guard to 'maintain order'? Are you kidding me?"

Thomas also defended the rights of the people of New Orleans to survive by any means necessary:

> If I was down there, and starving for five days, after suffering that type of devastation, and I saw some armed troops coming down not with food or water or supplies but with guns drawn, trying to enforce a curfew or whatever they were doing, I would have reacted the same way many of them reacted, with hostility. I am not saying that I condone shooting at the police or firemen; I'm just saying that I understand their frustration. This is unfortunately a direct reflection of the entire Republican platform. The rich are awarded all of the rights, privileges, respect, et cetera...in this country and the poor are pushed to the side. You see that with education, health care, court justice, and every other aspect of society. If this had hit a higher economic area, Bush would have reacted much quicker and more effectively. It's a sad reminder of the reality that is our society.

Thomas was not alone. Saints All-Pro receiver Joe Horn gazed at the place where he has set receiving records and said that football couldn't be farther from his mind. "It's devastating to us. I've cried three or four times. Seeing kids without any food, elderly people dying, and the government saying that help is on the way—that's the most shocking part."

"The Round Mound of Sound," Charles Barkley, never too shy to comment, focused on the broader context:

We need to look at the big picture now, and get these people back on their feet. We got to get them jobs and got to get them housing. That's the most important thing. America is divided by economics.... If you are poor and black, or poor and white or Hispanic, you are going to be at a disadvantage. You are not going to have the best neighborhoods or best school.... [I]f you don't get education and you are poor, then you are at the mercy of this government.

Barry Bonds asked why Congress had time to investigate steroids while people were dying in New Orleans.

William Rhoden, the *New York Times* sports columnist and author of *$40 Million Slaves,* describes his experience traveling to the Gulf with a group of NBA and WNBA players bringing supplies.

Horrifying images underscored the reality that there are multiple tiers of life in America. The images of death, desperation, hopelessness, and poverty, flushed into full view, made many of us wonder where this America had been hiding. We did not recognize it. Some of us did not even realize this America existed.

The hurricane was also a wake-up call for this group of NBA athletes, because the hardest hit were black and poor.... Many of the athletes were raised in Mississippi and other parts of the South. They knew firsthand what it meant to live by a slender thread. Justin Reed, a forward for the Boston Celtics, said he saw himself in the faces of young storm victims. "I come from a single-parent home, and once upon a time we were homeless," he said. "I know how hard it is to start from scratch, to have to build and build and wonder if you're ever going to be able to live like you once lived."

Dallas Mavericks center Erick Dampier also spoke about the need to "pull together as a group." The instinctive desire to come together was real, but we—and the people of the Gulf—are still waiting for it to ripen and cohere into the new kind of Civil Rights Movement so needed.

When athletes speak out for social justice, they break what Howard Cosell called "Rule number one of the 'Jockocracy'— that athletes and politics don't mix." But history also shows that when the iron wall of the Jockocracy is dented, it's usually the sign of deeper discontent in society. As I wrote in my first book, *What's My Name, Fool? Sports and Resistance in the United States,* Jackie Robinson, Muhammad Ali, and Billie Jean King were exceptional individuals, but also products of social movements that shaped them and which they in turn helped shape.

The response to Katrina, among other rumblings and grumblings in our SportsWorld, demonstrates that struggle and its relation to sports is a question not of the past but of the future. For the last generation, sports have been suffocated by corporate greed, commercialism, and military cheerleading. They have become our own personal Terrordome, and there is no exit. Our only option is to stay and fight. That is what *Welcome to the Terrordome* is about: if we wish to reclaim sports, we must look at history, learn from the role sports play in our world, and listen to the athletic rebels of today who are so often ignored by the media.

James Baldwin once said, "America is a nation devoted to the death of the paradox." In other words, to use the updated version by pro wrestler The Rock, "Know your role and shut your mouth." Stay in your box. If you're a cashier, a Wal-Mart employee, a sanitation worker, a teacher, that is how you are defined and all you can be. Don't think about being a cashier/artist, a firefighter/activist. We endure model/actresses and oil company executive/politicians but that is it. This book is dedicated to all athletes, sportswriters, and fans in the athletic industrial complex who defy the box. They are the hope for the future of sports.

CHAPTER ONE

Relearning Roberto Clemente

O nly once did I ever buy a rare baseball card. I was fourteen and the man on the laminated treasure was Roberto
Clemente. Clemente's story, in my young mind, held
the magic and poetry of folklore. He was the man who could
throw 400-foot lasers from right field to home plate. He
recorded his 3,000th hit in his last game, and then died in a
plane crash trying to get aid to earthquake-ravaged Nicaragua.
I knew that a friend of mine, a Nuyorican named Ray, had a
framed picture of Clemente in his house—right next to Jesus
Christ.

The card I bought was different. Unlike others, where players strike manly action poses, or smile goofily for the camera,
Clemente is looking down, deliberately, at his feet. It's the
baseball card equivalent of another doomed '60s icon, John
Kennedy, whose presidential portrait shows his face tilted in
eerie shadow. Unlike Kennedy, Clemente believed in a liberated, independent Latin America, but I knew nothing of that at
the time. There was something about Clemente's picture that
was undeniably charismatic, romantic, and defiant.

Clemente: A Latino Jackie Robinson?

Today, there is a controversial movement under way to have
Clemente's number 21 retired by every major league team.
Currently, the only player who holds that distinction is Brook-

lyn Dodger trailblazer Jackie Robinson. This has sparked a nasty war of words between those who want Robinson to hold the honor alone and the people who believe Clemente deserves an equal place on that pedestal.

This divisive fight occurs in the context of an urgent need for unity between African Americans and Latinos, given recent attacks on immigrant rights. Rather than turning into a turf battle over who is more worthy, the campaign to retire Clemente's number could be seen as an opportunity to unite around a common interest: the need for baseball to treat all players like human beings regardless of their backgrounds. The flap is somewhat ironic, considering that Clemente's emergence as a baseball star, as we will see, owed a great deal to Robinson and the Civil Rights Movement. Ironic considering that Clemente was also very inspired by the Black Freedom struggle and helped shape how it came to be reflected in the world of sports. Clemente is actually a terrific example of the collective strength and confidence that Black and Brown unity can inspire.

The comparison to Robinson is an interesting one. Unlike Robinson, Clemente broke no obvious barrier of race or language. He was not the first Latino player or even the first darkskinned Latino player. But the similarities to Robinson outweigh the differences.

Like Robinson, Clemente played with a fire and flair that transcended statistics. Like Robinson, Clemente was an armed forces veteran struck by the gap between the ideals he fought for and the reality on the ground. Like Robinson, Clemente was brought to the major leagues by legendary baseball executive Branch Rickey. Like Robinson, Clemente was told by Rickey to "ignore the abuse" that would come from racist fans. Like Robinson, Clemente possessed a fierce pride with no patience for bigotry or prejudice. Like Robinson, Clemente was

someone who came to represent something far more important, vital, and political than just a ballplayer. And, like Robinson, Clemente's legacy has grown more powerful over time.

Despite the fact that he played in Pittsburgh, a minor media
market, a football town, and a city slow to embrace baseball heroes of color, Clemente's legend has only mushroomed over
time. As David Maraniss wrote in his excellent book *Clemente:
the Passion and Grace of Baseball's Last Hero,* "Forty public
schools, two hospitals, and more than two hundred parks and
ball fields bear his name, from Carolina, Puerto Rico, where he
was born, to Pittsburgh, Pennsylvania, where he played, to far
off Mannheim, Germany." Maraniss could have added a bridge
in Pittsburgh to that list, as well as countless children. Much of
Clemente's lasting legacy has to do with the way he died, but it
is also intimately connected with who he was as a player. He
wasn't the first Latino, but he was the first Latino star. He was
the first to wear his Latino heritage proudly. He was the first to
speak out on the way racism in the United States affected
Latino ballplayers. He was the first Latino to find the hearts of
white baseball fans but never by checking his culture, language, or heritage at the door. He is an icon of gathering
strength, as baseball becomes more Latino and the government's immigration policies demand a new civil rights movement in the United States.

But the most chilling similarity to Robinson is the way
iconography has robbed Clemente of politics, of his true self.

Clemente as a Player: Art, Not Science

Clemente's baseball bona fides are above reproach. He led the
Pirates to two World Series victories, in 1960 and 1971, was the
1966 National League MVP, and won four batting titles. Hitting
in an era that forced him to face Mount Olympus–worthy pitchers like Sandy Koufax, Bob Gibson, Juan Marichal, and Don
Drysdale, Clemente led the major leagues in batting average

throughout the 1960s. Swinging at the ball wherever it was pitched, Clemente sprayed line drives all over the field like a broken sprinkler. And even though he never hit more than twenty-nine home runs in a season, the 185-pound Clemente hit the ball as hard as anyone. Once he broke Bob Gibson's leg with a line drive and another time he literally took off the top of Don Drysdale's ear with a screaming single.

But it was on the field that Clemente was a man apart. He garnered twelve Gold Gloves with a platinum arm that may be the best the game ever saw. In a recent piece, the *New York Times* called Clemente the "Fielder of Dreams," saying that he "looked like a dervish expelling a cannonball" when he threw the ball in from right field. As the prideful Clemente said about his arm, "When they say Babe Ruth hit over 700 home runs, I keep my mouth shut. But when they talk about throwing the ball, I can't keep my mouth shut."

Despite his many strengths, Clemente was derided throughout his career for overreacting to the assorted bumps and bruises that most view as part of the game, and there is no question that, when it came to his health, Clemente was an eccentric. But he bristled, justifiably, when labeled a hypochondriac, knowing that the moniker had more to do with propagating the stereotype of the lazy Latino asleep in the shade of his sombrero than it did with questioning the legitimacy of his time on the DL.

Clemente may not have had the titanic statistics of contemporaries like Hank Aaron, Willie Mays, Ernie Banks, and Frank Robinson, but it doesn't matter because his play transcended the numbing number-crunching that is so intrinsic to baseball. As Maraniss put so well,

> There was something about Clemente that surpassed statistics, then and always. Some baseball mavens love the sport precisely because of its numbers. They can take the mathematics of a box score and of a year's worth of statistics and calculate the case for

players they consider underrated or overrated and declare who has the most real value to a team. To some skilled practitioners of this science, Clemente comes out very good but not the greatest; he walks too seldom, has too few home runs, steals too few bases. Their perspective is legitimate, but to people who appreciate Clemente this is like chemists trying to explain Van Gogh by analyzing the ingredients of his paint. Clemente was art, not science. Every time he strolled slowly to the batter's box or trotted out to right field, he seized the scene like a great actor. It was hard to take one's eyes off him, because he could do anything on a baseball field and carried himself with such nobility. "The rest of us were just players," Steve Blass would say. "Clemente was a prince."

He was a prince, as we will see, who wanted to collectivize the crown.

His Era, Politics, and Roots

Clemente played right field for eighteen seasons, from 1954 to 1972, years that encompassed a panorama of fantastic changes in both Major League Baseball and U.S. society. His career spanned the entirety of the Black Freedom struggle from the Montgomery bus boycotts to the urban ghetto rebellions, from Martin Luther King to the Black Panthers.

Thanks to Jackie Robinson, Clemente broke into the big leagues alongside the first post-color-line wave of young, brilliant, African-American ballplayers. But while there was room for Black stars in the 1950s, teams had informal quotas to make sure that color was kept to a minimum. They also thought nothing of continuing to hold spring training in the segregated South. And the fact that baseball was moving, albeit slowly, toward acceptance of African-American players did not mean that the same courtesy was extended to Latinos.

In 1964, Giants manager Alvin Dark banned the Spanish language from the clubhouse. Dark was openly hostile to Latino players, but his loudly boorish rules were tacitly enforced in clubhouses around the league. Nevertheless,

Roberto Clemente poses in his Pirates uniform, 1967 (AP)

throughout the '60s, the changes occurring in society gradually bled onto the ballfield. Most players were passive participants in this process, but not Roberto Clemente. His was a voice impatient for change. Clemente was a populist in the best Latin American tradition. He was a Bolivarian, someone who believed in a united Latin America that could serve the interests of the region's poor. His heroes were Martin Luther King Jr. and Puerto Rican leader Luis Muñoz Marín. Marín—a name known to many people in the United States as the San Juan airport they fly into for spring break—was the first democratically elected governor of Puerto Rico. Early in his long political career, he was a member of the Puerto Rican Socialist Party and a strong advocate for independence.

Throughout his life, Clemente believed in economic and social justice. He also had an instinctive solidarity with people fighting for their rights. When his friend Osvaldo Gil chided Clemente for being controlled by his wife, Clemente said, "The way you think about women is what happened with the major leagues and black players. They were afraid that if they let black players in, they'd take over. That's the way you are with women."

The youngest of four children, Clemente was born August 18, 1934, in Carolina, Puerto Rico, and raised "by people who knew what it meant to struggle." Compared to others in depression-era poverty in Puerto Rico, the Clementes had stability: a roof over their heads, electricity, and food on the table. But even this meager living was a family project. Clemente's father, Melchor, earned only $12 a week. All the children worked, either in the sugarcane fields or by bringing ice water to the cane workers in exchange for pennies.

Despite the arduous labor, there was always time for sports. Roberto Clemente was not the only athlete in the family; his older brother Matino had major league dreams that were dashed by Jim Crow. Roberto always maintained that Matino was the better ballplayer. Once again a comparison to Robinson suggests itself. Just as Jackie was motivated by the aspirations of his brother Mack, a silver medalist at the 1936 Olympics, whose professional athletic aspirations were thwarted by racism, Roberto was inspired by Matino, who coached him throughout his career.

Dodgers Disgrace: Jim Crow vs. Brown Pride

Being raised in a proud Puerto Rican household did not prepare Clemente for the racism he encountered in the United States. Even as a dark-skinned Puerto Rican, Clemente never knew of the existence of race. He would tell reporters that he learned that dark skin "was bad over here." As an eighteen-year-old prodigy, Clemente leaped at the chance to play with the Brooklyn Dodgers, taking significantly less money than other major league teams offered. The Dodgers were the team of his beloved Jackie Robinson, and for a moment, it was a dream fulfilled. But Clemente languished in the Dodgers farm system for two years as they attempted to hide him from other teams until there was a "spot" for him on their big-league roster. The Dodgers most likely took this course of action because they had already reached their informal quota of dark-skinned players. But try as they might, they couldn't keep him hidden, and Pittsburgh Pirates team president Branch Rickey, who still had a mole or two in the Dodgers farm system, bought his contract in 1956 for $5,000.

This was not joyous news in the Clemente household. The Pirates were the saddest franchise in the game, having finished forty-four games behind the Dodgers in 1954. Even the legendary Rickey was failing to resuscitate the franchise. But Clemente had more on his mind than this pitiful team during his first spring training.

The Pirates spring games were in Fort Myers, Florida, which even by the standards of 1950s Florida was deeply segregated. Years later, Clemente's only memories of that first spring training consisted of eating on the bus with other players of color while his white teammates dined inside both fancy restaurants and greasy spoons. He also believed his Black teammates felt—probably correctly—that if they made waves they would find themselves out of the game. For someone who had never heard of Ol' Jim Crow, these were painful times. Clemente's friend Vic Power, a highly skilled Puerto Rican player for the Kansas City Athletics, was dragged off his team's bus that spring for buying a Coke from a whites-only gas station. Clemente seethed at the humiliation, feeling it as if it were his own. Power tried to calm Clemente down. His approach was humor. Power liked to tell the story of a waitress telling him, "We don't serve Negroes," and responding, "That's okay. I don't eat Negroes."

But Clemente just couldn't handle it that way. He recalled,

They say, "Roberto, you better keep your mouth shut because they will ship you back." [But] this is something that from the first day, I said to myself: "I am in the minority group. I am from the poor people. I represent the poor people. I represent the common people of America. So I am going to be treated like a human being. I don't want to be treated like a Puerto Rican, or a black, or nothing like that. I want to be treated like any person that comes for a job."

Clemente was too good to be kept off the club, and for years was the only dark-skinned player consistently in the Pirates' starting lineup. Not that there was any shortage of players of color; African-American pitcher Bob Veale once said that there were so many Black players on the Pirates minor league Carolina team, the Wilson Tobs (short for Tobacconists), that many fans thought they were a traveling Negro League team.

But Clemente's talent could not be ignored. The press tried to report on the young prodigy with a howitzer for an arm, but they insisted—to Clemente's fury—on quoting him phonetically, which made him sound like a Latino Stepin Fetchit. Headlines would read, "Clemente says: 'I Get Heet.'"

Clemente would respond by taking the press on directly like a man on a mission. "I attack [the press] strongly, because since the first Latino arrived in the big leagues he was discriminated against without mercy," he said. "It didn't matter that the Latino ballplayer was good, but the mere fact of him not being North American [made him] marginalized. They have an open preference for North Americans. Mediocre players receive immense publicity while true stars are not as highlighted as they deserve."

Yet for all his sensitivity, Clemente was not petty. Writers who were used to being spat on by players who didn't like the media were shocked to receive handwritten apologies from Clemente when he had flown off the handle or if he decided, in retrospect, that he had been unfair. It's impossible, however, to separate Clemente's simmering anger from his galactic ability on the field. He said, "If I would be happy, I would be a very bad ballplayer. With me, when I get mad, it puts energy in my body."

The Pirates Get Good

As the 1950s wound down, the Pirates dumped Branch Rickey and hired Joe Brown as their new president. The team was getting better every year, and in the 1960 World Series, they beat the Yankees in seven games, capped by Bill Mazeroski's walk-off home run in the final contest. Clemente was the only player to get a hit in all seven games, batting .310 for the series. This should have been his finest hour, but Clemente was outside the party. While players gargled champagne, he quietly packed his bags to return home. Despite Clemente's stellar series, Mazeroski was named MVP. But what really wounded Clemente's pride, what made him wonder if things would ever change, was when he came in eighth in the voting for league Most Valuable Player. Several teammates with worse stats, including winner

Dick Groat, finished ahead of him. Although racism prevailed in the league as a whole, Clemente was appreciated at home: Pittsburgh fans voted him their favorite Pirate.

The next spring, Clemente went public with his disgust at the official segregation he and other players of color had to endure in Fort Myers. He openly slammed the segregated spring baseball life saying, "There is nothing to do down here. [Players of color] go to the ball park, play cards, and watch television. In a way, it's like being in prison."

These statements may seem tame and several steps behind the sit-ins that were sweeping the South. But in the musty world of baseball, they were electric. Clemente even went to Pirates boss Joe Brown and, speaking for every Black player on the squad, said that they wouldn't take the team bus if they had to eat in their seats while the rest of the team stopped at restaurants. Brown got them a station wagon so they could drive on their own. In baseball in the early 1960s, this qualified as progress.

And Clemente's spring actions helped open the dam. That All-Star Break, elected representatives from every team met and agreed unanimously to demand an end to training camp segregation. This is at a time when there was no real union to speak of and the majority of reps were white. It was a watershed moment, proving in practice that players could unite. 1961 was also historic for Clemente at the plate. He won his first batting title with a .351 average. Fellow countryman—and close friend—Orlando Cepeda won the home run and RBI titles. In the Caribbean, this was known as the Puerto Rican Triple Crown.

By 1964, Clemente, a ten-year veteran, was becoming a mentor to other Latino players. This couldn't have happened without the loosening up of the informal quotas that existed against players of color. Finally the pipeline from the minor leagues was becoming unclogged, and Black and Latino players began to see big-league daylight. Young future All-Stars like Willie Stargell began to remake the Pirates. Teammates, Black and white, began to stick up for Clemente in a way they never did in the 1950s. Years later, teammate Don Leppert recalled his response to press treatment of Clemente. "They tried to make a buffoon out of him. I was sitting there one night when [Les Biederman of the Pittsburgh press] was asking Clemente something, and Biederman had a little smirk on his face. I went off on Biederman: 'Why the hell don't you ask him questions in Spanish?' I didn't endear myself to Biederman, but didn't give a rat's ass. They tried to take advantage of every malaprop."

Despite the racism of the press, Clemente had never been more confident professionally or personally. On November 14, 1964, he married Vera Cristina Zabala in Carolina, Puerto Rico. They went on to have three sons: Roberto Jr., Luis Roberto, and Roberto Enrique. Proud of their heritage, the couple arranged for all three sons to be born in Puerto Rico. Comfortable at home and at work, Clemente began to speak out for his dream: a sports city for impoverished Puerto Rican children. He began to look at land, collect investors, and talk rhapsodically of helping the poor. "I'd like to work with kids. If I live long enough," he would say.

During the 1966 off-season, Clemente's "adopted American sister" Carol was in Puerto Rico with Clemente and his family. In Puerto Rico, Clemente didn't have to be the intense, perpetually irritated star forever alert to any slight to his skin color or language. Only by seeing him relaxed and among his own people can we understand the mythical dimensions Clemente acquired in death. As Carol described to Maraniss,

> I came back being in awe of what a humble man he was. What a regular man he was [away from Pittsburgh]. But just so connected to the people. If children recognized him, or the most humble-looking person somewhere on a mountain hill where we

were driving approached him, wherever we were, it ended in a long conversation. I never remember a moment when Roberto didn't take the time to talk to somebody who came up to him. There never was a time when he didn't stop. I never remember him walking away or cutting someone off. And especially if it was someone young…. You could see him [in that setting] like a prophet.

Clemente would talk of his own death casually, believing he would die young and that it would happen while flying. Nevertheless, he would never be nervous while flying with his wife because he was also certain that she wouldn't die this way. Vera remembered, "He always said he would die young—that this was his fate."

Syndicato: Clemente Carries on King's Legacy

Another person considered a prophet and plagued with premonitions of death, Martin Luther King Jr. was assassinated the following spring. On April 3, King gave a speech saying, "I may not get there with you. But I want you to know tonight, that we, as a people, will get to the Promised Land. And I'm not fearing any man. Mine eyes have seen the glory of the coming of the Lord." The following day, April 4, 1968, King was shot and killed.

Clemente had met and spoken with King on numerous occasions. He idolized King, becoming more enamored with him as he adopted positions against the war in Vietnam and structural poverty in the United States. As Clemente recalled,

When Martin Luther King started doing what he did, he changed the whole system of American style. He put the people, the ghetto people, the people who didn't have nothing to say in those days, they started saying what they would have liked to say for many years that nobody listened to. Now with this man, these people come down to the place where they supposed to be but people didn't want them, and sit down as if they were white and call attention to the whole world. Now that wasn't only the black people, but the minority people. The people who didn't have anything, and they had nothing to say in those days because they didn't have any power, they started saying things and they started pick-eting, and that's the reason I say he changed the whole world.

Clemente was devastated by the news of King's death but didn't suffer in silence. Instead, he led a charge to prevent the Pirates and Astros from opening their season on April 8, the day before King's burial. Opening day was moved to April 10, and Roberto Clemente had put sports in its proper perspective in a way that no one could miss.

Clemente took King's legacy forward when he became the players' representative for the Pirates. The Players Association had changed decisively when steelworkers organizer Marvin Miller was brought in to head the union in 1966. In 1968, play-ers reached their first-ever collective-bargaining agreement with the owners. The pact improved health benefits and raised the minimum salary to $10,000 a year. But, more importantly, the contract included an agreement by the owners to "examine the reserve clause" that bound players to teams like chattel, opening the door for Miller's dream of defeating the hated clause. All-Star Curt Flood, who was being radicalized by the changes in society, stepped forward to challenge it. Miller be-lieved there was a direct relation between the Black Freedom struggle and the fact that it took an African-American player to make the challenge. He said, "It was definitely related. Black and Latin players like Roberto Clemente were at the forefront. This was not just the color of their skin. Flood, for example, did not grow up in the South. He grew up in Oakland, California.... When a player of his temperament and pride was sent to the South not being able to stay in the same hotels and motels, playing in Georgia and Mississippi, I think it made a very big difference in his outlook on the world." It was an outlook shared by Clemente.

In December of 1969, Flood presented his case to the reps alongside Miller and asked for their support in what would be an ugly court case against Major League Baseball. Flood was proud of his background but saw his struggle in broader terms. "I am a black man and we have been denied rights. But in this situation, race should not make a difference. We're ballplayers all with the same problem." Many of the reps were initially nervous, asking Flood and Miller about the "dangers" of challenging the bosses and of "going too far." Clemente was the first to stand up for Flood, saying, "So far no one is doing anything," and pointing out that Flood's solitary stance, rather than going too far, was a clear sign that players had not gone far enough. Tim McCarver, Flood's teammate, agreed with Clemente, saying, "We have no choice" but to support Flood.

But Clemente wasn't done. In his heavily accented English, he told the reps his own story: of taking less money to sign with the Dodgers because he dreamed of playing in New York; of being "bought" by the Pirates for $5,000. "He had me," Clemente said of team boss Joe Brown: a $5,000 investment in a player who would make the Pirates millions. It was a strong statement because Clemente was one of the few players in the game making more than $100,000 a year. Other players in this "class," such as Carl Yastrzemski, opposed an aggressive union. But Clemente's leadership was appreciated by all. As Dick Moss, the Players Association counsel, said, "Roberto was respected by everyone. He was very important to us."

El Noche Clemente

In 1971, Clemente was entering the twilight of his career. The team was competitive and had just moved from Forbes Field into Three Rivers Stadium. That year, the Pirates became the first team in history to field nine Black and Latino players at the same time, with Dock Ellis on the mound, famous for throwing a no-hitter while tripping on acid. The squad had come a long way from 1960 when Clemente was the only starting player of color on a team with hard quotas. But that didn't mean the team was beloved by fans. The team averaged about 33 percent attendance—about 15,000 people.

That changed for one glorious game: Roberto Clemente Night on July 24. A fleet of planes filled with Clemente's Puerto Rican compañeros came to the game, courtesy of the club. There were nearly 45,000 in attendance, many wearing the traditional peasant clothing of their island home. For the first time in major league history, the game was conducted bilingually, with ceremonies and announcements done in English and Spanish. It's worth noting that with the current stream of English-only initiatives and anti-immigrant hysteria, an event of this nature today—even with a team like the Mets, which is majority Latino—would be a radical act. But at the time it sprang naturally from all that Clemente represented, both to his own people and to Pirates diehards.

When Clemente tried to address the crowd, he broke down in tears, with no pretense of machismo. His tears flowed so freely that his baby son waddled down the first-base line to make sure he was all right. But Clemente gathered himself and said,

> I've sacrificed these sixteen years, maybe I've lost many friendships due to the effort it takes for someone to try to do the maximum in sports and especially the work it takes for us, the Puerto Ricans, especially for the Latinos, to triumph in the big leagues. I have achieved this triumph for us, the Latinos. I believe that it is a matter of pride for all of us, the Puerto Ricans as well as for all of those in the Caribbean, because we are all brothers. And I'd like to dedicate this triumph to all Puerto Rican mothers...[and] as I've said, for all those Puerto Rican athletes, for all those who have triumphed and those who have not been able to. And that is why I don't have words to express this thankfulness.

It may not have been Lou Gehrig, stricken with disease, saying good-bye to the Yankee faithful, but—given what we know of Clemente's death and legacy—it is no less substantial, no less important. Clemente left the game to a standing ovation in the eighth. Afterward, awed reporters who had had no idea of the breadth of Clemente's following asked him how it felt to be out there. Clemente recounted his emotions, how his entire life passed before his eyes while looking at the field. He then said in a fit of poetry, "In a moment like this, your mind is a circular stage. You can see a lot of years in a few minutes. You can see everything firm and you can see everything clear."

The World Series

"Roberto Clemente Night" was part of a baseball tradition of easing baseball greats out to pasture. After all the accomplishments, Clemente was nearing the end of his career, but not before providing one more flash of greatness on the game's biggest stage.

The 1971 World Series was supposed to be a pitiful mismatch. The Baltimore Orioles—with four twenty-game-winning pitchers—were to make short work of the Pirates. One writer wrote about Pittsburgh's chances, "Now they'll learn about agony. Now they'll have to play the reigning champions of the universe and the light and dark sides of the moon." Sure enough, the Orioles crushed the Pirates in the first two games of the series in Baltimore. As Jim Murray, a *Los Angeles Times* sports columnist renowned for his subtlety, wrote, "This World Series is no longer a contest. It's an atrocity. It's the Germans marching through Belgium, the interrogation room of the Gestapo. It's as one-sided as a Russian trial.... To enjoy it, you'd have to be the kind of person who goes to orphanage fires or sits at washed-out railroad bridges with a camera. They're taking the execution to Pittsburgh today. Unless the Red Cross intervenes."

Despite the Orioles' success, Clemente had been stellar, extending his World Series hitting streak to nine games. The most famous play of his career took place in game two, when the thirty-seven-year-old right-fielder barehanded the ball on one hop and threw a 400-foot screamer to third base that never got more than seven feet off the ground. The runner was actually safe, but the throw was so otherwordly, so defiant of basic physics, that Pirates third baseman Richie Hebner said, "After that play was over, I was like, wow." Clemente spoke about the throw in great detail after the game. *New York Post* columnist Dick Young, a proud Archie Bunker type who railed against the counterculture, quoted Clemente phonetically, saying, "Eef I have my good arm thee ball gets there a leetle quicker than he gets there." In previous years, Clemente would have seen that and steamed. But at this point in his career, playing on a multicultural, multilingual club, he was too much of a team leader to care. Instead of reacting, he stayed loose and kept his flailing team up by telling everyone, "We're gonna do it. We're going back to Pittsburgh. We're gonna do it."

In Pittsburgh, Clemente was unstoppable, knocking hits at will. He was so hot, the team organist played "Jesus Christ Superstar" when he came up to bat (something else that might get you ejected from the park in today's major leagues). He was the oldest man on the field, outplaying opponents and teammates almost half his age. Even Dick Young wrote, "The best damn ballplayer in the World Series, maybe in the whole world, is Roberto Clemente." Young's base may have choked reading those words.

Clemente led the Pirates all the way back, winning the series in seven games. He smacked a hit in every game, finishing with a .414 average and the series MVP. Clemente cemented his legend and transcendence in Latin America in the post-game celebration when television reporters asked for comment: "Before I say anything in English, I would like to say something in Spanish to my mother and father in Puerto Rico." His words were simple: *"En el día más grande de mi vida, para los nenes la benedición mia y que mis padres me échen la benedición."* [In the most important day of my life, I give blessings to my boys and ask that my parents give their blessing.] Not exactly the "I Have a Dream" speech, but it didn't have to be. It was simply Roberto Clemente including an entire culture and redefining the word "America" in "America's pastime."

Clemente's Dream

That off-season, Clemente used his fame to speak to audiences about his desire to build a sports city for Puerto Rico's poor. This wasn't a dream of charity but of social transformation. In one speech Clemente said,

> The World Series is the greatest thing that ever happened to me in baseball. It gives me a chance to talk to writers more than before. I don't want anything for myself, but through me I can help lots of people. They spend millions of dollars for dope control in Puerto Rico. But they attack the problem after the problem is there. Why don't they attack it before it starts? You try to get kids so they don't become addicts, and it would help to get them interested in sports and give them somewhere to learn to play them.

Clemente would cry openly and without shame as he talked about this dream, saying that he would "quit baseball tomorrow" if he had the money to oversee the project. In Puerto Rico, he urged his audiences—particularly working poor audiences—to help him with the project. Their full participation in the overhaul of society was a vision that Clemente embraced, and it endeared him to an audience fully aware that Clemente now had the money and fame to live in a mansion and never see them again.

Clemente's last season, 1972, started with a players' strike, the first of the new association. It was a strong victory. The Pirates, in a union town, were union supporters, a position helped by Clemente. He lived with the rookies in spring training—before the strike was official—and talked to the young players about the union and their responsibilities to their fellow players. That season would not be magic for the Pirates, but it did include Clemente's 3,000th hit, a frozen-rope double on September 29. Clemente was only the eleventh player to reach that number. It was a guarantee that he would become the first Latino to be enshrined in the Hall of Fame. He also won his twelfth Gold Glove that year and became the all-time leader in games played for the Pirates, surpassing Honus Wagner. Not bad for someone execs feared was an injury-prone head case. There were rumors that Clemente would retire, but he said that, whatever he did, it wouldn't be for the money. "I only want to have my health so I can work. I don't care if I'm a janitor. I don't care if I drive a cab…. I can be a person like me because I live the life of a common person…. I just worry that I be healthy and live long enough to educate my sons and make them respect people. And to me, this is my biggest worry: to live for my kids."

Unnatural Disasters

That December 23, an earthquake gutted Nicaragua. It hit 6.5 on the Richter scale, crushing 350 square blocks while killing and injuring thousands. The horror of this natural disaster was compounded by the unnatural nexus of Richard Nixon and Nicaragua's military leader Anastasio Somoza. Somoza was an anticommunist zealot whose family has stolen 25 percent of Nicaragua's wealth over the years, murdering and torturing anyone who got in their way. All of this was done for decades with the full financial and moral support of the U.S. government. It was Somoza's father about whom, legend has it, President Franklin D. Roosevelt remarked, "Somoza may be a son of a bitch, but he's our son of a bitch." Somoza Jr. was certainly Nixon's SOB. Somoza had even written a letter earlier in 1972 nominating Tricky Dick for the Nobel Peace Prize.

Thanks to Nixon's elaborate obsession with audio technology, we know that his immediate concern after the earthquake was not the horrific loss of life in Nicaragua, but rather that the country would "go Communist" in the ensuing chaos. Instead of providing relief, he sent in paratroopers to help the Nicaraguan National Guard keep order. Somoza had issued "shoot to kill" orders against anyone foraging for food, but not before shutting down all the service agencies that were feeding people and preventing them from respecting his curfew. One doctor reported, "I had more individuals that I treated who were shot [than who were injured by effects of the earthquake]. They were shot for looting. It was amazing. Young kids. I remember operating on young kids to remove bullets."

Roberto Clemente had many friends in Nicaragua. He also was haunted by the thoughts of the children he had visited there over the years. Were they dead? Alive? He had no idea. In twenty-four hours' time, Clemente had set up the Roberto Clemente Relief Committee for Nicaragua. Fear for his friends was supplanted by fury when he heard stories of Somoza's troops seizing aid for their own enrichment. One friend returned to Puerto Rico with a story that he stopped Somoza's troops from seizing his supplies by saying, "If you take this, I will tell the great Roberto Clemente what you did!" Clemente took from this that he himself would have to go to Nicaragua to make sure the aid got where it was supposed to go.

On December 31, 1972, he boarded a ramshackle plane, with more than 4,000 extra pounds on board. A friend tried to warn Clemente that it was unsafe, but in the urgency of the crisis his phobia of planes seemed to have left him. "You [could] even die riding a horse," he responded. The plane went down a thousand yards out to sea and Clemente's body was never recovered. His young boys were six, five, and two. The outpouring of emotion was overwhelming, and thousands of mourners flocked to the Clemente family home. Eleven weeks later, Clemente was elected to the Baseball Hall of Fame, joining

Gehrig as one of the only players who didn't have to wait five years for enshrinement. Vera gave the speech, her three sons looking on. One writer said of Clemente that he was so graceful and beautiful that "he made me wish I was Shakespeare." Puerto Rican poet Elliot Castro wrote that "the night Roberto Clemente left us physically, his immortality began."

Legacy

When Jackie Robinson broke Major League Baseball's color line in 1947, baseball ceased to be just a game. In the dark years of McCarthyism, as his biographer Arnold Rampersad wrote, "only Jackie Robinson insisted day in and day out on challenging America on questions of race and justice." As Martin Luther King said of Robinson, "He was a sit-inner before sit-ins. A freedom rider before freedom rides." In 1997, on the fiftieth anniversary of Robinson's rookie season, MLB commissioner Bud Selig marked Robinson's achievement by taking the unprecedented step of retiring his number, 42, from the league.

Recently, Hispanics Across America (HAA) appealed to the league to retire Clemente's 21, as well. But the effort to honor Clemente in this way has met resistance from a surprising source: Jackie Robinson's daughter Sharon. In January of 2006, she said, "To my understanding, the purpose of retiring my father's number is that what he did changed all of baseball, not only for African Americans but also for Latinos, so I think that purpose has been met. When you start retiring numbers across the board, for all different groups, you're kind of diluting the original purpose."

The place of Blacks and Latinos in baseball is a highly sensitive one. Twenty years ago, African Americans comprised 27 percent of the game's players; today they represent just 8.5 percent. In 2005, the Houston Astros became the first team since the days of Robinson to make the World Series without one African-American player. Latinos, according to 2005 rosters, represent 37 percent of players. Honoring Clemente, the HAA feels, is a way of honoring the role they play in today's game. HAA president Fernando Mateo responded to Sharon Robinson quite sharply, saying, "We as an organization and a community are surprised that Jackie Robinson's daughter would publicly address the retirement of Roberto Clemente's number or say it should not be retired. We believe it is self-serving of her to inject her personal views simply to keep her legendary father's number the only one in retirement."

Sergio Rodriguez, host of ESPN Radio's *Orlando Sports Caliente,* told me,

> This shouldn't be about pitting one group of people against another. Racism in this country did not end the day Jackie Robinson put on a Dodgers uniform. Robinson accomplished something phenomenal. But Roberto Clemente continued and carried that same achievement. People should realize that twenty years from now the majority of major league players are going to be Latino. Where did this all begin? It starts with Clemente. Every Latino superstar who plays now—Carlos Beltran, Alex Rodriguez, Carlos Delgado—owes this debt to Clemente. He is the one who broke down the doors to this modern era.

The heroic circumstances of Clemente's death merit special recognition, according to his supporters. As Rodriguez says, "Clemente was proud to be Puerto Rican, but even when he was alive he was about uplifting all of Latin America and the Latin American community. That's why he died going to Nicaragua with supplies, a country far from his own. He was a Hall of Fame player and a better human being."

Yet there are people who feel that Robinson holds a unique place in baseball history that needs to be honored uniquely. Richard Zamoff, who teaches a course at George Washington University called "Jackie Robinson: Race, Sports and the American Dream," told me,

Jackie Robinson as a historical figure stands alone. While both Robinson and Clemente were trailblazers, Jackie knew from the beginning that he had the weight of an entire race on his shoulders. Clemente came to this role near the end of his baseball career, and he was one of many Latin players to share the trailblazing role. Perhaps an honor that would speak more directly to his contribution would be to give one player in each league the privilege of wearing number 21 on his uniform to honor Roberto Clemente's legacy and his commitment to the ideals of national and international service.

In my view, Clemente and Robinson should be honored identically because it would cut against the idea that Blacks and Latinos need to compete with each other for equality—an idea that serves the owners and those who would pit them against each other and not the players or minority groups more generally.

We should support the retiring of Clemente's number because it could move fans closer to accepting the contributions made by Latinos to the game. It could be a statement against the current climate in baseball where many Latino players often feel mocked and marginalized. It could also be a counter to the anti-immigrant hysteria in Congress and provide inspiration to those building new movements for civil rights.

These are goals that I believe Jackie Robinson would have supported as part of his life's work to make baseball and the United States a more inclusive place. They are also goals for which Roberto Clemente lived and died. He, like Robinson, was far more than a number. He represents the idea that we can inspire each other's battles for social justice as well as the idea that unity, not division, is the natural logic of struggle. This is seen very clearly in an obituary that appeared in the days after Clemente's death—an obit that ran in the newspaper of the Black Panthers. The Panthers thanked Clemente for supporting the breakfast programs and health clinics operated by their Philadelphia chapter. They wrote, "Roberto unhesitatingly donated to the Survival Programs and showed a keen interest in their progress."

They end the obit by writing, "It is ironic that the profession in which he achieved 'legendry' knew him the least. Roberto Clemente did not, as the commissioner of baseball maintained, 'Have about him a touch of royalty.' Roberto Clemente was simply a man, a man who strove to achieve his dream of peace and justice for oppressed people throughout the world." If we can't recapture and reorganize this kind of unity today, it will remain a dream deferred.

CHAPTER TWO

Béisbol: How the Major Leagues Eat Their Young

"Marines shouldered bats next to their rifles when they imposed imperial order in a region by blood and fire. Baseball then became for the people of the Caribbean what soccer is to us."

—Eduardo Galeano

The prodigal holiday hath returned. In 2006, mass May Day protests came back to the United States with a delicious twist: they were led by people born beyond its borders. May Day 2006 was called the "Great American Boycott," "A Day Without Immigrants," or "A Day Without Latinos." It was a day when immigrant laborers and their allies removed their labor and purchasing power from the economic workings of the United States and hit the streets to stand up for their rights.

While countless worksites were hampered by these actions, one multibillion-dollar enterprise that could have been humbled emerged unscathed: "The Great American Pastime" itself, Major League Baseball. This is a shame. The ballpark could have been the scene of "A Day Without Pujols."

MLB is adored by politicians of all stripes since throwing out the first pitch is a surefire way to get good press and cheap applause from a friendly crowd. (Unless you're Dick Cheney and can't throw a ball twenty feet. Then it's lusty boos for you and "wiretap day" for all 30,000 people in attendance.) Right-wing pundits like George

Will, who normally see immigrants, if they see them at all, as something to demonize, love writing about baseball being "the fabric of our nation." Without Latinos, this fabric would fray. Without Latinos, baseball would be about as interesting as being trapped in an elevator with, well, the aforementioned Mr. Will.

Of the top twenty hitters in the National League in 2006, eight were Latino, including 2005 Most Valuable Player Albert Pujols. In the American League, seven of the top ten were born outside the United States, five in Latin America. Latinos dominate the pantheon of the game's superstars like never before. Six of the last ten American League MVPs were Latino (and, in addition, there has been one Canadian, 2006 MVP Justin Morneau, and, in 2001, the Japanese Ichiro Suzuki). In the thirty years before that, the number was four (Jose Canseco, Willie Hernandez, George Bell, and Rod Carew). The 2006 World Baseball Classic showcased a U.S. team that couldn't compete with its Latin American or Asian rivals. The new reality was laid bare: a profound demographic shift that has saved Major League Baseball from the sporting scrap heap.

As of Opening Day 2005, 204 players born in Latin American countries were on Major League Baseball rosters, accounting for nearly 25 percent of all players. According to ESPN *Deportes,* this number will reach 50 percent in the next twenty years.

Of course, much of this is a function of major league owners searching for talent on the cheap, setting up baseball academies south of the border where players can be signed in their early teens for pennies and then discarded if they don't make the cut. As one player said to me, "The options in the [Dominican Republic] are jail, the army, the factory, or baseball." Many prospects make it to the United States for minor league ball and then stay, illegally, to chase the dream of being worked to death in a factory. The outer boroughs of New York City are filled with semipro teams of men on the other side of thirty still thirsting for that contract, praying they can stay hot at the plate before the revamped and recently renamed Immigration and Customs Enforcement (ICE—formerly the INS) comes knocking on their door.

No major league player came out publicly to join the national boycott. Doing so would have been more than a mere act of solidarity. Despite the prominent role they play in the game, few Latinos hold prominent positions off the field. *Very* few: one owner, one general manager, and a handful of managers. Players routinely speak about being denigrated by the press and mocked by reporters for their lack of English skills. As All-Star Moises Alou said last year, "In the minor leagues, people think all Dominicans, Mexicans, and Venezuelans are dumb. You think if a guy doesn't speak English, it's because he's stupid. You go to the Dominican and try to have conversation in Spanish, and see how easy it is."

Today, players born outside the States are in a position to play a stronger role in shaping the future of the sport, due to their numbers and the quality of their play. They are in a position to demand inclusion but also respect. They have the ability to determine how their "cultural capital" is spent.

If they don't, if the owners continue to hold a monopoly on the future of the sport, we will be subjected to more ugly nationalist forays like the World Baseball Classic. The WBC was an unprecedented tournament, involving sixteen nations with players representing the countries of their birth. It was meant to be a kind of World Cup of baseball. According to MLB commissioner Bud Selig, "The reason for the [World Baseball Classic] is to further promote grassroots development in traditional and nontraditional baseball nations. The tournament's primary objectives are to increase global interest and introduce new fans and players to the game."

Despite Selig's intentions, what the WBC provided was a terrific example of the clumsy way baseball is trying to be a player in the globalization of sports. And although the stated goals of the project ring amazingly hollow—like saying George Lucas created Jar Jar Binks to promote multiculturalism—the significance of the heavily hyped tournament demands examination. The WBC was baseball's way of coming to terms with its own identity crisis. Baseball, as we are endlessly told, is "America's pastime." Yet increasingly, baseball's "America" is not from California to the New York islands but from Caracas to Saipan.

This stubbornly provincial sport now has an international roster of superstars. But unlike the NBA, the Major League Baseball brand is financially nonexistent as a global commodity. The sport of baseball may be thriving in different parts of the world, but where it does it eludes major league corporate control. The World Baseball Classic was meant to be a step toward changing that reality. Yet, as they extended their hands to the world, Selig and company also wanted the WBC to showcase U.S. might, assuring fans that while the face—and language—of the game is changing, the homegrown talent reigns supreme. There was only one problem: the rest of the world didn't get the memo. In fact, the U.S. talent pool on display was exposed as dangerously shallow. As sportswriter Jeff Passan wrote, "Don't call them Team USA anymore. They're not worthy.... [T]his is Team U, which could stand for Underperforming or Uninspired or plain-old Ugly."

The team floundered despite a setup so rigged it might as well have been sponsored by Diebold. The U.S. squad was in a bracket where it didn't have to play the powerhouse teams from Latin America until the later rounds. On top of this, 67 percent of the umpires were from the United States, *and* the team had home-field advantage throughout. They simply choked on their silver spoon.

But the U.S. belly flop was not the only storyline of the WBC.

Like all sporting events that pit countries against one another, political posturing was on display even before the games began. The White House Gang, through the Treasury Department, initially denied the Cuban team entry into the United States. After the Cuban minister of sports pledged that any money received from the tournament would be donated to victims of Hurricane Katrina, and in the midst of international derision for such profound pettiness, the White House backed down. Former Bush spokesman Scott McClellan—always good for a chuckle—said, "Our concerns were centered on making sure that no money was going to the Castro regime and that the World Baseball Classic would not be misused by the regime for spying. We believe the concerns have been addressed."

This WBC controversy snowballed when the Cuban team played Puerto Rico and a fan held up a sign that read "Abajo Castro" ("Down with Castro") behind home plate. Angel Iglesias, vice president of Cuba's National Institute of Sports, tore the sign from the fan's hands. Iglesias was shuttled to a nearby police station where the Puerto Rican police, according to the Associated Press, "lectured him about free speech."

The irony is rather thick. During the WBC, ESPN's broadcasts closely resembled propaganda that would shame Castro's minions. The "worldwide leader of sports" incessantly and mind-numbingly referred to Cuba as the "only country here that is under a dictator." They even had a Cuban defector doing commentary. And while Cuba was called a nation "under a dictator," China was given a political pass. As a colleague of mine said, "The only time it seems politics are allowed to intrude is when the sentiment is anti-Castro." Washington's bipartisan post–Cold War standard of the carrot for China and the stick for Cuba was once again reflected in sports coverage.

In the end, the United States finished eighth, behind Japan, Cuba, Korea, the Dominican Republic, Puerto Rico, Mexico, and Venezuela. Far from exporting the Major League Brand, the WBC only served to remind the world how dependent the future of Major League Baseball is on international players. This presents an opportunity for the Latino baseball world to make demands on how players from Latin America are both treated and compensated from their first signing. These are demands that are desperately needed if young Latin American players are to be treated like human beings and not global commodities: easily acquired, easily disposed.

The Death of Super Mario

If Selig would dare allow himself to see the human costs of Major League Baseball's global sports dystopia, he would have to look no further than the late Mario Encarnación. In early October 2005, thirty-year-old Mario Encarnación, who played for Taiwan's Macoto Cobras, was found dead in his Taipei dormitory room from causes unknown. His lonely and mysterious death, with the lights on and the refrigerator door open, ended a tragic journey that began in the dirt-poor town of Bani in the Dominican Republic, and concluded on the other side of the world. In between, Encarnación, or "Super Mario," as he was known on the baseball diamond, was the most highly touted prospect in the Oakland A's organization, once considered better than American League Most Valuable Player Miguel Tejada. Tejada, also from Bani, paid the freight to bring his friend home from Taiwan. It's hard to imagine who else from their barrio could have managed to foot the bill.

Encarnación's death was not even a sidebar in the sports pages of the United States. A thirty-year-old playing out his last days in East Asia might as well be invisible. But if Selig and company won't bear witness to Mario Encarnación, we should—because the Dominican Republic now stands as the leading "exporter" of international baseball talent. Just five years ago, there were sixty-six Dominican-born players on opening day rosters. In 2006, there were more than one hundred. This means roughly one out of every seven major league players was born in the D.R., by far the highest number from any country outside the United States. In addition, 30 percent of players in the U.S. minor leagues hail from this tiny Latin American nation, which shares an island with Haiti and has a population roughly the size of New York City's.

All thirty teams now scout what baseball owners commonly call "the Republic of Baseball," and, as noted earlier, a number of teams have elaborate multimillion-dollar "baseball academies" in the D.R. The teams trumpet these academies in a typically enlightened fashion; as one executive put it, "We have made Fields of Dreams out of the jungle." But unmentioned is the fact that for every Tejada there are a hundred Encarnaciós. And for every Encarnación toiling on the margins of the pro baseball circuit, there are thousands of Dominican players cast aside by a Major League Baseball system that is harvesting talent on the cheap with no responsibility for those who get left behind. Unmentioned is what Major League Baseball is doing—or not doing— for a country with 60 percent of its population living below the poverty line. As American sports agent Joe Kehoskie says in *Stealing Home,* a PBS documentary, "Traditionally in the Latin market, I would say players sign for about 5 to 10 cents on the dollar compared to their U.S. counterparts." He also points out that "a lot of times kids just quit school at ten, eleven, twelve, and play baseball full time. It's great, it's great for the kids that make it because they become superstars and get millions of dollars in the big leagues. But for ninety-eight kids out of one hundred, it results in a kid that is eighteen, nineteen, with no education."

Considering both the poverty rate and the endless trumpeting of rags-to-riches stories of those like Sammy Sosa and Tejada, it's no wonder the academies are so attractive to young Dominicans. Most young athletes in the D.R. play without shoes, using cut-out milk cartons for gloves, rolled-up cloth for balls, and sticks and branches for bats. The academies offer good equipment, nice uniforms, and the dream of a better life.

Sacramento Bee sportswriter Marcos Bretón's book, *Home Is Everything: The Latino Baseball Story,* highlights the appeal of the academies:

> Teams house their players in dormitories and feed their prospects balanced meals. Often it's the first time these boys will sleep under clean sheets or eat nutritious meals. The firsts don't stop there: Some of these boys encounter a toilet for the first time. Or an indoor shower. They are taught discipline, the importance of being on time, of following instructions.

Competition to get into these "baseball factories" is fierce. In *Stealing Home,* sports anthropologist Alan Klein describes the scene in front of one of the academies:

> Every morning you would drive to the Academy, you would see fifteen, twenty kids out there, not one of them had a uniform, they all had pieces of one uniform or another, poor equipment, they would be right at the gate waiting for the security people to open up the gates and they would go in for their tryout. If they got signed, they were happy. If they didn't get signed, it didn't even deter them for a minute; they would be on the road hitchhiking to the next location. And they would eventually find one of those twenty-some clubs that would eventually pick them up. And if not, then they might return to amateur baseball.

Yet even the ones who make it through the academy doors often find themselves little more than supporting players in a system designed to help pro teams ferret out the few potential stars. As Roberto González Echevarría, a Cuban baseball historian who also appears in the documentary, says,

> I take a dim view of what the major leagues are doing in the Dominican Republic with these so-called baseball academies, where children are being signed at a very early age and not being cared for. Most of them are providing the context for the stars to emerge; if you take a hundred baseball players in those academies, or a hundred baseball players anywhere, only one of them

will play even an inning in the major leagues. The others are there as a supporting cast.

What's more, little is done to protect the select few who make it into a major league farm system from the likely fall to the hard concrete floor of failure. Brendan Sullivan III, a pitcher who played five seasons for the San Diego Padres, told author Colman McCarthy,

> Sure, they were thrilled to have gone from dirt lots to playing in a U.S. stadium before fans and getting paychecks every two weeks. But once a team decides a Dominican won't make it to the big leagues, he is discarded as an unprofitable resource. That's true for U.S. players, but at least they have a high school diploma, and often college, and thus have fallback skills. Most Dominicans don't. They go home to the poverty they came from or try to eke out an existence at menial labor in the States, with nothing left over except tales of their playing days chasing the dream.

Major League Baseball seems unconcerned and uninterested in a situation it had a central role in shaping. Boston Red Sox owner John Henry speaks of the "special relationship Major League Baseball has with the people of the Dominican Republic," but it's unclear whether he believes the BoSox and Major League Baseball have any responsibilities regarding the players they employ and the families left behind.

Al Avila, assistant general manager of the Detroit Tigers, whose father, Ralph, operated the Los Angeles Dodgers' Dominican academy for decades, told ESPN.com,

> Baseball is the best way out of poverty for most of these kids and their families. They see on television and read in the newspapers how many of their countrymen have made it. For parents that have kids, they have them playing from early on. The numbers show that the dream is within reach. And even if they don't make it, these Dominican academies house, feed…and educate these kids in English. They become acclimated to a new culture, which is always positive. At the very least, even if they don't make it as a player, they could get different doors opened, like becoming a coach.

The question we need to ask is this: Does baseball have a broader responsibility to the Dominican Republic and these ten- and eleven-year-old kids who think they have a better chance of emerging from desperately poor conditions with a stick and a milk-carton glove than by staying in school? Does a highly profitable organization like Major League Baseball have an obligation to cushion the crash landing that awaits 99.9 percent of D.R. kids with big-league dreams, or the 95 percent of players who are good enough to be chosen for the academy but are summarily discarded with nothing but a kick out the door? We can probably surmise where the family and friends of Mario Encarnación fall on this question.

The death of "Super Mario" went unnoticed in the U.S. press with one exception, a heart-wrenching column on October 6, 2005, in the *Sacramento Bee* by his friend Marcos Bretón, who wrote, "Mario wasn't a warped athlete like we've come to expect in most ballplayers. He was big-hearted, fun-loving, a good friend.… The pressure of succeeding and lifting his family out of poverty was a weight that soon stooped Encarnación's massive shoulders."

Another question that must be asked is: Should it have been Mario's responsibility to shoulder such a burden alone? These fifteen-year-old kids signed for a pittance must not be treated like speed bumps on the globalization express. If Major League Baseball is going to pull these kids out of their communities at such a young age, then they have a responsibility to provide them with a real education. If they are going to sign them to an amateur contract, then the money they make should be commensurate with what U.S. players are making. But any idea that reaches into the pockets of George Steinbrenner and his ilk will not be received with good cheer. This means that it won't happen without a fight and those who have made it to the majors—Pedro Martinez, David Ortiz, Miguel

Tejada, who unlike their young brothers are unionized—are in the best position to demand that baseball not merely strip-mine the D.R. of its baseball talent and ambition, but give something back to those who can't turn on a 96 mph fastball. That is what is called globalization from below: accept the new global commercial realities, but also demand that social justice and human rights accompany those realities.

◆ ◆ ◆ ◆

Players seeking change can gain inspiration from Latino stars who have had the courage to speak out, athletes who put out their necks and endure the heat. Unfortunately, a courageous leading light took a step backward in 2006 when Carlos Delgado, one of the most outspoken stars of his generation, allowed himself to be silenced.

Sometimes sports mirrors politics with such morbid accuracy you don't know whether to laugh, cry, or hide in the basement. Just as the Bush administration shows its commitment to democracy by operating secret offshore gulags, the New York Mets made it clear when Carlos Delgado joined them at the beginning of the 2006 season that freedom of speech stops once the blue and orange uniform—their brand—is affixed to his body.

For the previous two years, Delgado had chosen to follow the steps of his personal hero, Roberto Clemente, and use his athletic platform to speak out for social justice. Clemente, as we saw, never accepted being treated as anything less than human. Delgado's contribution to this tradition was to refuse to stand for the singing of "God Bless America" during the seventh-inning stretch. This was his act of resistance to the war in Iraq. "I think it's the stupidest war ever. Who are you fighting against? You're just getting ambushed now," Delgado told the

Toronto Star in 2004. "We have more people dead now, after the war, than during the war. You've been looking for weapons of mass destruction. Where are they at? You've been looking for over a year. Can't find them. I don't support that. I don't support what they do. I think it's just stupid."

Delgado's antimilitarist convictions grew from spending time and money to help clean up the small island of Vieques in his native Puerto Rico. The U.S. Navy had used Vieques for decades as a bombing-practice target, with disastrous results for the people and environment. When asked by the *Star* if he was concerned about taking such a public stance, Delgado, then a player for the Toronto Blue Jays, responded, "Sometimes, you've just got to break the mold. You've got to push it a little bit or else you can't get anything done."

But then Mets management pushed Delgado back into the shadows. The shame of this is that, despite a guaranteed contract and support in the streets, Delgado didn't push back. He said at the press conference announcing his trade to the Mets from the Florida Marlins, "The Mets have a policy that everybody should stand for 'God Bless America' and I will be there. I will not cause any distractions to the ball club.... Just call me Employee Number 21." And we saw him grin and bear it when Jeff Wilpon, son of Fred Wilpon, Mets CEO and owner, said, "He's going to have his own personal views, which he's going to keep to himself."

If opposition to the war were a stock, Delgado bought high and sold low. There couldn't be a better time than when 70 percent of the country opposes the war, a better place than New York City, or a better team than the Mets for Delgado to make his stand. Instead, he had to hear baby-boy Wilpon say to reporters, "Fred [yes, he calls his father "Fred"] has asked and I've asked him to respect what the country wants to do." One has to wonder what country the Wilpons were talking about. At the time, polls showed Bush and his war meeting with subterranean levels of support. Delgado could have been an important voice in the effort to end it once and for all.

He also might have received significant organizational support from Mets general manager Omar Minaya, the first Latino GM in major league history, and from Willie Randolph, the first African-American manager for the Mets. Randolph even told reporters, "I'd rather have a man who's going to stand up and say what he believes. We have a right as Americans to voice that opinion." Minaya merely commented curtly, with an arctic chill, "This is from ownership." But Delgado still caved.

Ever true to their own hypocrisy, the mainstream media attacked Delgado for refusing to continue his act of protest. If they had supported his stance to begin with, it would not be so galling to see, for example, *New York Newsday*'s Wallace Matthews write, "Even if you disagree with his politics, Delgado's willingness to break out of the mold corporate America loves to jam us in set him apart from the thousands of interchangeable young men who thrive athletically and financially in our sports-crazed culture.... But no. One of the few pro athletes who had the guts to say no is now a yes man. And the silencing of his voice, whether you agree with it or not, is not a victory for democracy but a defeat." But where was Matthews when the then-protesting Delgado was being booed as a visiting player in New York? When radio commentators suggested he "just shut up and play"?

Ironically, one of the parts of the press conference that was genuinely touching was Delgado's thrill at finally being able to wear the number 21, the number of his hero, the great Roberto Clemente. To Clemente, the Wilpons of the world were little more than mosquitoes buzzing about his ears. Delgado could have been our Clemente. Instead, to use his own words, he is just Employee Number 21.

This could still change. In an interview with *Vibe* magazine, Delgado said,

Let me make one point clear: I haven't changed my mind. It's not like I don't think the same way. I still feel the same way about the war [against Iraq]; I am against the war. But there are a couple of things that you have to consider. I am a baseball player and I want to have a chance to win. I am going to a team that has certain rules, but those rules aren't going to change the way that I think. I have to be smart with what I do. Drawing attention will distract from what I am trying to do which is win. Obviously people are going to criticize you one way or the other, but like I said you have to make a decision. That doesn't mean that I now agree with playing "God Bless America" especially in conjunction to war celebrations, I still think one thing doesn't have to do with another and I still feel the same way. Obviously I kind of want to be careful about drawing attention to myself. I am not going to put myself in front of the team. That doesn't change the way that I think.

But thoughts without deeds wither on the vine. Also, remember that Clemente won two World Series, Kareem won six championships, and Bill Russell won eleven. The idea that politics are a "distraction" to the goals of winning is pure fiction. And it is a fiction that any supporter of Clemente should know well.

◆ ◆ ◆ ◆

If 2005 saw Delgado sit out this round of struggle, it fortunately also saw seventy-year-old Giants manager Felipe Alou show the young folks how it's done. In a climate of anti-immigrant, Latino-bashing, border-patrolling, right-wing intolerance, Alou stood up. For those who know him, this came as no surprise. Alou, who has stared down the U.S. Marines, the Jim Crow South, and Major League Baseball, will give no quarter to racism, especially when it's coming from just another dime-store, right-wing microphone jockey trying to make a name on his back.

Former San Francisco KNBR "radio personality" Larry Krueger learned this when he described the San Francisco Giants as "brain-dead Caribbean hitters hacking at slop nightly" and then characterized Alou as having "cream of wheat in his brain." Krueger thought that his comments would pass unnoticed. But in taking on Alou, Krueger proved painfully overmatched.

Alou was the first Dominican player ever to play in the majors. Couple that with his dark complexion and a minor league stint in Louisiana, and Alou's intro to the United States afforded him "a depth of racism I never saw in the Dominican Republic." While the rest of his team dined in segregated restaurants and stayed in "whites-only" hotels, Alou ate meals on the team bus and scrounged for housing. But Alou never let it beat him down. "I was never scared. Some of my [Black] teammates were, but I was proud of who I was and where I was from." As a minor leaguer in Louisiana, Alou wouldn't listen when bus drivers would tell him to take his seat in the back, pretending not to speak English and refusing to budge.

This didn't stop in the minors. When Felipe played for the Giants with his brothers Jesús and Matty, it took just one losing streak for manager Alvin Dark to say, "We have trouble because we have too many Negro and Spanish-speaking players on this team. They're just not able to perform up to the white players when it comes to mental alertness."

Alou struck back by campaigning for Major League Baseball to hire a person in charge of ensuring the welfare of Latin American players. He succeeded in 1965, when Commissioner William D. Eckert hired Cuban-born Bobby Maduro for the newly created role. "Felipe went through a lot of trouble not just for Matty and me but a lot of Dominicans as a black Latin player," remembers Jesús. "He went through a lot to clear the path for others."

Alou's politicization continued when he experienced first-hand the U.S. Marine occupation of the Dominican Republic in 1965. "Hopefully it will be the only time I will have to confront soldiers from another country," he said in a recent interview.

"We lived for months under occupation from foreign soldiers. You just can't ignore that."

Not surprisingly, then, Alou's response to Larry Krueger was immediate, political, and refreshingly unforgiving. "It made me sad to know that 40, almost 50 years later, we have comments like that, especially in San Francisco," he said. "There are more countries [represented] in San Francisco now than when I was a player here and I never heard anything like that. I heard it in the South and in some other cities, but not here. A man like me and the Latin guys out there, we have to be aware now that [racism] is not over yet. It is coming back."

His son Moises, as we've already seen, also has voiced these frustrations. The pent-up anger felt by many Latino players explains why Felipe Alou rebuffed Krueger's efforts to apologize. "I know this individual came to apologize to me. Are you kidding? There is no way to apologize for that kind of thing. If I say I accept it, the Latin players will never forgive me. There's no way to apologize for such a sin." Alou also asked people to consider how many countries comprise the Caribbean, and said, "All of these people were offended by that idiot."

In case anyone missed the point, Alou also said that he would no longer do his pregame radio spot with the station. "My voice and the voices of others can't be coming out of the same wave," he said. "No way. I am a man of principle. I always have been and always will be."

Thanks to Alou's principles, Krueger got canned. And now Alou, in the eyes of certain representatives of the sports industrial complex, is—bizarrely, shamefully, and predictably—the bad guy and Krueger has been morphed into Mario Savio with gravy stains: a free-speech martyr sacrificed on the altar of "political correctness."

When Krueger was given the boot, Alou was sympathetic but remained firm. "I feel bad about people being fired. It wasn't my intention, but I didn't start it and I took a stand. I want people to understand that [racism] is a social issue. I want to make people aware of that so they will know that in the United States, it won't be tolerated."

But it is exactly this antiracism that met with a tide of intolerance. The mainstream media called Alou "divisive," "venomous," and even "Machiavellian." In one theory that oozed its way through talk radio, Alou masterfully used the uproar to draw attention from the Giants' hideous season. The real students of Machiavelli, however, are those who reframed the debate to be about Alou instead of the issues he was striving to bring to light.

As Chuck Carlson wrote in the Reno *Gazette-Journal*,

> Felipe Alou's bizarre reaction has only hurt his case for racial sensitivity in this country.... [I]n this instance, Alou looks like an overwrought bully who may need his own course in sensitivity training. Should Krueger have said it? Of course not. It was a dopey comment said for a cheap laugh and it's done a thousand times a day in a thousand different places.... [T]he truly strange part of this story is how Alou has reacted.

Carlson is absolutely right that racism raises its ugly head "a thousand times a day in a thousand different places." But to him and his ilk, injustice is the tolerable status quo. To actually speak out is "truly strange" and "bizarre." It's like George W. Bush whining at Cindy Sheehan for ruining his vacation.

Meanwhile, Krueger has been called a "sacrificial lamb" destroyed by "political correctness." In the words of Gary Radnich, a San Francisco television sportscaster, "Felipe Alou got rolling, got a head of steam up, and in this politically correct world, you don't get a second chance any more."

Another writer claimed that Krueger is being railroaded because he is some kind of populist hero. "KNBR is the Giants' flagship station but Krueger's opinions aren't always popular with the suits and ties. It makes you wonder if the Giants are trying to rid themselves of their most outspoken critic."

San Francisco Giants manager Felipe Alou looks on at a 2006 game against the Cincinnati Reds (AP/Al Behrman)

This, simply, is a rotten red herring. The issue is not whether Alou "went too far," but the banal, persistent, thudding reality of racism in the United States. Every day, on both sports and talk radio, gallons of racist spew are projected across the airwaves. Every day we condition ourselves to just ignore it, absorb it, and move on. Alou, to his eternal credit, refused to play that game.

He stood tall and attempted to shine the brightest light possible on some deeply ugly ideas. One of the points that had his detractors in a lather was when he called Krueger a "messenger of Satan." Asked if he didn't think the statement about Satan was too harsh, Alou explained, "I didn't call him Satan and I never would. I said he was a *messenger* of Satan, because his message was a message of division. We should be past all that after so many years."

I was asked on sports radio if the Satan remark was somehow "worse" than the statement about "brain-dead Caribbean hitters." The feeling was that Alou was somehow "meaner" than Krueger and therefore worthy of equal contempt. Once again, this goes back to having the most basic understanding of what racism is and is not. Racism is not about hurtful words, bruised feelings, "political correctness," or refusing to call short people "vertically challenged." Racism is about power. To be Latino in the United States today means living with a bull's-eye on your back. In California, it means living in a state where the Republican governor welcomes an armed militia to hunt you down at the border. In New Mexico, it means Democratic governor Bill Richardson declaring a "state of emergency" to appeal for the National Guard to stop "the flood" of "illegals." Right now, anti-immigrant fearmongering is political gold. Alou referenced this racist renaissance when he said, "We're not out of the woods yet, and the thick wood is coming." To ignore the "thick wood" means to invite a knock on the head. Our hope for the future lies in doing exactly what Alou did: calling out racism as loudly and sharply as possible, without regret and without a pause. As Alou's friend, Hall of Fame slugger Orlando Cepeda, said, "Trust me, you have to fight. When people are wrong, you've got to let them know it."

This idea that justice and unity must confront both racism and the cold march of commerce applies not only to the treatment of Latinos, but also the African-American baseball talent pool in the United States. It's a pool drying up from neglect. This came to light in gutsy fashion in 2005, from the mouth of then–L.A. Dodger Milton Bradley. Bradley, who has been mandated in the past to attend anger management classes, has been called everything from "perennially enflamed" to "certifiably insane." But in 2005, he was as calm as the Dead Sea when addressing reporters. Bradley sounded almost weary as he detailed the racial insensitivity of teammate Jeff Kent. "The problem is he doesn't know how to deal with African-American people," Bradley said. "I think that's what's causing everything. It's a pattern of things that have been said—things said off the cuff that I don't interpret as funny. It may be funny to him, but it's not funny to Milton Bradley."

Kent—who wears a wispy 1970s-style mustache that makes him look like someone who splashes on some Hai Karate before strutting to the free clinic—did himself no favors by using the "some of my best friends" defense: "If you think that I've got a problem with African Americans, then go talk to Dusty Baker. Go talk to Dave Winfield, who took me under his wing. Go talk to Joe Carter. All the guys…who taught me how to play this game."

Fortunately for Kent, the sound of his words faded quickly while Bradley's next comments echoed in Major League Baseball's executive suites: "Me being an African American is the most important thing to me—more important than baseball.

White people never want to see race—with anything. But there's race involved in baseball. That's why there's less than 9 percent African-American representation in the game." Then Bradley looked around the Dodgers clubhouse, where the air was once breathed by Jackie Robinson, Roy Campanella, and Don Newcombe, and muttered, "I'm one of the few African Americans that starts here."

The sports media, with a predictability rivaled only by the setting sun, proved Bradley's point by rushing to condemn his attempt to launch a "taboo discussion" about race. In Ryne Sandberg's baseball column, the recently minted Hall of Famer ran a letter from a fan that read, "[Bradley] says being black is more important to him than baseball. If it is, then he should leave baseball and get into something 'more black' that he feels comfortable with."

But in their rush to smear the messenger, the media ran roughshod over a critical message. African-American players indeed make up a mere 8.5 percent in the major leagues. In 1975 that number was 27 percent. Five teams—the Boston Red Sox, Baltimore Orioles, Houston Astros, Atlanta Braves, and Colorado Rockies—had no African Americans on their active rosters in 2005. At the end of the 2006 season, there were no African-American catchers and only five starting pitchers. This is a crisis that extends beyond "the talent pool" and "urban marketability." It's a crisis of history.

Today's baseball leadership says that they desperately want to reverse these trends, but the "leadership" of the major leagues has an uncanny ability to not actually lead. Commissioner Bud Selig, doing his best impression of Mr. Magoo, commented, "I've been puzzled [by the diminishing African-American base] for years, both in terms of talent and those attending games. There are no easy answers. It is a very complex issue."

Actually, it's not that complex. There are two main factors that have led to the decline of the African-American baseball player. The first is economic. As longtime major leaguer Royce Clayton said, "Many Black families can't afford for their children to play the sport, which requires the purchase of gloves, balls, bats, and other equipment as well as money to maintain playing fields." A low-priced set of baseball gear—a bat, a ball, some spiked shoes, a glove—costs about $75, while a $20 basketball or football can serve ten or more players. Then there is city upkeep of fields and leagues. In Washington, D.C., where I live, the public baseball diamonds are nobody's idea of fields of dreams. Instead, they're swamped in broken glass and neglect, with kitten-sized rats waddling around the bases, always heading for home.

Baseball's owners could have stepped in at any point in the last thirty years, as cost-cutters slashed city budgets and private investment in youth programs and upkeep remained modest. But they didn't, because MLB has all the new blood it needs flowing north in the form of cost-effective players from Latin America.

Sports sociologist Dr. Harry Edwards got it right when he said, "I'm convinced that the increase in Latin players is not because all of a sudden the leadership and hierarchy of baseball developed a love for Latins. It's about money.... I'm convinced, as Michael Corleone used to say, it's not personal. It's just business."

Baseball belatedly attempted to start a program in the inner cities similar to those it has set up in the Dominican Republic, opening a "factory" in South Central, Los Angeles, but this may be a case of too little too late. As Edwards said of such programs, "It's like pumping air into the lungs of a dead man. He needs life; he doesn't need air." In other words, building a baseball factory on top of the dilapidated infrastructure of today's inner cities is like putting a cherry on top of a melted ice cream sundae.

As Byron Jones, a Little League coach in Gary, Indiana, said to me:

> It breaks my heart seeing our pitchers dodging large indentations in the mound to keep from breaking their ankles; pitchers including my own son. Yes, it's definitely the economics that is keeping African Americans on the outside looking in. There's a lot of lip service from corporations and major league teams about fields they have built or refurbished, but that isn't even a drop in the bucket. Even on a small scale, it's a losing battle. I don't have to look further than the Gary Southshore Railcats Stadium. The Railcats, to their tremendous credit, established the Home Field Advantage Foundation, which has been invaluable in keeping baseball alive in Gary. Last year they donated $50,000 to Gary Youth Baseball, money that was desperately needed.
>
> But the Railcats play in a stadium that cost over $50 million. For a minor league stadium. Let that marinate for a moment.... 50 Million! With an *M*! For just 1 percent of that we could build a centralized youth complex for baseball and softball. When they play in such luxury while we wallow in the muck and mire of fields decades old, it just leaves a bitter taste in my mouth. The bottom line is we just want to provide our kids with a decent place to learn and play this game, a game I love and respect. We just want to give our kids the same chance as anyone, a level playing field, pun definitely intended.

If baseball really wants to see more African Americans in the sport, they can start by calling a cease-fire on their perpetual efforts to strafe our cities with sweetheart stadium deals. Getting teams to put private money into urban centers instead of taking public money out would help get to the root of the problem.

Owners can also start where they have the most direct control: the front office. Sixty years after Jackie Robinson broke the color line, there is only one African-American general manager in all of baseball, Kenny Williams of the Chicago White Sox. Until owners stop bleeding our cities dry and actually hire

African Americans for positions of power, all the hand-wringing in the world won't amount to a hill of black-eyed peas.

The present dynamic of young African-American players getting starved out of the game while Latino players are sucked into a system of indentured servitude screams for the kind of Brown-Black unity exemplified in the last chapter by Clemente. These are the lessons of history that hold the potential to turn the tide and restore the humanity of those trying to make the big leagues. This isn't a game; it's about fighting for a model for globalization that doesn't, as Dr. King put it, "thingify" human beings and turn them into widgets.

CHAPTER THREE

Soccer: The Perilous Practice of Political Projection

Learning from Soccer

"You are asking which is more important—Brazil or a U.S. invasion?" a Haitian fan said to an American reporter in 1994. "We are hungry every day. We have problems every day. The Americans talk about invading every day. But the World Cup only comes every four years."

Imagine for a moment Tom Brady throwing the game-winning touchdown in the Super Bowl, removing his shirt, and having an antiwar slogan scrawled on his chest. Or see if you can envision Dwyane Wade tearing off his Miami Heat jersey Hulk Hogan style to expose a demand in support of striking South Beach janitors. Such actions are almost beyond the imagination of the U.S. sports fan. In soccer, it's how they roll. Now imagine your favorite NFL star celebrating a victory by giving a fascist salute. Italian star Paolo Di Canio did just that—while his fans waved swastika flags in the background.

Soccer is the redheaded stepchild of U.S. sports. Calling yourself a soccer fan in some quarters is an act of daring and principle. You must be prepared to defend your love with an almost political zeal. And it's understandable why. Some on the right fringe, in between burning Harry Potter books and getting the Teletubbies banned, think being a soccer fan means you wear a red, white, and blue thong and take French lessons between trips to the neighborhood madrassa. Like clockwork, whenever the World Cup rolls around, the right-wing press puts out a spate of columns with all the delicacy of a John Birch tract opposing water fluoridation.

As Stephen Moore wrote in the *National Review:*

> After watching the first two soccer games of my six-year-old son, Justin, this spring, I finally understand why Europeans riot at soccer matches. For the same reason inmates riot in prisons: sheer boredom. There is no surer sign of the decline of America's culture than the craze over this awful European sport. Drive past a park or a schoolyard on a clear spring afternoon and you're likely to witness a depressingly unpatriotic sight: the baseball diamond lies empty and crab grass grows in the infield [Then why don't you tell your president to stop cutting rec programs?], while herds of American children dressed in preposterous polyester uniforms run around kicking a white and black ball in no particular direction and to no apparent end.... I am convinced that the ordeal of soccer teaches our kids all the wrong lessons in life. Soccer is the Marxist concept of the labor theory of value applied to sports—which may explain why socialist nations dominate in the World Cup [Socialist nations, huh? Like Brazil and Argentina?]. The purpose of a capitalist economy is to produce the maximum output for the least amount of exertion. [Spoken like someone who never exerted himself at anything.] Soccer requires huge volumes of effort but produces no output. What makes peewee soccer particularly insidious is that boys and girls play together. At this level, the sport has become a giant social experiment imposed upon us by the same geniuses who have put women in combat. No one seems to care much that co-ed soccer is doing irreparable harm to the psyche of America's little boys.

John Derbyshire, in a column called "The Longest, Awfulest Game"—a title that continues the *National Review's* decades-long assault on good grammar—wrote,

> What really needs explaining is not why Americans do not care to watch soccer, but why the rest of the world does. With the probable exception of cricket, it is the most boring game ever devised.... American soccer fans have not yet been infected by the spirit of hooliganism.... [If] the game ever does take off here, though—if it seeps down into the great American underclass—

be prepared for scenes that will make the disturbances following
the L.A. Lakers game last month look like schoolyard scuffles....
America: be warned!

This lovely tract ignores that there already is violence at
United States stadiums—some of which actually have court-
houses in the bowels of the building for the easy expediting of
drunken brawlers. There is even a U.S. fan group called Sam's
Army that drapes itself in a militarism that would make some
Euro-hooligans blush. But the dirty little secret that Derbyshire and Moore try to smother with their patrician whines
is that this is a soccer-mad country.

It is often remarked that soccer is the sport of the future in
the United States and it always will be. It already is the most
popular youth sport in the United States. That means the same
folks bashing the game as an act of treason take their kids to
play on weekends, compounding their hypocrisy with apparent
child abuse—please note that in Moore's passage above, he
takes no responsibility for the "irreparable damage" being
done to little Justin's psyche. Also, people from Eastern Europe, Latin America, and the West Indies are bringing their
love of the game to an increasingly multicultural United States.

An amazing sight in Washington, D.C.—our segregated
capital—is that of a group more multiracial than a meeting of
the UN playing soccer on weekends. On the brown and green
fields of local area high schools, every Sunday without fail, the
games are on. The groups are mostly always men, and almost
all share an oddly disjunctive body type: bellies that jiggle gen-
tly against the seams of their shirts above legs as thick and
firm as oak. And U.S. soccer madness is by no means limited
to D.C.; journalist Simon Kuper made the point that "there is
probably one city in the world where a [match] between El Salvador and Copenhagen can draw 30,000 fans. It's not San Salvador and it is certainly not Copenhagen. It's Los Angeles."

Not everyone who hates soccer, however, is someone who longs for the days when women couldn't vote and movie cowboys didn't make love by the campfire. The "big" sports—football, NASCAR, baseball, basketball, golf—control the airwaves while soccer bashing, certainly in the world of commentary, has become as popular as the sport itself. As always, the big-sports lovers sneer at the importance of soccer in the lives of its fans—and in particular at the way that soccer has been a critical stage in the athletic development and participation of an entire generation of women athletes. Especially in the United States.

Women, Soccer, and the United States

In most of the world, soccer is more men's only than Augusta National. But this is far less the case in the United States, where it is the most popular youth sport among girls. It's not difficult to understand why. It is one of the few team sports to have produced female athletic role models. The 1999 women's World Cup team of Mia Hamm, Julie Foudy, and—the shirtless one—Brandi Chastain became an important and historic showcase for women's sports.

The significance of the 1999 summer of love with women's soccer has been undermined in two ways. First, in the mainstream press, the 1999 team was dismissed as a tempest in a Martha Stewart teacup. The women's soccer wave was a fad, as proven by the crash-and-burn demise of the first U.S. women's pro soccer league, the WUSA. Second, as packaged by the press and the president, the spectacle seemed to carry the queasy message that "girls can deliver the jingoistic goods as well as the boys!" Never shy to ooze toward an opportunity, Bill Clinton trumpeted the 1999 team with patriotic overkill that developed into a Cold War atmosphere as the U.S. played China in the final, flying fighter planes over a packed Rose Bowl to create a scene reminiscent of Red Square (or a Yankees game).

But both these views miss the fifteen-year struggle of this team for recognition and respect, as well as the squad's significance as a physical, artistic representation of the landmark legislation known as Title IX. Even CNN had to admit, "Team USA's dramatic victory in the women's soccer World Cup might never have been if not for Title IX." Title IX was the landmark legislation passed in 1972 barring sex discrimination in school sports and academics. Today, one out of three girls plays some form of sports. Before Title IX, it was one out of thirty-five. The number of women participating in intercollegiate sports in that same span has gone from about 30,000 to more than 150,000. In the last twenty years alone, the number of women's college teams has nearly doubled. From 1987 to 1999, the number of girls age six and over playing soccer increased by 20 percent to 7.3 million. Women's soccer is now of-

Mia Hamm battles Norway at the 2003 Women's World Cup (AP/Al Behrman)

fered on nearly 88 percent of college campuses compared to only 2.8 percent in 1977. Despite this record of achievement, Title IX is subject to constant attack. Like all of the 1960s reforms that improved the lives of women, people of color, and the poor, Title IX has been the focus of a well-organized and well-funded backlash.

The members of the women's soccer team grew up together in a time when women's soccer was at best a sideshow. Women's sports meant tennis or golf: country club sports both economically prohibitive and highly individualistic. Team sports were an afterthought. As one member of the team remembers, "Growing up, my idols were 8-foot-tall basketball players and 300-pound-football players and I don't remember ever having a woman that I pointed to and said that's who I want to be some day."

In the 1980s, the national team existed without either a World Cup or a spot in the Olympics. They received $10 a day in meal money and practiced on fields showing more wear and tear than the golf course at the end of *Caddy Shack*. "Men's soccer got all the money and respect. That's just the way it was," 1999 team cocaptain Michelle Akers once said. This began to change with a new generation of teenage players, fifteen- and sixteen-year-olds who grew up with the opportunity to play. They included Julie Foudy, Joy Fawcett, Brandi Chastain, and future legend Mia Hamm.

Their breakout finally happened at the 1996 Olympics in Atlanta, but not before a very underpublicized struggle. In the lead-up to the Atlanta games, the players knew that an Olympics on U.S. soil was their best shot at amplifying their sport. They also knew that they were getting a raw deal. The women players were getting $1,000 a month, with a promise of a bonus only if they won the gold. The men were set to get a bonus no matter how they medaled. The players met and went to get advice from someone who knew something about fighting for equal pay and respect: Billie Jean King. King, in addition to being a feminist pioneer in the world of tennis, was also the founder of the first-ever women's athletic union. "I told them, you just don't play. That's the only leverage you have."

The players unified and basically had what one called a "wildcat strike," refusing to report to practice. As Foudy remembers, "[King] taught us that this wasn't an issue for the federation to handle. The team could handle it ourselves."

The soccer powers—backed by the United States Olympic Committee—brought in a group of scab players, some of whom stayed on the team after the strike ended victoriously. One of those scabs was a player who had left the team and was trying to return: Brandi Chastain.

The 1999 World Cup was the culmination of this struggle. The team sold out Giants Stadium and the Rose Bowl—and did it by marketing the sport straight to fans, in clinics for young girls around the country. The crowds were very young, and very female. As Sally Jenkins astutely put it, "One problem with mainstream American sports today is that they have gotten so far from the people who watch them. This team came back to the audience." The final game against China ended, of course, with Brandi Chastain's penalty shot, and the Nike ad heard round the world. The initial popularity of the team was strong. The "reluctant superstar," the painfully shy Mia Hamm, was in Gatorade commercials with the icon of commercial himself, Michael Jordan. The team became the first group of women ever named *Sports Illustrated*'s Sportsperson of the Year.

There was an effort to capture the popularity of the moment with the creation of the women's pro soccer league, the WUSA, but an absence of corporate sponsorship spelled its doom. This was a profound disappointment, but it shouldn't blind us to the larger significance of that summer: Mia Hamm carried through her play the symbolic weight of everything about Title IX that is indomitable and will not be turned back. In honoring the retiring Hamm, along with teammates Julie Foudy and Joy Fawcett, former U.S. national team coach April Heinrichs said, "Think of it this way: Imagine that Magic, Larry Bird, Michael Jordan, Shaq, Kobe, and LeBron were all on one team for 15 years. That's what we have had with our women's national team. They had an impact on America's consciousness, on women's sports, on women's voices." Heinrichs was asked if the feminist movement could in fact take credit for their World Cup triumph and she said, apart from scoring the goals, "Yes. Absolutely."

Because of the efforts of the women's team—as well as cyberspace access to teams, leagues, and scores—soccer in the twenty-first century has attracted new legions of fans. Globalization has taken the game and run with it like a Ronaldo breakaway. But this has created a debate among soccer purists the world over about the current state of the game.

Soccer Today

Soccer at present contains all the contradictions of globalization. On the one hand, Internet-savvy fans have immediate access to scores around the world, and teams are able to scout globally, creating squads more gifted, more multicultural, and more dynamic than ever before. On the other hand, the sport has been increasingly commercialized, breeding a crushing uniformity into the game that some observers say could destroy it.

Two books by soccer writers of boundless passion represent the opposing sides of the twenty-first century soccer debate: Franklin Foer's breezy *How Soccer Explains the World* and Eduardo Galeano's *Soccer in Sun and Shadow*. Foer writes for the *New Republic,* a magazine that I enjoy picketing. In case you haven't heard of it, it's a shoddy-looking, highly influential, centrist rag that pines for the day when Democrats can just stop the pretense of giving lip service to their "base" and we can all be a happy one-party state. It's perhaps best known for letting young journalist Stephen Glass write pure fiction and pass it off as fact, as well as joshingly calling for the death of internationally renowned author and peace activist Arundhati Roy. Not exactly a proud place to call home. That said, *How Soccer Explains the World* sees in soccer all the dynamism that makes globalization a big virtual party for the wired among us. Foer praises globo-pornographer Thomas Friedman's "world is flat" ethos and writes,

> As a soccer fan, I [understand] exactly what [Friedman means]. It wasn't just the ways that the internet and satellites had made the world of soccer so much smaller and more accessible. You could see globalization on the pitch. During the '90s Basque teams under the stewardship of Welsh coaches, stocked up on Dutch and Turkish players; Moldavian squads imported Nigerians. Everywhere you looked it suddenly seemed had been swept in the dustbin of soccer history.... [I]n the end, I found it too hard to be too hostile to globalization. For all its many faults, it has brought soccer into the far corners of the world and into my life.

What are those Brazilian peasants, Nigerian oil workers, and Uwa Indians thinking? Globalization is great because Franklin Foer gets to watch soccer!

Galeano's view of the current state of the game is more negative. "The journey of soccer in the 20th century," he writes, "is the journey from daring to fear":

> For many years soccer has been played in different styles, expressions of the personality of each people, and the preservation of that diversity is more necessary today than ever before. These are days of obligatory uniformity in soccer and everything else. Never has the world been so unequal in the opportunities it offers and so equalizing in the habits it imposes: in this end of the century world, whoever doesn't die of hunger dies of boredom.... Soccer is now mass-produced, and it comes out colder than a freezer and as merciless as a meat-grinder. It's a soccer for robots.

Galeano longs for the days when a team's style reflected national identity with space for individual creativity. He writes about the spread of soccer to Brazil by traders and missionaries:

> No longer the possession of a few comfortable youths who played by copying, this foreign sport became Brazilian, fertilized by the creative energies of the people discovering it. And thus was born the most beautiful soccer in the world, made of hip feints, undulations of the torso and legs in flight, all of which came from capoeira, the warrior dance of black slaves, and from the joyful dances of big city slums.... There are no right angles in Brazilian soccer just as there are none in the Rio Mountains.

Now, although teams are more multicultural, the play itself, instead of reflecting a pastiche of cultures and influences, has—surely to Tom Friedman's joy—"flattened."

Galeano also can't stand cheering for players who don't have a stitch of clothing not papered with ads, another function of globalization. Players receive stiff fines for writing antiracist slogans or solidarity statements across their chests, but logos are everywhere. In the 1950s, star player Obdulio Varela wouldn't wear product names on his shirt, saying, "They used to drag us blacks around by rings in our noses. Those days are gone." Valera was beating against an irresistible tide.

Yet what Galeano (and I) love about soccer is its ability—despite the corporate control—to surprise us, to dare us to imagine and reimagine teamwork, as well as its ability to excite passions that transcend the sport itself. It was that intersection of sport, politics, adrenaline—and having the good fortune to study in soccer-mad South America—that converted me from provincial soccer bigot to internationalist soccer fan.

Conversion in Chile

In 1995, I lived in Chile for a year as a twenty-year-old college kid studying overseas. By the mid-'90s, Chile had existed uneasily under a nominal democracy for four years. Yet there was no reconciliation and no reckoning for the victims of the Pinochet era. In a country of 13 million people, an estimated 2.5 million had been "visited" by his secret police, yet no one had answered for these crimes. The Old General, as a condition of stepping down from power, was allowed to rewrite the constitution to make himself and his cohorts immune from prosecution. He was also still in charge of the army and held martial troop processions every time civil society threatened to seek justice.

I wanted to study in Chile because I believed—and still believe—in what the people of Chile were fighting for under Salvador Allende's 1970–73 left-wing presidency. I had dreams of meeting with the era's surviving firebrands for social justice and recording their history. What I found instead were good people who managed haunted lives. I met torture victims who couldn't bring themselves to walk outside at night. I met men who drank themselves unconscious, seething that their torturers walked among them. I met women whose forcibly broken bones never set correctly and who used leg braces out of the nineteenth century. Every week there were protests, with grieving parents clutching yellow-edged photos of their children, demanding to know their fates, pleading for some closure.

It was, frankly, more than I could handle. It's one thing to witness a person's pain. It's another to know that your country bankrolled the torturing of their bodies and minds and did so proudly. I was bit of a wreck.

One morning, in an effort to get me out of the house, my host family took me to a soccer game. It seemed innocent enough, and I was eager for a little mental escape courtesy of my old friend, sports. The weather that morning was all sun and light breeze, the sky a color that locals call "Chilean blue." But my joy turned to dread when I learned en route that we were headed toward Chile's National Stadium. I didn't care that Colo Colo was playing Universidad de Chile—affection-ately known as "La U"—in the match of the year. After the Pinochet coup, the National Stadium's bleachers were filled with dissidents of every stripe, turning it into a mass waiting room for execution and torture, where compañeras were raped for the crime of wearing pants. In nearby Chile Stadium (a smaller, indoor facility), the great Víctor Jara, the Bob Dylan of Chile—or is Dylan the Víctor Jara of the United States?—had his fingers mutilated in front of thousands of prisoners and, with his hands bloody stumps, still tried to sing a song of protest, only to be gunned down, shot dead as thousands in the stands tried to join in chorus. I didn't want to watch a soccer game in either stadium any more than I would want to watch a baseball game in Auschwitz.

When we arrived at the stadium, it was difficult not to no-tice the hulking security police at every turn. It was especially hard to ignore the flaming brick tossed in our direction as we walked toward La U's "cheering section." To wrap a brick in kerosene-soaked rags, light it on fire, and then pick it up to throw, takes some serious conviction. Finally, we arrived at our seats, for the most part unscathed, except I couldn't stop think-ing, "My God. This is Chile's National Stadium."

I almost walked out, but the son of my host parents, a U of C fanatic, tried to make me understand. He told me that Pinochet, a rabid soccer fan, had nicknamed himself "Presi-dent of Colo Colo" during his reign. He explained to me how Pinochet hated La U—not the team but the school. He told me about how his father's classmates were tortured, murdered, disappeared, or, if they were lucky, expelled from the country. He told me of the students who remained, forced to study in the gray conformity of dictatorship. He told me of programs called "limpiezalas cabezas" (head-cleanings) where students were forced to listen to lectures on neoliberal economics from disciples of Milton Friedman.

It finally made sense why the stadium had a La U section, a Colo Colo section, and a narrow, middle "neutral" section. It made sense why someone would take the time to set a brick on fire, pick it up, and toss it in our direction. This was so much more than a game. It was catharsis. In a country where public expressions of emotion are frowned upon, a land nicknamed "the nation of lawyers," it was a place to scream to the heavens, to howl at injustice, and feel a moment of supreme satisfaction.

It was also the place where I finally understood soccer's appeal. The insane endurance on the field, the powerful fakes, twists, and turns, the explosion of cheers at every goal. As a basketball junkie, I saw why this, and not hoops, was the beautiful game. Basketball, at its best is about teamwork, balance, and acting in concert with others. No coincidence that two of my all-time favorite players, Steve Nash and Hakeem Olajuwon, at one time were both soccer players. But, too often, hoops is one person making a move while four stand around and watch. That day, I didn't see anyone on the pitch just standing around. It probably helped that I was arm-in-arm with people whose politics I shared, dancing with their children in the aisles, as La U stomped Colo Colo. Imagining old man Pinochet hearing about this game and gnashing his capped teeth also helped.

Of course, no one in my section believed that this was somehow an actual "victory." It was symbolism, pure and simple. But it would be rank condescension of the worst kind to say the game meant nothing or was merely entertainment for a broken people. It was an expression of humanity, of resilience, and of release.

Now Pinochet is dead, never forced to take residence in the spider hole he so richly deserved. He was forced, however, to sit by and watch while Chile Stadium was renamed Víctor Jara Stadium in 2003. And, as a Chilean friend emailed me soon after the dictator's death, "In Chile, we have always known the truth about this evil man. It does my heart well, that jail was his immediate future...and that the bastard knew it." He is right. Any public humiliation Pinochet received at the end was the result of a movement by ordinary folks who never gave up. If the cheers for La U acted to give even a shard of sustenance to those who felt their cause was just, then it was worth every last shout.

This is the case around the world. People project their political aspirations on soccer. Sometimes it becomes the stage for political satisfaction. Often it can lead to terrible disappointment. Soccer is not a substitute for struggle, and its great players aren't necessarily Martin Luther King in cleats. Sometimes they rise to the occasion and justify the political hopes people project on them, and sometimes they do not. We can see how both sides play out in the stories of soccer greats Diego Maradona and Ronaldo.

If there were a Mount Rushmore of international soccer, Diego Maradona's face would be on it. In 2000, FIFA placed him beside Pelé as one of the two greatest players in the history of the sport. But in his native Argentina, Maradona is a lightning rod for love, hate, brutal criticism, and passionate defense. He is Muhammad Ali in 1968—and, for Maradona, 1968 has lasted for twenty years.

Maradona was in the eye of a media storm for participating in a rally against George W. Bush and U.S. trade policy while Bush met with Latin American leaders at the Fourth Summit of the Americas in Mar del Plata, Argentina. Surely many casual CNN viewers wondered why this stocky, five-foot-six former athlete was so adored, so incendiary, and so intimately involved in a protest against the American president.

Maradona went from soccer superstar to Argentine folk hero during the 1986 World Cup, when he "avenged" the 1982

British defeat of Argentina in the Falklands War. Argentina trounced England again four years later with two Maradona goals—one with his foot and one with the sly help of his hand, a score that has become known as "the Hand of God."

His brilliance on the pitch inspired Galeano to write,

Maradona, with Venezuelan president Hugo Chávez (not shown), raises a fist in protest of George Bush's appearance at the Fourth Summit of the Americas, November 4, 2005 (AP/Marcelo Hernandez)

No one can predict the devilish tricks this inventor of surprises will
dream up for the simple joy of throwing the computers off track,
tricks he never repeats. He's not quick, more like a short-legged bull,
but he carries the ball sewn to his foot and he's got eyes all over his
body. His acrobatics light up the field.... In the frigid soccer of the
end of the century, which detests defeat and forbids all fun, that man
was one of the few who proved that fantasy can be efficient.

In later years, Maradona struggled with an addiction to
hard drugs. He was suspended from the sport for twelve
months in 1991 after testing positive for cocaine. Then he was
banned for another fifteen months for taking ephedrine during
the 1994 World Cup. In 1997, he tested positive again, and
eventually slouched to retirement, withdrawing into a shell of
drug dependency and obesity.

His real sin, however, at least in the eyes of the soccer au-
thorities, was a tendency to speak truth to power. He agitated
for international labor standards to be applied to soccer and
asked team owners to "open the books" so players could know
the profit margins inked with their blood and sweat. Corporate
media treated his drug addiction like a national spectacle. His
1991 arrest for possession was played live on Argentine television.

Mocked by the media for drug dependency (they called
him "Maracoca"), weight problems, and psychiatric distress,
Maradona was in and out of Cuban health clinics for much of
four years. Now clean and sober, he has experienced a public
resurrection as the host of a popular Argentinean talk show, *La
Noche del 10.* In the weeks leading up to the Summit of the
Americas, Maradona urged his viewers to join the protests.
This included airing parts of a five-hour interview with Cuban
leader Fidel Castro, who said, "We are in solidarity with you
and with Argentina. We have fought for decades, and we will
be happy knowing that you are there."

Maradona arrived at the mammoth stadium protest wearing
a "Stop Bush" T-shirt and said, "I'm proud as an Argentine who

can travel in this train to oppose the human rubbish that Bush is." At the packed rally, Maradona sat shoulder-to-shoulder with Venezuelan president Hugo Chávez, who had come to the conference vowing to "bury" Bush's proposed Free Trade Agreement for the Americas (FTAA). Maradona embraced Chávez to rapturous cheers as he shouted into the microphone, "Argentina has its dignity! Let's throw Bush out of here!"

Of course, his stance opened him up to the oh so intelligent criticism of the op-ed pundits. John Tierney, conservative columnist for the *New York Times,* slammed Maradona as a hypocrite who benefited from lucrative endorsement deals with global corporations, yet now condemns the excesses of global capitalism. But what Tierney and his ilk don't understand is that this only further endears Maradona to his people. The poor of Argentina know from bitter experience that, unlike Maradona, they will never taste the fruits of globalization. The fact that he now stands alongside them only cements his greatness.

Bush left Argentina after the summit embarrassed, off-message, and without a trade deal. That's hardly surprising. When a former Major League Baseball owner like Bush squares off against a soccer deity in Latin America, you don't need the sports pages to discover who has the greater claim to the hearts and minds of the people.

The Fourth Summit of the Americas will be remembered as a moment when a certain smirk was wiped off the face of the American president by those who oppose U.S. trade policies— with a little help from the "Hand of God." But there was no hand of God present to challenge the iron fists of the United States and Israel when Ronaldo went to Palestine.

Ronaldo, for the uninitiated, is a Brazilian soccer player who is arguably the most famous athlete in the world. However, due to the pro soccer blackout in the U.S. sports media, Ronaldo's name-recognition among American sports fans hovers somewhere between that of the WNBA's Lisa Leslie and the Whizzinator.

Soccer-heads know that Ronaldo, far from being an athletic footnote, matters. Ronaldo matters because his global recognition and social import stretches far beyond any NBA or NFL superstar. To soccer-obsessed children, especially in the impoverished global South, Ronaldo is a demigod. And his worshippers don't need expensive sneakers or equipment—just a ball and some friends—to imitate the utterly distinctive moves and motions of their hero.

But heroes don't always rise to the level of heroism. This was seen when Ronaldo traveled to Palestine in his official capacity as Goodwill Ambassador for the United Nations. He inaugurated a youth center in Ramallah and announced to a crowd of 1,500 people that his visit was part of a campaign for Middle East peace. He told a news conference, "I hope that the sports movement will be revived in Palestine, and I hope to see a Palestinian soccer team when there will be peace." Then the star went to Tel Aviv and gave the same kind of speech to an Israeli audience, preaching "sports, love, and understanding" like a thick-thighed Elvis Costello.

This was in many ways a highly scripted trip. But reality intervened when Ronaldo's plan to visit the occupied Gaza Strip was thwarted by Israeli armed checkpoints. The checkpoints prevented Ronaldo from granting the wish of a twelve-year-old Palestinian boy in the Rafah refugee camp, named Hamad al-Nairib. Hamad once dreamed of becoming "the Ronaldo of Palestine," and wrote the following letter, urging Ronaldo to defy the travel ban on the Gaza Strip, so the two of them could "shake hands." (Note: This letter has been widely published in European and Middle Eastern papers but did not appear in the mainstream press in the United States.)

Dear Ronaldo,

My name is Hamad al-Nairab, I am 12-years-old, live in the Refugee Camp of al-Shabboura in the southern Gaza Strip city of Rafah. I like football very much, and love you very much. I am one of the supporters of the Brazilian football team. Everyday, I watch football matches on TV to see you while playing football. I used to play football in our quarter. I used to wear the yellow shirt with number 9. I hoped to visit Brazil to see you there, play with you and to take picture with you.

I had a dream to be older and older and to become a famous professional footballer like you, I had a dream to be the Ronaldo of Palestine. Dear Ronaldo, I cannot play football because I lost my left leg. On May 19, 2004, me and my friends participated in a peaceful march in Rafah. The Israeli helicopters hit us with missiles. A lot of friends were killed and others wounded. On that day, I lost my leg and my dreams dead. No more playing football.

I was so pleased and surprised when I heard that you are visiting our homeland Palestine. But, unfortunately, I will be not able to see you because of the Israeli checkpoints and my health condition. All of my friends love you so much, and love football, they hope just to see you even for seconds. Seeing you is one of their big dreams.

I invite you to visit Rafah and beg you to agree, to award me the opportunity to shake hand with you and to take pictures with you. And to see how much the people here love you. All of them talk about you and about your visit. I hope you will not disappoint the children of Rafah and all the people here who love you. We are waiting for you,

Hamad al-Nairab

Hamad is still waiting, as defying travel bans was not on the goodwill agenda. It's hard to comprehend how deeply soccer is loved around the world. It is perhaps harder for us to digest that U.S.-made weapons are blowing the legs off of twelve-year-old boys with familiar dreams of athletic glory. It is intolerable that Hamad's dreams—dreams to meet Ronaldo, dreams to play soccer, dreams to walk—are little more than collateral damage to the U.S. and Israeli governments.

CHAPTER FOUR

The 2006 World Cup:
The Politics of Play Personified

T he World Cup is by sheer numbers the most important sporting event on earth, creating the closest thing we have to a united global audience. More than one in four human beings viewed the final game in 2006. That means, outside the United States, just about anyone with access to a television tuned in.

Politics cannot be separated from the World Cup any more than it can be extracted from the Olympics or distilled from Chile's National Stadium. Sometimes this is for the best. For example, Africans throughout the continent exulted in Senegal's shocking upset of its former colonizer, France, in the first game of the 2002 Cup. In 2006, however, it was for the worst. German and U.S. politicians seized on the tournament to intensify the saber rattling aimed at Tehran. Citing Iran's efforts to develop a nuclear program and the anti-Israel pronouncements of Iranian president Mahmoud Ahmadinejad, several leading politicians in both countries called for the Iranian team to be banned from the World Cup. In this spirit of tolerance and peace, Berlin's "liberal" daily *Der Tagesspiegel* ran a cartoon in February 2006 that depicted Iranian soccer players as suicide bombers.

Germany's conservative chancellor, Angela Merkel, stoked this sentiment by likening Iran's nuclear plans to the threat posed by the Nazis. Christian Democrats further upped the ante by asserting that Tehran would slip some suicide bombers into a game, disguised as regular fans. Calls for a ban, or at least for a travel ban against the Iranian president, intensified in Germany as the games approached. Leading Conservative and Social Democratic officials were quoted almost daily, decrying a possible visit by Ahmadinejad. British conservatives, perhaps distraught over their own team's dwindling prospects after an injury to their best player, got in on the act. In early May, a German newspaper reported that officials of Germany, France, and Britain were hoping to orchestrate a scheme banning travel through the European Union that would prevent high-ranking Iranian officials from attending any of the games. Not to be left out, Italian reform minister Roberto Calderoli of the anti-immigrant Northern League called on FIFA to exclude Iran and other "rogue states."

Following Italy's lead, on May 12, a group of European Union representatives presented a letter to FIFA demanding that Iran be evicted from the games. The hypocrisy is overwhelming: according to this logic, Iran deserved to be banned because its leaders indulge in belligerent rhetoric and attempt to develop a nuclear energy program, yet no one advocates the exclusion of the United States, even though it was engaged in two military occupations, and President Bush has refused to rule out a nuclear strike on Iran.

Despite its general tendency to demonize and isolate Iran, the United States was slower than its German counterparts to recognize soccer as a useful tool in its campaign—not surprising, given the sport's pariah status in the United States. But a few politicians craftily picked up on it. On April 6, Senator John McCain—aka "Mr. Maverick"—introduced a resolution to the Senate Foreign Relations Committee advocating a World Cup ban on Iran. To its credit, FIFA rejected all of these demands. (In November 2006, however, it suspended Iran's team from the Asian Cup, only to lift the ban in December after an international outcry.)

The Iranian people are perhaps even more enthusiastic about soccer than most of the rest of the world; they held a national day of celebration when their team qualified for the Cup. The team performed in surprisingly poor fashion in the Cup, losing to Portugal and Mexico and drawing a tie with Angola to finish at the very bottom of World Cup Group D with just one point. One wonders how they would have performed without the swirl of controversy and saber rattling that encircled their team.

But much of this anti-Iran campaign had less to do with banning the top-level Middle Eastern team than with grooming public opinion for aggression.

Middle East expert Juan Cole pointed out in a May 3, 2006, post on his blog that Ahmadinejad's overheated oratory is hardly the gravest threat to world peace. Cole argues,

> Ahmadinejad is a non-entity. The Iranian "president" is mostly powerless. The commander of the armed forces is the Supreme Jurisprudent, Ali Khamenei. Worrying about Ahmadinejad's antics is like worrying that the U.S. military will act on the orders of the secretary of the interior. Ahmadinejad cannot declare war on anyone, or mobilize a military. So it doesn't matter what speeches he gives. Moreover, Iran cannot fight Israel. It would be defeated in 72 hours, even if the U.S. didn't come in, which it would…. What is really going on here is an old trick of the warmongers. Which is that you equate hurtful statements of your enemy with an actual military threat, and make a weak and vulnerable enemy look like a strong, menacing foe. Then no one can complain when you pounce on the enemy and reduce his country to flames and rubble.

"I would rather people built a clear wall between sport and politics," Iran's Croatian-born coach Branko Ivankovic once said. But the 2006 Cup reminded us all, and the Iranian people in particular, that while soccer may be a beautiful game for us, it's little more than a political weapon for others.

The aggressive efforts to ban Iran were not the only ugly gray clouds hovering over the start of the 2006 World Cup. The tournament also opened amid fears that an open and violent racism could upstage the games, humiliate its German hosts, and provide an international platform for neo-Nazi swill. The rising number of attacks on nonwhites in Germany, combined with a spate of racist sloganeering and taunting of Black soccer players throughout Europe, set the stage for an unprecedented display of racism in front of a global sports audience.

The issues of race and racism continue to be at the heart of some of the most polarizing political battles in soccer, particularly in Europe. In Britain, soccer "hooliganism" has a long and ugly history of commingling with hard right-wing forces, as demonstrated by one of their "fight" songs:

> *Stand by the Union Jack*
> *Send those niggers back*
> *If you're white, you're alright*
> *If you're black, send 'em back*

In the former Yugoslavia, soccer clubs were organizing centers for some of the deadliest sectarian violence of the early '90s. In Germany, Hitler salutes are not uncommon, particularly at international matches. An analysis of the political attitudes of German fans revealed that 20 percent feel close to neo-Nazis. All of this is further complicated, exacerbated, and combated by the increasingly international face of Europe's top teams.

Twenty-five percent of European players are of color, yet despite soccer's popularity only a minute fraction of that diversity is reflected in the stands, mostly because of fear for personal safety. As a writer from Britain's Social Issues Research Centre explains, "The attractions of football matches to far-right groups are obvious. Football grounds provide a useful platform for the groups to make their voices heard. From them their views can be directed into millions of homes. It also seems as if football grounds can be a means to recruit young support." This has led some to actually blame soccer itself—

but once again, to go back to the font of Galeano, that is like blaming the handkerchief for the tears.

Fortunately, racism breeds antiracism, expressed through actions large and small. In soccer—imagine this—clubs are responsible for fans' behavior and teams can face punishment ranging from a fine to a stadium ban (where no one is allowed to enter the bleachers to watch a game) or a deduction of league points for fan infractions. Britain even passed a law in 1991 called the Football (Offences) Act that made racist chanting at soccer matches unlawful. But this kind of top-down legislation is largely unenforced and ineffectual. The most stirring and effective displays come from the bottom up, from players and fans demanding change.

An example of this is when Treviso players blacked up their faces as a show of support for a Nigerian teammate hit by bananas. Another was when Gramoz Palushi, a twenty-year-old Albanian man, was killed in fighting that broke out between Greek fans and Albanian immigrants hours after Albania's squad upset Greece. More than 2,000 immigrants and members of antiracist groups marched on parliament in Athens, holding banners reading, "Stop the racist attacks" and "Stop racism and xenophobia," and chanting, "No to racism—yes to unity."

Organizations such as the Commission for Racial Equality (CRE), the Football Supporters' Association (FSA), and the Professional Footballers' Association (PFA) are explicitly antifascist and openly appeal to fans for help. In 1993, the CRE and PFA launched the Let's Kick Racism Out of Football campaign "with the aim of highlighting anti-racist and equal opportunities messages within the context of football." Aiming to encourage clubs and supporters' groups to launch their own organizing against racism, the campaign stated that "if football is to be played and enjoyed equally by everyone, whatever the colour of their skin, and wherever they come from, it is up to us all, each and every one of us, to refuse to tolerate racist attitudes, and to demand nothing less than the highest standards in every area of the game."

The conclusion for some, like John Derbyshire, is that the sport itself breeds these problems: they are European problems brought on by the sloth of the social welfare system and "socialist principles" (the social welfare system in Europe has also been blamed in the *National Review* for gout, male pattern baldness, and William F. Buckley's unfortunate chin). More liberal commentators, like the aforementioned Mr. Foer, blame soccer violence on the uncertainties created by the globalized world: the rise of violent "tribalism" as the nation-state withers away. But the fact is that neither racism nor "hooliganism" is a European, non-American issue. Brawls between players and fans, player-on-player pregame brawls in American football, and fights in the stands between fans are as much a part of American sports as F-14 flyovers and eight renditions of the national anthem. And though far-right groups in Europe have historically used soccer games as opportunities for recruitment, and saw their influence rise during the economic crises of the '70s and '80s, they have since been challenged. As the riots in France in November 2005 showed, people can only take being mocked and marginalized for so long before demanding to be heard. Soccer players of color, their teammates, and antiracists are making the same point.

Still, the bigots love the idea of using soccer as their platform and will do so whenever they get the opportunity. That's why the sewers where neo-Nazis nestle were bubbling with the idea of turning the World Cup into their stage from the day Munich was awarded the 2006 games. They had reason to be optimistic.

The games took place in the shadow of some of the worst "football racism" seen across the continent in years. In late February 2006, Cameroonian FC Barcelona star Samuel Etó almost walked off the pitch after being showered by "fans" with monkey chants and peanuts. In November 2005, Messina's Marc Zoro picked up the ball and threatened to leave the field because of racist chants from followers of Inter Milan. Afterward, in tears, he told the press, "I cannot stand it that people go to the stadium to insult players instead of to enjoy themselves. I have had enough. The rules are there and they should be applied. That's why I asked the referee and the fourth official to stop the game, but they didn't listen to me." As a show of solidarity, players took a five-minute moment of silence before running onto the field. It was a stirring display of unity against what was clearly not an act of isolated ignorance, but rather one with strong roots in the Italian game and beyond. In Italy, a Jewish player, Ronnie Rosenthal, was unable to play even one game for Udinese because of massive pressure from neo-fascist circles, and Aaron Winter, a native of Suriname of Hindustani extraction, was subject to attacks when playing the Lazio squad involving cries of "Niggers and Jews Out." The Nigerian goalkeeper Alloy Agu, who plays in Belgium, offered an explanation: "There's still an idea here in Europe that Africans can't do anything better than whites. Don't look at color. Look at what we can do! Black, white, yellow, we're all the same. Still, if you're black, you're well dressed, you drive a nice car, they want to see your papers."

These were only the best publicized stories, but the fact is that players of African origin continue to give accounts of being treated, in the words of one, "worse than dogs" on a regular basis. The problem became so pronounced in advance of the Cup that even the soccer- and racial-awareness-challenged U.S. media had to take note, as U.S. star DaMarcus Beasley reported being greeted with monkey noises and tossed banana skins every time his foot touched the ball.

The rise of anti-immigrant sentiment in Europe—which has, of course, become de rigueur in the United States as well—aggravated the situation leading up to the Cup and continues to do so today. Shaun Harkin, who played for Coleraine FC in the Northern Irish League and captained Brown University's soccer squad to the NCAA quarterfinals, now works as an immigrant-rights activist in Chicago. He points out that

> the racist abuse players have faced across Europe is an aspect of the growing backlash against immigrants more generally. Immigration from former European colonies has grown. As in the United States, immigration has been necessary for many European economies and a source of cheap labor—but immigrant communities have also been a convenient political scapegoat in a continent riddled with unemployment and increasingly anxious conditions for workers dealing with the repercussions of deepening neoliberal policies.

In the run-up to the Cup, the German government wanted to have its schnitzel and eat it too: foment anti-Muslim bigotry, tighten immigration restrictions, and attack asylum seekers, on the one hand, and on the other deny any racism that would sully the nation's reputation and diminish the grandeur of the highly profitable spectacle that is the World Cup. Dutifully ignoring the Reich rumblings, they focused instead on the corporate bonanza that accompanies the Cup, never lifting their faces from the Euro-trough to recognize the repercussions of their own rhetoric.

Their complacency lasted until a man named Uwe-Karsten Heye, a former spokesman for the Social Democratic-Green coalition government, told the press that "there are small and mid-sized towns in Brandenburg and elsewhere where I would advise anyone [in the country for the World Cup] with a different skin color not to go. They might not make it out alive." Heye, a cofounder of an antiracist group called "Show Your Face!," was slammed for his comments. In Brandenburg, State Premier Matthias Platzeck, a fellow Social Democrat, called his words an "absurd slur of a whole region that is no way justifiable." Wolfgang Bosbach, a leading Christian Democrat parliamentarian, denounced Heye for singling out Brandenburg. But Bosbach was at least equally alarmed by the prospect that such comments would damage the tourist industry, saying it would be "fatal" if Heye's comments kept people from Germany. Heye's experience was alarmingly similar to Felipe Alou's, as discussed earlier. Confronting racism spurs accusations that you are in fact perpetuating it. Across an ocean, a culture, and a language, the method of the backlash is globalized as smoothly as the Nike swoosh.

The German government found, however, that, unlike their counterparts in the States, the German press was more concerned with the message than the messenger. As a columnist in Berlin's daily *Die Tageszeitung* wrote, "the fact that non-Germans or non white Germans can barely move around in safety is [the real] scandal," not Heye's comments.

Spurred to action, Interior Minister Wolfgang Schuble promised that his government would "not tolerate any form of extremism, xenophobia, or anti-Semitism." Schuble's solution, from the Dick Cheney school of diplomacy, was to station tanks outside soccer stadiums. Schuble, it should be noted, "balanced" his promises of combating racism by adding, "Blond and blue-eyed Germans can also become the victims of violence, sometimes attacked by those who don't have a German [family] background."

Meanwhile, FIFA made toothless pledges to combat racism at the Cup. They held two "antiracism days," during which banners reading "Say No to Racism" were hung high and proud—until the beginning of the game, when they were taken down. This is what a FIFA spokesperson called a "clear message." Thank goodness some players took stronger stands. At the European club championship, French superstar Thierry Henry sported an armband promoting an antiracist campaign called

Stand Up Speak Up. Henry pushed his sponsor Nike to produce black and white intertwined armbands that demonstrate a commitment against racism; they sold more than five million before the Cup even started. "That's important in making the very real point that racism is a problem for everyone, a collective ailment," Henry said to *Time* magazine. "It shows that people of all colors, even adversaries on the pitch, are banding together in this, because we're all suffering from it together." In addition to Henry's initiatives, Muslim and Christian religious leaders organized a very successful Berlin game in early May.

Other than some fringe incidents—like fans of the Spanish team making monkey noises at the French squad as they arrived at the stadium—much of the racism in European soccer was held at bay for the duration of the Cup. This would not have happened without the efforts of grassroots organizations, including Football Against Racism (FARE), a Europe-wide network that has pressured FIFA to take concrete measures. FARE speaks for the majority of the world when they say that they want "to see the 'beautiful game' played without the cancer of racism."

Yet just when FIFA officials were uncorking the champagne and patting themselves on the back for holding a hate-free Cup, there came the mouth of Materazzi and the head butt heard around the world.

At the 2006 World Cup final, the French national team captain, the great Zinedine Zidane, competing in his last professional match, was kicked out in overtime for crushing Italian player Marco Materazzi with a head butt to the chest. Zidane, or Zizou, as he is known, became the first captain ever ejected from a World Cup championship match. The announcers denounced him for committing a "classless act" and the French team withered in his absence, eventually losing to—in my view—a demonstrably inferior Italian squad. The following morning, the international tabloids, with their typical grace, gave Zizou a new nickname: "Butt-head." They seemed to forget that Zizou had literally carried a lightly regarded French team to the finals, that he had been grabbed, kicked, and fouled all game by the vaunted Italian defense, and that he had almost left minutes before the "act" due to injury, his arm hanging from his shoulder like a wet leaf of spinach. An unholy amount of pressure is the primary reason the thirty-four-year-old veteran snapped and planted Materazzi into the pitch.

What Materazzi could have possibly said to send him over the edge is a question still debated. Here is how ABC News summarized Zidane's press conference following the match:

> Various translations claimed Materazzi insulted Zidane as the son or brother of a terrorist whore. Others suggested insults around Islam, incest and sexual preference. Speaking in front of a television showing the incident, he wouldn't specify exactly what was said.
>
> Zinedine Zidane (translated): "It is very offensive, very personal. It affects my mother, my sister. These are very hard words. So you hear it once and then you try to walk away, and I do walk away. Then he repeats that for a second time. And the third time, well, I'm a human being. There are some words sometimes, which can be harder than.... Well, I'd rather have received a right-hand punch in the face rather than hear that."

Materazzi, in an answer that can only be called Clintonian, responded by saying, "It is absolutely not true. I didn't call him a terrorist." Of course he didn't comment on what he *did* call him. Even if "all he did" was call Zidane, an Algerian, the "son of a whore," it is still racist and sexist as well. If you can't see that, then you need to put yourself in Zidane's shoes and ask how you would process such comments, given everything happening in the world and given the racist culture in soccer. And it is certain that racism has played a central part in the aftermath: racist chants about Zidane in Italy, a racist statement by a former member of Italian prime minister Silvio Berlusconi's cabinet ("The French team is made up of Negroes, Islamists, and Communists"), and reports of racist slurs and chants from as far afield as the North End of Boston, where Italian-American fans were watching the game on an outdoor big screen. In other words, people were ready to champion the butted Materazzi for all the wrong reasons.

We still do not know beyond the shadow of a doubt what was said, but we do know that Zizou has sparred verbally with Europe's far-right political machine for more than a decade. He is an antiracist on a team that has defined itself by its multiculturalism and stubborn insistence on standing up against bigotry both inside and outside the sport. Materazzi, on the other hand, will be playing this year for the Italian team Lazio, formerly coached by his father. Lazio's fan club, The Ultras, is notorious for its fascist-friendly politics. Lazio's hardcore Ultras, known as the "Irriducibili," have members in Italy's extra-parliamentary far right and try to use the club to recruit. The group frequently carries racist and anti-Semitic slogans, one time hanging a 50-foot banner that said their opponents were a "team of niggers."

It would be wrong to blame Materazzi for the actions of Lazio's fans, but there is more.

When Marc Zoro famously picked up the ball and walked off the pitch in protest of the monkey chants raining down on him from Inter supporters, many of the Inter players immediately showed support for Zoro's actions. But one opponent yelled, "Stop that, Zoro, you're just trying to make a name for yourself." And that opponent's name was Marco Materazzi.

While Materazzi received more initial support following the head butt, Zizou in the long run has come out on top. Despite the *International Herald Tribune*'s comments that Zidane's head butt "not only brought down the career of one of the game's greatest players, [but] sullied the image of the game

Zidane colliding with Matterazi during the 2006 World Cup's final game
(AP/Christophe Ena)

when it needed a lift and should have been celebrating its biggest occasion," many people understood and were willing to forgive. France embraced him upon his return with a poll published that showed 61 percent of French people forgave him. His sponsors pledged to stand by him. A French tune with an East African beat called "Coup de Boule" (or "Head Butt"), celebrating Zidane, became a surprise continent-wide hit.

And in another expression of political projection, I have seen people at antiwar rallies wearing Zidane jerseys. I asked one Northern Virginia Arab-American teenager why he wore it, and he said to me, "I am not even a French fan. But I felt like that was a head butt for dignity, a head butt for the greater good." I can see readers thinking this to be beyond ridiculous. But as we see, people project their politics onto sports. If that head butt not only propelled Materazzi back a few feet but also propelled this young man to an antiwar demonstration, then it was clearly an act with repercussions beyond the pitch.

CHAPTER FIVE

The NBA and the Two Souls of Hip-hop

The NBA uses hip-hop the way Tony Montana treated a mountain of blow. It's a commodity: the gateway to riches and relevance. It's something you stick your whole snout in and abuse with delirious pleasure. It's also something that makes you eight steps beyond paranoid.

After twenty years of using rap music as the league's unofficial soundtrack, the NBA has gone from CL Smooth to C. Delores Tucker faster than you can say "backlash."

Hip-hop and the NBA have very similar lifelines, reflecting their dual modern roots in the Black community and urban America. They are also both possessed by the Cain and Abel of modern culture: the blood fight between commerce and artistic expression. In the late 1970s, the NBA was on its deathbed. Basketball was played inside half-empty arenas, the finals were shown on tape delay, and most people associated the game with drugs, violence, and decrepitude. The league was too thuggish, too rugged, too BLACK to cross over. Concurrently, hip-hop was being developed in the South Bronx at a time when unemployment was 80 percent in a borough that had lost 600,000 industrial jobs over the previous generation. The South Bronx defined despair, even garnering a visit from Mother Teresa.

Conditions in the South Bronx foreshadowed urban life across the country, as Reagan came to office promising a

"Morning in America" and preparing to lay an ax into the victories of the 1960s. He announced his bid for the presidency in Philadelphia, Mississippi—the infamous site where three civil rights workers were murdered in 1964—with the rallying cry "The South will rise again." Myths of welfare queens riding around in Cadillacs were spun out of Pennsylvania Avenue and ascendant think tanks by young comers like Jack Abramoff and Lee Atwater. "Wilding" teens, crack babies, Willie Horton: it was a decade of fear, reaction, and racism. As Lady Liberty clutched her pocketbook, brutal cuts came down on our cities, sending unemployment to Depression-era levels. Recreation centers were shuttered, after-school and jobs programs became as passé as the Bee Gees and bell bottoms, and African Americans in places like the South Bronx were invisible.

But invisibility had its privileges. Without state-sponsored employment or grant-generous artistic opportunity, a protective hothouse developed where, unencumbered by the reach of commercialism, the four elements of hip-hop—DJing, emceeing, break dancing, graffiti writing—were able to gestate future legends like Kool DJ Herc, Afrika Bambaataa, and Grandmaster Flash. They made history every weekend before a crowd of dozens. As Jeff Chang wrote in *Can't Stop Won't Stop: A History of the Hip-Hop Generation,* "If blues culture had developed under conditions of oppressive, forced labor, hip-hop would arise under conditions of no work."

This dynamic also began to have a seismic, generational impact on African Americans and sport. With the destruction of rec leagues, youth teams, and public school phys ed programs, the once thriving culture of urban American baseball suffocated, leading, as discussed in chapter two, to today's pitiable presence of African-American players in the major leagues.

The "beneficiary" of the starving of urban sports was basketball: cheap, easy, and creative. The rise of both hip-hop and basketball was beautiful proof of the creative spirit in dire circumstances: to paraphrase Tupac, they were flowers growing through cracks in the concrete.

These two uniquely urban art forms found their first synthesis in the rhymes of the legendary Kurtis Blow. Don't feel bad if you've never heard of Mr. Blow. He rapped so long ago, there was no old school or new school. Just school. In 1984, Kurtis Blow recorded the classic anthem "Basketball," in which he extols his love of all things hoop and rhymes "microphone" with "Moses Malone." Hip-hop was in its swaddling clothes, but that didn't stop the floundering NBA from using Blow's rallying cry at games. They even created a video that pieced together clips of every player mentioned on Blow's track from Earl Monroe to Tiny Archibald, Larry Bird, Bernard King, and "Number 33 my man Kareem, the center on my starting team." Also on the 1983–84 NBA Entertainment–produced season retrospective, there is the camp classic "14 Johnsons," which is not the name of a pornographic film but a rap that pays tribute to Magic, Marques, Eddie, Gus, and all the other "Johnsons" in the NBA.

The rhyme redefines terrible, but it was the equivalent of the NBA buying shares of Microsoft when Bill Gates was working out of his garage learning to steal software. The NBA, led by an ambitious young commissioner named David Stern, saw how hip-hop—at the time being dismissed by most as a fad or gimmick—came from the same earth as a new generation of players lighting up the league. Stern saw how the beat could revive the NBA for a new generation. As Todd Byrd wrote on ESPN.com, "1984 was not only the infamous year invoked by that George Orwell novel, but it marked the beginning of the modern era in the NBA. For the first time that year, Magic Johnson and Larry Bird faced each other in the NBA finals…transform[ing] the NBA from being perceived as a league of 'overpaid black drug addicts' to its current status as a preeminent sport around the globe."

The hip-hop/basketball connection took a quantum leap forward the very next season when a bald-headed Brooklyn-born kid with a wagging tongue took the court and redefined the parameters of gravity. His name was Michael Jeffrey Jordan. Jordan's talent would have captured the imagination in any era. But the corporate synthesis of a struggling shoe company called Nike and a "hip-hop aesthetic" director named Spike Lee sent him into the commercial stratosphere. As Chang wrote, "Spike and Mike's ads helped propel Nike past Reebok and the company never looked back. Not only did Nike's success confirm that niches were the future, it also confirmed that a massive shift in tastes was occurring—from baby boomer to youth, from suburb to city, from whiteness to Blackness." The NBA, more than any other league, recognized this trend and ran with it. With Stern pulling the strings, the league was set to become the "hip-hop league"—not running from associations with urban culture but marketing them to death.

In the late 1980s, rap music transitioned in the eyes of the U.S. culture czars from dismissible fad to political TNT: a wellspring of debate, polarization, resentment, and racial resistance. In other words, it wasn't something you merely *liked* or *disliked.* It was something you were either *for* or *against.* The top stars—from Public Enemy to Ice T to N.W.A.—were attacked by Congress, police organizations, and parent and religious groups. The stars themselves thrived on controversy and lived by the Jungle Brothers' line of wearing "black medallions, not gold." It was a time before bling, before Dom, when EPMD could rhyme, "Rappers come along making that noise you see/Still I have yet to see any rapper living comfortably." The NBA once again was ahead of the curve. While hip-hop was under siege, they promoted Michael Jordan to host the season premier of *Saturday Night Live* in 1991. The musical guest? Public Enemy.

Hip-hop also allowed the league to perpetuate either a dazzling slight of hand or a shameless fraud, depending on what side of the table you are on. Over the course of the 1990s, the NBA raised the volume on its soundtrack of the streets and expanded its urban cool. The league also jacked up ticket prices far beyond a typical "urban family" salary and pioneered the idea of "corporate seating" (selling the prime tickets to companies to use or discard). Execs or clients could now order drinks and sushi from their seats. They also opened new arenas like the Palace in Auburn Hills in the suburbs of Detroit, out of urban environs and on the taxpayer dime. It all happened with a dope bass line and two turntables.

While geographically and financially distancing itself from the city, the league kept its rep, as Air Jordans, and whatever kicks were selling that month, became something people lived and died for on the city streets. Hip-hop music began to reflect this chasm as well, developing its "bling-bling" wing in which materialism trumped politics—and in turn gave cover to a league "just trying to get theirs." For me personally, a low point of the '90s was when a friend told me of arguing with a guy in Harlem against the injustice of a world that allows Bill Gates to get so rich while poverty spreads like a virus and being called a "playa hater."

It became common to see rap stars like Diddy, Nelly, and Jay-Z courtside, not merely as window dressing for a league addicted to cool, but as actual financial partners in the process. But, not unlike the rap game, while the NBA went global and grew fat, the product suffered. The average team's scoring went from 108 to 93 points. The league had spent so many years marketing individual "stars" like Magic, Bird, and Jordan that the play became a nearly insufferable, predictable formula.

The offensive end became a place where a player went one-on-one while four teammates stood and watched, as young players were raised on this individualized style of play. The defensive end began to resemble the Ultimate Fighting Championship. Ironically, one of the pioneers of this approach was then-Knicks coach Pat Riley, who in the '80s helmed the run-and-gun, endlessly entertaining Showtime Lakers. But his '90s Knicks were led by Patrick Ewing and Charles Oakley, two guys who couldn't hurdle a magazine. Their most dynamic player was John Starks, a CBA veteran who head butted more people than the Junkyard Dog. They were tough as week-old steak, and about as enjoyable.

AI: Nothing Artificial

The NBA's very profitable and hyper-controlled dance with hip-hop was unsettled by the arrival of a young man from Virginia named Allen Iverson. AI has always defied every expectation. He is listed at six feet, 165 pounds, both of which are generous, but he scores in the paint as much as most seven footers. His moves are filthy, utilizing a crossover dribble that has broken more ankles than Paulie Walnuts. He is a former MVP, a lifetime 27-points-a-game scorer, and simply the most dominant little man in league history. He is also perhaps the toughest, throwing his body around, slamming into the floor, and getting up for more, fitting for someone who was also a star football player in high school.

Iverson is someone who entered the league reflecting the state of race and polarization in the United States. In high school, after a large bowling alley brawl that pitted white against Black, the high-profile Iverson was the only one who ended up in jail. Iverson's teenage incarceration was an act so reeking of southern justice it was profiled on *60 Minutes* and in *Sports Illustrated*, with Iverson eventually receiving a pardon from Virginia governor Douglas Wilder. Iverson then spent two years at Georgetown where coach John Thompson, a man known for being a conservative defensive-minded strategist, let

Allen Iverson, during a game in which he scored 44 points and made 10 assists, drives to the hoop (AP/David Zalubowski)

Iverson loose to run opponents ragged. As Thompson said, "Allen had been in prison, confined. I didn't want him to feel that way on the court. I wanted him to be free." Iverson was the top pick in the NBA draft in 1996 by the Philadelphia 76ers, the shortest ever chosen number one. In his first game against Jordan, AI crossed him over, perhaps the first time the then-thirty-three-year-old Jordan had ever looked slow. But it was after the game when the media hordes asked AI how it felt to light up his hero that ripples became waves. "He's not my hero," AI said. "My heroes don't wear suits." Envision, at that moment, a red phone ringing in Stern's office. Articles came out about Iverson's lack of work ethic, about his "boyz" and his "posse," written by mainstream sportswriters rummaging through their Ebonics dictionaries. Iverson was immediately transformed by the media into a young "thug" more interested in scoring than winning. At the end of the season, the rookie set a record by getting at least 40 points in four straight games. Critics pointed out that the 76ers didn't win any of those games. His cornrows, his goatee, and his tattoos were fodder for league-wide hand-wringing, best exemplified when *Hoop* magazine, the NBA's official publication, put Iverson on the cover and airbrushed his tattoos off his arms, a combination whitewash and blackout.

Iverson also had several run-ins with Philadelphia's notoriously racist police department, and then had the temerity to go public. He said that despite his wealth and fame, local cops wanted him six feet under. He said, "I heard about police officers toasting to Allen Iverson's next felony conviction. I'm hearing about them saying I'm involved with one thing or another, and it scares me. I know that if there's a crooked cop out there, they could do anything to me. He could do anything. Allen Iverson could wind up dead tomorrow if a crooked cop wants him dead. It's as simple as that." The league and media called AI's charge ludicrous, with one writer penning, "Allen Iverson isn't a victim, just a complete embarrassment." AI's concerns resonated, however, with his base in Philly—those who had tasted the Philadelphia police's brand of "brotherly love" firsthand.

Then Iverson took a step beyond just representing hip-hop and entered the music studio. Under the name "Jewelz," he attempted to release a track called "40 Bars" that he pulled before it hit stores, after the lyrics were lambasted by the media and David Stern because of their combination of violence and homophobia. Iverson's response to the criticism was confusion, not understanding how people could get so upset. "It's something I always wanted to do. It was a childhood dream of mine, just like basketball," he said. "But I feel like people took it the wrong way. It kind of took all the excitement out of it."

One thing is certain. Iverson's rhyme reflected another side of hip-hop: not the bling, and not the "14 Johnsons" side:

> *Hats off to the hardcore niggaz FUCK the rest*
> *In my guess y'all useless, just talkin music*
> *Never mistake me for a fake MC*
> *You got the wrong idea nigga I'm CT fool*
> *Get murdered in a second in the first degree*
> *Come to me wit faggot tendacies*
> *You'll be sleepin where the maggots be....*

> *Everybody stay fly get money kill and fuck bitches*
> *I'm hittin anything in plain view for my riches*
> *VA's finest fillin up ditches, when niggaz turn to bitches*
> *die for zero digits; I'm a giant yall midgets....*

Iverson's rhyme, with all its homophobia, sexism, and violence is unquestionably a part of the hip-hop landscape and also unquestionably something the league didn't want any part of. Hip-hop artists ranging from Kanye West to Queen Latifah have challenged these kinds of politics, particularly the homophobia and sexism; it is something rap has had to wrestle with for years. But according to David Stern, who called "40 Bars" "coarse, offensive, and antisocial," AI was the problem, and hip-hop was, for the first time, an aggravating factor, a league liability.

League offices were concerned that the "hip-hop mentality" would alienate fans. This concern became a full-blown frenzy when Ron Artest and other members of the Indiana Pacers entered the crowd in Auburn Hills and both fans and players gave physical expression—in the form of punches and thrown drink cups—to the resentment that had been building in NBA arenas between the executive ticket-buying fan base and players. The league's response was to look around with mock shock and outrage, hand against their hearts, and say, "I do declare, the league has become too hip-hop." This idea has been backed by a pliant press, who treat Stern like the *Vatican Times* treats the pope, echoing his claim that it's not low scoring, poor officiating, high ticket prices, or incomprehensible defensive rules that are at the root of declining ratings and half-empty arenas, but rather hip-hop and its sundry pathologies.

As Bryan Burwell wrote in the *St. Louis Post-Dispatch,* "[NBA marketing people] thought they were getting Will Smith and LL Cool J. But now they've discovered the dark side of hip-hop has also infiltrated their game, with its 'bling-bling' ostentation, its unrepentant I-gotta-get-paid ruthlessness, its unregulated culture of posses, and the constant underlying threat of violence." The *Tampa Tribune* wrote a whole piece corroborating the league's claim that "hip-hop" was "alienating" older fans, providing ideological cover for racism and the entailing discomfort with seeing young Black men fronting a billion-dollar enterprise. Or as *Sports Illustrated*'s Frank Deford put it, "The rapper-style look is off-putting to many of the sports fans—and sponsors—that the NBA is trying to reach."

◆ ◆ ◆ ◆

Eventually the conflict found formal expression on two fronts: the NBA dress code instituted for the 2005–06 season and a collective-bargaining agreement that prevents players from coming into the league straight out of high school. The dress code promotes the insipid idea that whatever is ailing the league can be cured with a dollop of tweed. You don't need Miss Cleo to figure out which image problems the Commish wants to ditch. The NBA higher-ups fear that "the public" views pro ballers as one step removed from the yard at Riker's Island. They are concerned that "Main Street USA" thinks the league is too gangsta, too hip-hop, too urban, all of which is code for "too young, Black, and scary." So now everyone from Jason "White Chocolate" Williams to Darius Miles must wear business casual clothes for all team affairs or risk substantial fines. That means a sports coat and slacks. No jeans, no sneakers, and no medallions, black or gold.

As Stern said, "We want our players to look like the fans buying the tickets to our games." This move away from the trappings of urban youth culture—and away from the majority of fans, who cannot afford tickets to NBA games—has been in the works since Stern hired Matthew Dowd, the PR brain behind the Bush administration, to give the league "red-state appeal." The dress code, like a sleazy campaign ad, has Dowd's fingerprints all over it, and with his help, the NBA is distancing itself from a style and culture they have sold by the pound for a generation. Stern runs the marquee sport for both the inner city and suburbanites looking for that big-city fix. He has been able to do this not only because of what players do on the court, but their image off of it. As Suns guard Raja Bell put it, "I understand they're making it out to make us look better to corporate and big business. But we don't really sell to big business. We sell to kids and people who are into the NBA hip-hop world. They may be marketing to the wrong people with this."

But the dress code doesn't just make bad business sense, it is morally repellent. Trying to control what NBA players wear off the court gives weight to people's worst stereotypes about the young, Black, and gifted among us. It sends a message that players are "out of control" and need some kind of external discipline or the league will go to hell. It also gives credence to the deeply reactionary idea that you can profile antisocial behavior through clothes. If someone wears baggy jeans and a chain, they must be on drugs, packing a gat, or on their way to see one of their twenty babies. This is a slap in the face to every baller who lives clean and, as a grown man, chooses to wear what he damn well pleases—not to mention the young urban audience that the NBA depends on.

As proof of this, the dress code proposal has made it open season for high-profile pundits to spew stereotypes like broken fire hydrants. *New York Post* columnist Phil Mushnick wrote, "NBAers are showing up to speak at schools and in airports and for TV interviews looking like recruitment officers for the Bloods and Crips."

Presidential lickspittle Tony Snow, back when he was anchoring a show on Fox News, spoke to how offended he was by the players' dress, saying,

> You see the bling, what is it? It's a reference to a hip-hop culture that glorifies violence and glorifies sexism. And I don't care if it has to do with somebody's roots, but if you're making $15–20 million a year, perhaps you need to be a role model rather than someone filled with nostalgia of back in the old days when guys were popping each other back in the neighborhood.

Snow says this with a straight face, as if the patriotic militaristic fanfare that—with his blessing—surrounds sports doesn't glorify violence. And it's not just reporters. Lakers coach Phil Jackson also seems to have decided that rap is the root of all evil. "I don't mean to say [this] as a snide remark toward a certain population in our society, but they have a limitation of their attention span, a lot of it probably due to too much rap music going in their ears. The players have been dressing in prison garb the last five or six years. All the stuff that goes on, it's like gangster, thuggery stuff." This is nothing but racism—particularly galling coming from Jackson, who spent the '60s and '70s dressed like a roadie for Country Joe & the Fish.

Mushnick, Snow, and Jackson all speak the language of the backlash. But their comments have provoked a response. Writer Scoop Jackson came back at Coach Phil with a tenacity that should be recognized, writing:

> At what point did Phil Jackson feel that it was his place to take derogatory and demoralizing shots at a culture and walk around as if we were too "illiterate" to understand the subliminal, covert messages behind his comments and beliefs? At what point did he feel nothing would be said? In the words of SNCC: I AM A MAN. In the words of KRS-One: I AM HIP-HOP. And just like any subculture inside of America—rock 'n' roll, grunge, heavy metal, country, bluegrass, electronica, reggae, merengue, punk, funk, rave, classical—that has been given birth through music, there are both good and bad sides. All open not only to judgment, but interpretation.
>
> But when a Hall of Fame–bound, messiah-like respected coach who is a child of a subculture of imperfection feels that he needs to go out of his way to defame and slander another culture and its music while making an irrelevant point about music and basketball, someone has to [do a] Kanye West: Stand up!... Last I looked, I had on an oversized pair of Sean John jeans, an L-R-G white tee with a black L-R-G hoodie resting on my shoulders. AF1 LE's that cost $300 on my feets. Every time I get dressed for work, this is what I wear.... Last I looked, I could retain information, hadn't missed a deadline, haven't been fired from a job, haven't been unemployed or unemployable, haven't been mistaken for a thug or bank robber, haven't been accused of a crime, haven't sold out or sold my soul, and last week was able to get a point about self-esteem across to an auditorium full of kids at a college that made them cry. I recited Nas and Tupac lyrics. My jeans were hanging off my ass. They asked me to come back.

Scoop Jackson is absolutely right. It is ridiculous and pro-foundly hypocritical for David Stern and Phil Jackson to try to define what hip-hop is and isn't and enforce it through a dress code. Take a player like Etan Thomas. Everything Etan wears is against the dress code: the baggy jeans, the medallion, the shades. Etan is also someone who spends more time in D.C. public schools than some principals. Compare that to Jordan who always wears his Sunday best and runs a division of Nike that employs people in conditions that would make Andrew Carnegie blush. I know who I would want my child to emulate. Stern probably knows who he'd want his kids to be like, too.

But at least Stern is consistent. Charles Barkley, on the other hand, vacillates wildly between being someone who tells uncomfortable truths about race and class in the United States to being a Bill Cosby-esque scold, saying, "If a well-dressed white kid and a black kid wearing a do-rag and throwback jersey came to me in a job interview, I'd hire the white kid. That's reality. That's the No. 1 reason I support the dress code."

The problem with Barkley's formulation is that it rests on wrongheaded blame-the-victim excuses for why we live in a country where Black unemployment is three times that of whites. Two recent studies show the racist obstacles African-American applicants face, which have nothing to do with a predilection for baggy jeans. The University of Chicago found that job applicants with "Black-sounding" names—such as LaKisha or Jamal—were twice as likely not to be called back for an interview as applicants with "white-sounding" names. Another study found that even white applicants with prison records were called back more frequently about jobs than African Americans with no prison record at all. Unemployment today for young Black men ages sixteen to nineteen tops out at more than 30 percent, double that of young white men in the same age category. In spite of that appalling statistic, Bush announced that he will cut funds for urban job training programs by 70 percent, from $225 million to $45 million. Another recent study conducted by Cornell University found that "nine out of 10 Black Americans, or 91 percent, who reach the age of 75 spend at least one of their adult years in poverty," compared to 52 percent of whites. The study goes on to say, "that by age 28, the Black population will have reached the cumulative level of lifetime poverty that the white population arrives at by age 75."

It is a slap in the face to say that this unemployment exists because African Americans are showing up to job interviews in do-rags.

If Barkley doesn't get it, many players do; overall, the announcement of the dress code sparked more threats of resistance than pledges of compliance. Operation Penny Loafer today is about as popular as a team trip to the Grand Ole Opry. Allen Iverson commented to the *Philadelphia Daily News*, "I really do have a problem with the dress code.... It's just not right. [Eliminating the dress code] is something I'll fight for." Stephen Jackson agreed: "I think it's a racist statement because a lot of the guys who are wearing chains are my age and are black. I wore all my jewelry today to let it be known that I'm upset with it." Even Wally Sczerbiak, who no one is about to confuse with Trick Daddy, said, "This whole dress code thing is a big ordeal right now. The NBA just snaps their fingers and proposes to change the entire dress code. They don't understand the cultures and what goes into all that stuff.... They're going to try to fine us if we don't. They're going to plant people around to be checking up on teams."

Right now the NBA is the ruckus at Auburn Hills: a reflection of deep antagonisms based on race, age, and class. By pushing the dress code, Stern took all of these tensions and rubbed them raw. Unfortunately, he has continued on this path with a series of moves that make you wonder if he doesn't see himself as a modern Rudyard Kipling, sent to tame the savages of his league by any means necessary. Since Auburn Hills, this has been seen not only in the dress code, but in the new rules regarding age restrictions, and the response to the brawl at Madison Square Garden, at the center of which stood one of the "faces of the new NBA," Denver Nuggets star forward Carmelo Anthony.

◆ ◆ ◆ ◆

After a 2005 game against the lowly Toronto Raptors, Indiana Pacers All-Star forward Jermaine O'Neal was asked a simple question about Stern's desire to see players banned from the NBA before their twentieth birthdays. A Canadian reporter queried, "Is it because you guys are Black that the league is trying to put an age limit on the draft?"

O'Neal, maybe because he was feeling the cool breezes of Canada's social democracy, responded freely, without censor, without filter, and without approval from his sneaker company. He said,

> In the last two years, the rookie of the year has been a high school player. There were seven high school players in the All-Star game, so why we even talking an age limit? As a black guy, you kind of think that's the reason why it's coming up. You don't hear about it in baseball or hockey. To say you have to be 20, 21 to get in the league, it's unconstitutional. If I can go to the U.S. army and fight the war at 18, why can't [I] play basketball for 48 minutes?

The belching scolds of sports radio descended on O'Neal as if he had tipped over Reagan's coffin in the Capitol Rotunda.

He was called stupid. He was told to "just shut up."

All of this because he spoke a truth that made much of the U.S. sports media squirm. But it was a question that needed to be asked. Seventy-six percent of NBA players are African American. But the percentage of players who came right out of high school that are Black is more like 99.9 percent (the one exception ever: Seattle's Rob Swift). In other words, a policy is being proposed that will hurt the ability of young Black men to make a living. Is this racist? There is no similar clamor for baseball, soccer, or hockey leagues to stop drafting high schoolers. The army sure isn't shutting down its high school recruitment booths around the country. No age restrictions are coming down the pike to prevent Dakota Fanning from acting. No law was passed that could have stopped Ashlee Simpson from singing before she was of age (although legislation on the latter could have saved the world from significant aural agony). And yet the NBA calls for change. The arguments in defense of Stern's proposal are painfully weak. Steve Kerr wrote, "So why is David Stern interested in an age limit? To improve the NBA's product; a better product on and off the court." A better product "on and off the court"? Would the league be a better product without instant high school to pro sensations LeBron James and Amare Stoudamire? Even considering players who have taken longer to develop like O'Neal himself or Tracy McGrady, it's the team's decision to draft "potential" over immediate dividends, and the player's right at eighteen to try to make a living.

The other Stern argument is that players who come straight out of high school are "unprepared" and they need "the guidance and discipline" of college life to ready them for the NBA. Anyone who thinks the life of a college athlete breeds "discipline" has turned a blind eye to the University of Colorado's "hooker slush fund" program or Maurice Clarett's exposure of Ohio State as a place where ruddy-cheeked boosters stuff $100 bills in your pocket for playing Xbox with their kids. But even beyond this ridiculous view of college as a Buddhist temple of austere discipline, this statement reeks of racist paternalism by implying that these young Black men need a father figure—often a white father figure—to set them on the right track. As one columnist wrote in defense of raising the age limit, "Perhaps Kobe Bryant would have dealt with adversity in a more positive manner had he spent a season or two playing for Mike Krzyzewski at Duke." It strains credulity that a season or two among the preppy wealth of Cameron Crazies and some fatherly pats on the head from St. Francis of Assisi himself, Coach K, would have altered Kobe's destiny.

The fact is that O'Neal is right. There is no economic reason, no reason with regard to the quality of play, and no reason with regard to the stunting of talent that justifies Stern's move. That leaves race. Stern is simply expressing in policy the long-held concerns of NBA executives that a league whose base of talent is America's bogeyman, the YBT (Young Black Teenager) is unsustainable.

The message is that young Black men are good enough to die in Iraq, but not good enough to play ball. This—no matter how you dress it up—is racism, and, far from stupid, O'Neal has every right to raise this and be heard. As Scoop Jackson wrote, "Let's define stupid. Stupid is Barry Bonds still working out with [his indicted trainer] Greg Anderson. Stupid is Mike Tyson still fighting for a title shot. Stupid is the Lakers not getting at least one All-Star in return for Shaq. An NBA superstar finding something racially motivated when the principals involved are specifically of one race? That's not stupid. That's conscious."

It's a conscious approach desperately needed. Today, much like hip-hop, the NBA is at a crossroads. Hip-hop is no longer something you are for or against. It has become so diverse that it has a left wing and a right wing. It can represent both the deeply progressive and the highly reactionary. It also still has the capacity to threaten power like no other art form. When Kanye West said on national TV that George Bush doesn't care about Black people, it created an unholy stir. If his stage mate at the time, the slack-jawed Mike Myers, or even another prominent African American, like Denzel Washington, had said the same, the reception would have been profoundly different.

In the NBA, the lines are less clearly drawn. Clearly there are players who resent the corporate direction of the league, especially because their dress and personal style have revived the sport. Stern's hard line ignores the fact that the league is on a new journey from the Riley-era Knicks. We are now in the era of seeing people like LeBron, Carmelo Anthony, Dwyane Wade, and Gilbert Arenas begin to reinvent and redefine the game once again. Scoring is up. Smart recent rule changes have put the power back into the hands of creative passers and motion offenses. Teams like the Phoenix Suns have turned back the clock to a style of pure entertainment, with a strategy that states, "We will score and score and dare you to score more."

But Stern's constant reflex of damage control—acting like Mr. Drummond on *Diff'rent Strokes* dealing firmly with a league of Gary Colemans—just feeds the backlash. This was seen when Carmelo Anthony, the Denver Nuggets' star forward, threw a punch last year during a game against the Knicks in Madison Square Garden. In basketball, a fight gets decidedly different treatment from baseball's bench-clearing brawls or the kinds of aggravated assault taken for granted on the hockey rink. It's debated and discussed like the 1992 Los Angeles riots—with an over-caffeinated mix of condemnation and concern. The NBA has become the spittoon for every racial anxiety aslosh in SportsWorld.

For those who have been living in Dick Cheney's bunker, here is how the Carmelo punch went down. The Nuggets were pounding the Knicks, up 19 points with a minute left, and rubbing the Knicks' noses in it. As Denver guard J. R. Smith went up for another highlight dunk, little-used Knick Mardy Collins yanked him down by the neck. This led to a scuffle between

Smith and the five-foot-nine Nate Robinson that spilled into the first row behind the basket. Just when things were starting to calm down, Anthony punched Collins in the face and then backpedaled across the floor quicker than Ginger Rogers. That was followed by several minutes of macho posturing as players preened for the cameras in bogus displays of bravado. Stern suspended Anthony for fifteen games—most observers expected five to ten. Robinson and Smith were banished for ten games each. That wasn't all. We were also deluged with articles about how, as a Yahoo! Sports headline described it, this is really "a black eye" for the entire league. The *Baltimore Sun*'s Childs Walker wrote that the brawl should spark a discussion "about the sociology of the NBA." MSNBC's Michael Ventre opined that "the terms 'NBA' and 'thuggery' have become inextricably linked in the minds of basketball fans the world over." The piece also calls the incident another example of "The NBA vs. Idiots."

Northwest Airlines pulled an issue of their in-flight magazine with Anthony on the cover. In a statement they said, "Northwest does not want to appear to condone in any way the behavior of some of the players during Saturday's game, including Mr. Anthony, by continuing to offer the current edition of *WorldTraveler*."

The responsibility for this lunacy falls back on Stern. It is lunacy because the hysteria flies in the face of facts. This approach, in my mind, is rooted in efforts to assuage the folks who can afford the pricey tickets at Madison Square Garden.

As *Washington Post* sportswriter Michael Wilbon wrote,

> Of the four major team sports in America, basketball has the least amount of fighting. The NHL sells fighting, promotes and glorifies it. Major League Baseball can't go two weeks without somebody rushing the mound to start a bench-clearing brawl, and suspensions are minimal. Pro football, in what seems almost an outgrowth of the mandatory contact, has its skirmishes and fights

all the time. Basketball hasn't had a fight in two years. So, fighting's okay in baseball but not basketball? Why? Fighting is cool for the NHL, but not the NBA? Why? Because the NBA is the only one of those leagues that's perceived as being a "black league."

Wilbon is absolutely right. But then he makes the jaw-dropping jump to defending Stern's handling of the situation: "You can sugar-coat this any way you want but the bottom line is: A black league has to be palatable to white patrons. And black multimillionaires swinging at each other isn't part of the equation. If Stern doesn't send the message that the league has zero tolerance, it's incredibly bad business."

For Wilbon, feeding the fires of racism is nothing more than a better business practice. Fear wins. It's an amazing scenario, in which the same African-American youth culture the league cozied up to is now treated like it needs to be either gelded or quarantined. Players are faced with the dilemma of either "playing ball" or bucking against the system—and risking all its attendant privileges. It's a dilemma young hip-hoppers today know all too well. But they also know that staying true to who you are carries its own rewards. It allows a person to be connected to a broader community: a connection worth more than Benjamins.

As hip-hop artist S.O.N. rhymed,

Everything I got my people worked hard for, scrub floor for, shot by 44 for, lynched by the neck and even burned alive for, so there's no reason to lie for, I'd die for my people though I know most would never cry for, let alone take the time to even ask why for.

There's too many triggers cause everybody knows that there's too many niggas and not enough dough, trickle down economics trickle down slow so there's less degreed bros than blacks with c.o.'s, shorty's get weeded out and end up being weeded out, and get cheated out of the life that they dream about, yeah, it's the same pain you get drunk to be without so I know you feel what I speak about when I blow your speakers out, representing shit that's hard to read about.

CHAPTER SIX

The Olympics: Gold, Guns, and Graft

The modern Olympic Games began in 1896 as a place for imperial rivals—in the process of carving up the world from Cuba to the Congo to the Philippines—to spur fevered nationalist frenzies through sports. In an age when people like Teddy Roosevelt expounded on the redeeming values of empire and the development of "muscular Christianity" through sports, the Olympics provided the perfect place for the rulers of imperialist nations to assert their right to symbolic domination. Over the years, little has changed. During the Cold War, the Games helped to fix ideas of the enemy in the minds of East and West. Today, they've taken a place at the corporate trough, helping multinationals soak cities and giving rise to Olympic-sized graft.

For more than a century, the Olympics have been run by the International Olympic Committee (IOC), a club for fossilized aristocrats with nostalgia for anything with epaulets. When French aristocrat Pierre de Coubertin launched the IOC at the end of the nineteenth century, its membership comprised five European nobles, two generals, and nine leading industrialists. Between 1894 and the turn of the century, de Coubertin added ten more barons, princes, and counts. But the days of de Coubertin seem innocent and carefree compared to what the IOC would become.

Following the 1917 Russian Revolution, when the threatened leisure class found comfort in the politics of fascism, the IOC became a place where the most reactionary of refuse could feel at home. The dominant Olympic figure of the twentieth century was not Jesse Owens, Carl Lewis, or Mark Spitz, but Avery Brundage. As IOC president, Brundage never failed to use his politics to sculpt who and what the Olympics would glorify. In 1936, when the Olympics were to be staged in Hitler's Germany, Brundage—then merely the president of the U.S. Olympic Committee—personally set out to quash a rising din of protest. He met with Hitler in Berlin, where they shared smiles and handshakes for the cameras. Brundage returned to the States with tales of a new Germany that treated Jews and other national minorities with exceptional care. He dismissed the anti-Hitler rumblings as the work of a communist conspiracy.

Brundage's steadfast support of Hitler earned him the respect of the other members of the International Olympic Committee. They voted to have him brought into the club, replacing American Ernest Lee Jahnke, who had called for a Berlin boycott. Unlike other prominent Nazi sympathizers like Henry Ford and Joseph Kennedy, Brundage never apologized for his Hitler leanings. As late as 1941, he was praising the Reich at a Madison Square Garden America First rally. He was even expelled from the right-wing anti–World War II America First Committee because of his endless love of all things Hitler.

But despite the cloud of controversy that surrounded him, Brundage remained chief of the IOC until 1972. Over the years, he used his position to speak out against women competing at the Olympics, continuously denigrating their contributions. He strongly opposed the exclusion of Rhodesia, South Africa, or any state that practiced forms of white supremacy. He was also prone to the most hackneyed, sanctimonious spew, such as, "The Olympic Movement is a 20th century religion. Where there is no injustice of caste, of race, of family, of wealth." Underneath the ponderous self-righteousness, he was an authoritarian leader, contemptuous of the concerns of Olympic athletes, who took to calling him "Slavery Avery."

This is why, when Black Americans attempted to organize their own boycott of the Olympics in 1968, the removal of Brundage was one of their primary demands. The genesis of the famed black-gloved salute of 200-meter gold and bronze medalists Tommie Smith and John Carlos was tangentially connected to Brundage, as African-American athletes brought the gloves because they didn't want to have to actually touch Brundage's skin if they needed to shake hands after medaling.

Brundage is perhaps most notorious for his decisions surrounding the 1972 Summer Olympics in Munich, Germany. On September 5, a Palestinian group called Black September took eleven Israeli athletes hostage. Brundage pushed the Olympics to continue while negotiations were taking place for their release. Even after all the athletes were killed in a botched rescue attempt, Brundage announced that the Games would not be halted. Overwhelming outside pressure forced the IOC to interrupt competition for one day and hold a memorial service of 80,000 spectators and 3,000 athletes in the Olympic Stadium. When Brundage spoke, he shocked observers by making no reference at all to the slain athletes, praising instead the strength of the Olympic movement; his position was that "the Games must go on," a stance endorsed by the Israeli government. Not everyone agreed, however, and many countries left in protest. American marathon-runner Kenny Moore, who wrote about the incident for *Sports Illustrated*, quoted a Dutch athlete saying, "You give a party, and someone is killed at the party, you don't continue the party, you go home. That's what I'm doing."

In a subsequent speech, Brundage stated that Rhodesia, despite its apartheid policies, should never have been excluded from the Games. He then said that the massacre of the Israeli athletes and the barring of the Rhodesian team were crimes of equal weight. Clearly Brundage, after standing astride the Olympics for most of the century, had become a liability. But when the IOC finally put him out to pasture, they settled on a replacement—after a brief interlude with a man named Lord Killanin—no different from Brundage: Juan Antonio Samaranch of Spain. In fact, the only point on which Samaranch and Brundage were at odds was their choice of all-time favorite fascist.

When appointed head of the IOC in 1980, Samaranch was known as a proud and open fascist. Born in 1920 to a wealthy factory owner in Barcelona, Samaranch knew with bloody clarity which side he was on. When General Francisco Franco's fascists fought the Spanish Republicans during the 1936 Spanish Civil War, the teenage Juan Antonio was already an active youth fascist organizer and professional strike breaker. Up until the dictator's death in 1975, Samaranch proclaimed himself "one hundred percent Francoist." As a sportsman, Samaranch believed in the Brundage ideal of the Olympics as a celebration of nationalism and power. As journalist Andrew Jennings wrote in his book *Lord of the Rings*,

> Samaranch schemed for years to be appointed to the Olympic committee, sending unsolicited letters to its president, Avery Brundage, eulogizing in one of them the American's "intelligence, laboriousness and love for [the] Olympic idea" and in another promising, "I will entirely devote myself to go with your personality and prominent work."

Jennings also observed of Samaranch,

> Three decades of devotion to fascism had taught Samaranch a peculiar language. All the institutions in Spain—the monarchy, politics, the church, industry and its workers—were forced into slavish obedience; the dictator and his mouthpieces called it "sacred unity." This has been one of Samaranch's contributions to Olympic jargon. He calls frequently for the "unity" of the Olympic movement and

hails the "sacred unity" of the committee, the international sports barons and the national Olympic committees around the world; all of course under his leadership.

Samaranch was also notoriously corrupt, overseeing the transformation of the Olympics from a Cold War spectacle to a corporate feeding frenzy of privatization and payoffs. Like Brundage, he had a titanic ego and loved issuing platitudes suitable for fortune cookies. Read today, they are delicious in their irony: for example, "We shall serve sport, not use it. Money generated by sport shall benefit sport."

In the peculiar language of Olympic-ese, sport is a synonym for graft. This heartless plundering has, in the post–Cold War era, become the Olympic ideal. It's not "faster, higher, stronger." It's "We'll make you an offer you can't refuse." But refuse, by any means necessary, is exactly what cities should do.

◆ ◆ ◆ ◆

Only those who want to see their hometowns bankrupted, militarized, and flattened should pine for the Olympic Games. Even *Sports Illustrated*'s Michael Fish, a writer who generally blows the Olympic bugle, wrote, "You stage a two-week athletic carnival and, if things go well, pray the local municipality isn't sent into financial ruin."

The evidence is overwhelming. People may remember the 1976 Olympics in Montreal where Nadia Comaneci stole our hearts. More than hearts were stolen. Three decades later, the people of Montreal are still paying for the majesty of the Summer Games, even though at the time one official said, "Olympics cause deficits as often as men have babies."

But there's no need to go back so far; one need only look to the 2004 Summer Games in Athens, which gutted the Greek economy. In 1997, when Athens "won" the games, city leaders and the International Olympic Committee estimated a cost of $1.3 billion. When the actual detailed planning was done, the price jumped to $5.3 billion. By the time the Games were over, Greece had spent some $14.2 billion, pushing the country's budget deficit to record levels.

This is why, in 2005, the people of New York City, in a largely spontaneous uprising, flooded local politicos and the Olympic offices with emails and letters asking—some politely, others with more, ahem, local flavor—to keep the Olympics out. In a town defined by savage inequalities and a police force ready to enforce them, the prospect of a local Olympics was chilling to many New Yorkers. More than 20 percent of the city's residents live below the poverty line. More than 50 percent of African-American youths in Harlem are unemployed. Losing the Olympics saved thousands of residents from being caught in the web of the criminal justice system.

New York City's loss was a bitter pill for Senator Hillary Clinton. Never one with shame, Clinton blithely exploited the terrorist attacks of 9/11 to make the case for her share of Olympic manna: "We're standing here a little less than four years from the time when we were attacked and we're telling you that New York City is the place to bring the 2012 Olympics because people of New York are resilient. They're extraordinary in their capacity to pull together and plan for the future." (Actually they did pull together, just not the way Clinton would choose.)

Perhaps the most dispiriting sight was that of the great Muhammad Ali shilling for the New York bid. New York City's mayor, billionaire Michael Bloomberg, called Ali the bid campaign's "secret weapon" as he led the largely incapacitated former boxing champion from photo op to photo op.

Remembering the Ali of 1960 paints the scene in even more tragic colors. That Ali, then eighteen and known as Cassius Clay, won Olympic boxing gold in Rome only to be turned away from a whites-only restaurant in his hometown of Louisville, despite the medal swinging from his proud neck. The young Clay then took his medallion of gold and as he said, "gave it a home at the bottom of the Ohio River." Cities should take his lead and jettison the Olympics, complete with cement shoes, into the nearest fetid swamp. The people of New York won a victory in keeping the Olympics out. But their gain was London's loss.

Blair's Olympiad

Upon finding out that the Olympics will be marching into New Britannia, London organizer Katie Andrews expressed both shock and anger. "There was no plebiscite. No vote. Now we have these Games being shoved down our throats." In a stunning upset, the IOC awarded London the 2012 games over heavily favored frontrunner Paris. French president Jacques Chirac had spent over $30 million on various inducements—otherwise known as graft—to lure the Olympics to France. Victory seemed assured, and Chirac had already lit a cigar, claiming that "the only contribution London has made to European agriculture is Mad Cow Disease." But beneath Chirac's snippy jingoism, a larger drama was playing out on the board of the IOC.

Avery Brundage once said famously, "The cardinal rule of the Olympics is no politics," which is like saying the cardinal rule of boxing is no punching. It's hard to believe that this year's decision is in any way exempt from geopolitical concerns. Fearing they won't get their piece of the Iraqi pie, the French government has been a thorn in the side of the United States' imperial objectives in the Middle East. Britain, meanwhile, has been only too happy to yip at the feet around the U.S. dinner table, hoping to be thrown a crust and maybe earn a pat on the head. France, which has been an Olympic bridesmaid three times in the last twenty years, stands humiliated while the U.S.'s favored poodle gets the gold.

The question now is whether the British left—which responded so brilliantly to the Iraq invasion with mass antiwar demonstrations—can mount a defense against the Olympic leviathan. To do so, they will need to break with Labor politicians who are dressing the Olympic rings in populist garb. Chief among them has been London mayor Ken Livingstone, who in another life—or an alternative universe—was known as "Red Ken." Livingstone has been a major player in whipping up public support—which currently stands in London at over 50 percent—for the Games. He has been quick to point out, in the words of one observer, that "anyone who is against the Olympics is against the investment and infrastructure and jobs which will help the poor." Yes, Red Ken has turned the Olympics into a social-welfare program. But in between cheers, Livingstone has also announced that each London Council taxpayer will have to pay £20 a year for twelve years (i.e., £240), even if the Games do not make a loss, which is about as likely as seeing the Queen wear leather pants. Already in London, property prices have started to rise. If there is anything we can count on, it's that the wealthy of Britain will make out like bandits, the poor will be squeezed, and Big Ben will end up in the back of a Lausanne pawnshop.

In a particularly groveling moment, Tony Blair told the IOC, "My promise to you is we will be your very best partners. The entire government are united behind this bid…. It is the nation's bid." Is it? It probably won't feel like the bid of those caught in the web of temporary martial law that accompanies every Olympics. Already in Britain, and in Beijing as they prepare for the 2008 Games, we are seeing a familiar script replayed every two years, with only the language changing. Political leaders start by saying that a city must be made "presentable for an international audience." Then the police and security forces get the green light to round up "undesirables" with extreme prejudice.

In 1984, Los Angeles Police Chief Daryl Gates oversaw the jailing of thousands of young Black men in the infamous "Olympic Gang Sweeps." As Mike Davis has written, it took the reinstatement of the 1916 Anti-Syndicalism Act, a law aimed at the revolutionary union, the Industrial Workers of the World, to make these Stalinesque jailings a reality. The 1916 bill forbade hand signals and modes of dress that implied IWW membership. The L.A. politicos of the '80s modernized the bill to include high fives and bandanas, making the case that Blood and Crip Joe Hills were overrunning the city. It was in the Gates sweeps that the seeds for the L.A. Rebellion of 1992, as well as the first music video by a fledging rap group called N.W.A., were planted.

The Atlanta Games in 1996 were no different. These Games were supposed to demonstrate what President Clinton called "The New South," but the New South ended up looking a lot like the old one, as officials razed African American–occupied public housing to make way for Olympic facilities.

Repression followed the Olympic rings to Greece in 2004. Psychiatric hospitals were compelled by the government to lock up the homeless, the mentally ill, and those who suffered from drug dependency. In addition, Greece actually overrode its own constitution by "allowing" thousands of armed-to-the-teeth paramilitary troops from the United States, Britain, and Israel into their country.

But the most heartless example of Olympic repression came in 1968 in Mexico City, where hundreds of Mexican students and workers occupying the National University were slaughtered in the Plaza de las Tres Culturas in Tlatelolco.

The Ghosts of Tlatelolco

"There was one Mexico before 1968 and one Mexico afterward. Tlatelolco was the dividing line."

—Luis Gonzalez de Alba

There was never a year when the worlds of sports and politics collided so breathlessly as 1968. It was the year Muhammad Ali, stripped of his heavyweight title for resisting the draft, spoke on 200 college campuses and asked the question, "Can they take my title without me being whupped?" It was the year Bill Russell's Boston Celtics became champions once again, yet the player-coach saw his house vandalized by bigots. This led Russell to call the city of Boston a "flea market of racism" and say "I am a Celtic, not a *Boston* Celtic." It was the year the Detroit Tigers won the World Series, playing in a city preoccupied by the specter of insurrection, with riots in the hood, snipers on the roofs, wildcat strikes in the auto plants, and Martha and the Vandellas' "Dancing in the Streets" ringing throughout the projects.

And most famously, it was the year that Tommie Smith and John Carlos took the 200-meter medal stand at the Mexico City Olympics to raise their black-gloved fists in a demonstration of pride, power, and politics. Smith and Carlos were part of the Olympic Project for Human Rights (OPHR), and they made their stand because of what was happening outside the stadium: the assassination of Dr. Martin Luther King Jr., the growth of the Black Panthers, the May strikes in France, and most recently in their thoughts, the slaughter of hundreds in the country where they were being feted with gold.

On October 2, 1968, right before the start of the Games, Mexican security police murdered as many as 500 students and workers at the Plaza de las Tres Culturas in Tlatelolco, Mexico City. The families of those murdered in 1968 may finally be finding justice. Mexican prosecutors have announced that they are finally acceding to a four-decades-long campaign, filing charges against former president Luis Echeverría for ordering the Tlatelolco bloodbath. Echeverría was interior minister and head of national security at the time of the massacre. "It has been almost 37 years of impunity and justice denied," prosecutor Ignacio Carrillo told Reuters. "Now for the first time it is possible that the justice system may perform its duty." On June 30, 2006, Echeverría was placed under house arrest for the duration of the investigation.

The Tlatelolco killings were fatally intertwined with the oncoming Olympics. This was a time of mass struggle from the Yucatan to Tijuana. Student strikes had rocked Mexico

Statues honoring Smith and Carlos unveiled in California in October 2005
(AP/George Nikitin)

throughout the year. As part of a rising tide of protests, students vowed to challenge the coming Olympic leviathan. They raised chants like "Justice, yes! Olympics, no!" and held banners that blared, "We Don't Want Olympic Games, We Want Revolution!" and, all too presciently, "Don't Shoot, Soldier! You're One of the People Too!" But despite these kinds of slogans, by all firsthand accounts documented in Elena Poniatowska's oral history, *Massacre in Mexico,* students and their worker allies had no idea what atrocities Echeverría's government was prepared to execute to secure "Olympic peace." On October 2, 10,000 marchers assembled peacefully in Tlatelolco Square at the Plaza de las Tres Culturas. Few realized they had been herded into the square by the military police. As the sun began to set, without warning, the police opened fire. At first, protest leaders said over loudspeakers, "Don't run! They are just firing in the air!" What was happening in front of their eyes was almost too unbelievable to contemplate: the police were methodically shooting to kill. After twenty-nine minutes of uninterrupted gunfire, an estimated 325 people were dead.

Echeverría's Olympic cleanup was responsible for the deaths, not panicked police, rogue officers, or indiscriminate trigger-happy shooters. Recently declassified documents paint a picture of a massacre as cold and methodical as Echeverría's instructions. Cold is to be very kind. On August 22, Echeverría had said, "The Government is most willing to meet with the representatives of teachers and students...connected with the present problems." But despite his willingness to meet in August, by October, Echeverría was ready to unleash hell.

As Kate Doyle, director of the Mexico Documentation Project, describes,

> When the shooting stopped, hundreds of people lay dead or wounded, as Army and police forces seized surviving protesters and dragged them away. Although months of nation-wide student strikes had prompted an increasingly hard-line response...no one

was prepared for the bloodbath that Tlatelolco became. More shocking still was the cover-up that kicked in as soon as the smoke cleared. Eye-witnesses to the killings pointed to the President's "security" forces, who entered the plaza bristling with weapons, backed by armored vehicles. But the government pointed back, claiming that extremists and Communist agitators had initiated the violence. Who was responsible for Tlatelolco? The Mexican people have been demanding an answer ever since.

Thousands of people have marched in the streets every year demanding justice for what is seen as Mexico's Tiananmen Square. And while it is certainly welcome to see Echeverría doddering in cuffs, this arrest should not be seen only as an epilogue of the past but a warning for the future. As mentioned, the Beijing Olympics in 2008 and the British Olympics of 2012 both hold the potential for crackdowns that could rival Tlatelolco. In China, where human rights and trade union organizing are a daily battle in normal times, the government will at the very least use the Olympics to crush even mild dissent.

A new Olympic Project for Human Rights is necessary so people in China and Great Britain who want to resist the state repression, which trails after the Olympics like so much detritus, have the political space to do so. It would be a true, living justice if the martyrs of 1968 can be resurrected to haunt a new generation of Echeverrías already planning security operations in Beijing and London.

Such organizing could also raise the profile of a counter-history to the Olympic Games, in which athletes have shown how sports can be a festival of excitement and achievement as opposed to a commercial free-for-all. In 1925, a year after the Paris Olympics, 150,000 enthusiasts attended the first Workers' Olympics in Frankfurt. Six years later they mustered 100,000 worker athletes for their next festival in Vienna. Again they gathered in 1936, this time in Barcelona, for their anti-Nazi games, but these were cancelled when Franco led his rebellion against the Spanish government. This killed the workers' games as surely as fascism ran over the spines of the workers' movements in these countries. But moments of resistance can be found throughout Olympic history in the actions of people like South African poet Dennis Brutus and Tommie Smith and John Carlos.

Words from the Dark Genius

"The Dark Genius of Dissent." This is how Frank Deford described Dennis Brutus in the pages of *Sports Illustrated* thirty years ago. Deford's characterization, which echoes Joseph Conrad's depiction of Africa, painted a picture of someone to be feared, the man responsible for the "dark clouds" of protest that were sullying the Olympic Games. It was 1976, and the Summer Olympics in Montreal had become a place where several dozen African nations threatened to boycott if South Africa was allowed to play. Their solidarity was a watershed moment, a critical nail in the coffin for South Africa's apartheid regime. Deford's ominous description is comical to anyone who has met Dennis Brutus, who resembles a cross between Gandhi and Yoda. Deford is however correct that, like Gandhi (and Yoda for that matter), Brutus is no one to be trifled with. But the rest he got wrong. Brutus's genius is actually his ability to shine light on true darkness.

No one has ever used sports to advance the cause of social justice quite like Dennis Brutus. The eighty-three-year-old Brutus is perhaps best known today as the former poet laureate of South Africa, a man called the "singing voice of the South African Liberation Movement." He spent decades fighting the apartheid system of white supremacy, earning a bullet in his gut and captivity at the notorious Robben Island Prison off Capetown, South Africa, for his troubles. It was at Robben Island that Brutus spent time breaking stones with a former boxer named Nelson Mandela.

But the least examined part of Brutus's legacy is how he used sports in general—and the Olympics in particular—to highlight the savage inequalities of South Africa's apartheid system: the gap between the purported level playing field of sports and the incredibly unlevel terrain of everyday life. This is why one observer described him as "more than any other single person...responsible for South Africa's and Rhodesia's exclusion from the Olympic Games."

Sports not only surrounded Brutus's childhood, as they do for many in sports-mad South Africa, but also catapulted his political understanding of the world. "I was very enthusiastic, but not very skillful," he said. "But I grew up in a ghetto, a segregated area. I went to a segregated school and the sport is all around you." For a young Dennis Brutus, access determined what he could and could not play. "Going to school we had very little track and field for Blacks, it was mostly for white kids and we would read about them going to the Olympics or whatever. But we were not ourselves able to participate. There were no tracks, no stadiums."

It was Brutus's organizational skills, not his athletic skills, that landed him in the middle of the South African world of sports. He became a sports club secretary, putting together matches, rosters, and schedules. This put him in position to coordinate many athletes and teams excluded from Olympic consideration. The injustice, the disappointment, the anger among those he worked with fueled his desire to fight apartheid. As he said to me, "If you want to know the origins of me as an activist and as an organizer, it really comes from my initial [involvement] in sport."

In 1960, Brutus founded SANROC—the South African Non-Racial Olympic Committee—which grew to challenge the most powerful of international bodies: the International Olympic Committee, and its leader, the imposing—and infamous— Avery Brundage. In a recent interview, Brutus recalled,

> In SANROC, as a matter of course, we would write to Brundage and we would consistently get no reply. Absolutely none. At the time, none of us were conscious of Brundage being the notorious bigot he was. We just didn't know. Later I learned all about it. At

that time I was assuming that he was open-minded—all that sort of thing. In the 1950s the [South African] prime minister makes the statement in Parliament that "we will never allow Blacks on any of our teams." I sent the statement to Avery Brundage in Chicago and wrote, "Hey, here's a country that says it will never allow Blacks on its teams. But you, as president of the IOC, guardian of Olympic values, should be able to say this is in violation of the Olympic charter."

In response to the pressure of SANROC, Brundage sent a fact-finding team to South Africa to investigate if there really was, in fact, racial discrimination in the country—just like the team he had sent to Berlin in 1936, the one that concluded that there was no anti-Semitism in Nazi Germany. Brutus, for his part, was threatened with arrest for expressing interest in attending the meeting between the IOC and the South African Olympic Committee, and was eventually arrested just for being in the vicinity of the meeting. Because of this, and other political activities, Brutus was on Robben Island in 1964 when the first suspension of South Africa's involvement in international play was announced.

As he remembered, "We were in a group with some political prisoners, and one of the new prisoners had read the papers.... [T]he new man announced to us all, 'Hey, have you heard? South Africa is suspended, you know.' So we all cheered and of course we got punished and got our food taken away. But it was an occasion for celebration and we cheered as the guards stood over us armed, with automatic rifles."

The South African issue—and SANROC's challenge to their participation—was a catalyst for transforming the entire structure of international sport. SANROC used the IOC's own charter to highlight the hypocrisy of the proceedings. This was not possible with the IOC's charter in its original form, which, according to Brutus, said something like,

"All countries are welcome to participate for the high ideals of the Olympic spirit." Which was actually a very unhealthy spirit to start with because it began in 1896 with the idea that military power could be replicated symbolically as athletic power. That's why marksmanship was an important sport and the ridiculous ability for instance to fire while on skis was part of it. Gymnastics, the whole athletic perfection, was really about making better soldiers. It fused sport and military for the twentieth century.

But SANROC received a boost at this time from "the grassroots struggles of the 1960s":

> By the '60s the question of South Africa and the question of racism in South Africa had become an issue of international debate, which forced the IOC to redefine the first chapter of the Olympic charter to make a more precise stand against racism. Changing the charter increased the pariah status of South Africa and in addition gave the IOC the power to take action.

But the IOC's "power to take action" was not accompanied by actual deeds. Pressure continued to build from 1964 to 1967 and culminated in that most political of Olympic Games: Mexico City, 1968. Brutus said,

> In Mexico there are all the pressures coming from three areas: Black Americans under the leadership of Dr. Harry Edwards who had formed the Olympic Project for Human Rights. They're getting pressure from the socialist bloc. And they're getting pressure from the South African bloc and our allies, which fortunately were not exclusively socialist. We were able to get allies in the Caribbean and in Asia and in South America. This was important because a common slur of pro-apartheid forces was that SANROC was funded by the USSR.

While many world-class athletes in the United States were silent on the issue of apartheid sports, Brutus was able to bring a select few into the fold, including New York Yankees pitcher Jim Bouton, basketball star Lew Alcindor (soon to be known as Kareem Abdul-Jabbar), and the athletes in the Olympic Project for Human Rights. The public attention proved to be a mighty embarrassment to the IOC. Brutus notes that even Mexico's politicians—who had invested millions in the games and couldn't afford for the Olympic spectacle to become an Olympic deba-cle—began to crank up the pressure on Brundage, as sixty countries threatened to boycott the games over the question of racial discrimination. The actions of the Black athletes from the United States were critical to shedding light on the conflict—al-though there were tensions between the South African and African-American organizers about how best to proceed. "The importance of the American Black Athletes revolt cannot be minimized," says Brutus.

> I have to say Harry Edwards [organizer of the Olympic Project for Human Rights] and I disagreed then, and we might even disagree now. But my whole approach was that, while I supported them, they were using the wrong line of argument. They were using the games to attack a laundry list of grievances, from treatment in the ghetto, [to] unemployment, racism in the laws, and so on. And Brundage had a straightforward answer. He said the Olympics have nothing to do with these issues. So however justified you are, I don't have to take any action on it. But when I said the charter says that every country must be free to participate with regards to race, religion, or politics, I was within the Olympic charter. So I think their line was not a good one in terms of the IOC. But their stance certainly helped us in South Africa. It meant a tremendous deal to know that there was pressure coming from the U.S. and I think it helped the U.S. to know there was pressure coming from South Africa.

Despite his own ability to use sports to expose the hypocrisy and racism of both South Africa and the Olympic Games, Brutus is pessimistic about the prospects today:

> Very often the sport nowadays is elitist. There's a lower level, of course, that goes back to the old-fashioned grounds of Eliza-bethan theater. The other thing that really scares me is the way that sport is used to divert people's attention. Critical political is-sues in their own lives. Their living conditions. The Romans used to say this is the way to run an empire. Give them bread, give them circuses. Now they don't even give you bread and the cir-cuses are lousy.... So my short answer [to the question of whether sports can be used as a site of resistance] is no. But the

power and reach of sports is undeniable. It's kind of a megaphone. People will hear athletes because their voices are amplified. Not always in a very informed way so it [often] ends up expressing the wrong things. Of course when there are exceptions, it can produce magic: Kareem Abdul-Jabbar for instance...[and] Muhammad Ali.... So it does help and they do have that megaphone: but all-important is content. All-important is politics. That is decisive.

When Fists Are Frozen: The Statue of Tommie Smith and John Carlos

The recent unveiling of a statue giving tribute to one of the best examples of Olympic resistance might give Brutus cause to be just a little more hopeful. Trepidation should be our first response when we hear that radical heroes are to be immortalized in fixed poses of bloodless nostalgia. There is something very wrong with seeing the toothy, grinning face of Paul Robeson staring back at us from a stamped envelope. Or the expression the U.S. Postal Service has affixed on Malcolm X—harmless, wry, inviting, and, by extension, slanderous.

These fears erupted in earnest when I heard that San Jose State University would be unveiling a statue of two of its alums, Tommie Smith and John Carlos. The 20-foot-high structure would be a commemoration of their famed black-gloved salute at the 1968 Olympics in Mexico City. I dreaded the thought that this would be the athletic equivalent to Lenin's Tomb: when you can't erase a radical history, you simply embalm it. These fears are not without foundation. Smith and Carlos's frozen moment in time has been consumed and regurgitated endlessly by the wide world of corporate sports. But this process has taken place largely without any kind of serious discussion about who these men were, what ideas they held, and what kind of the price they paid.

With palpable relief, I report that the statue does Smith and Carlos justice, and then some. It is a lyrical work of art, and a fitting tribute to two amazing athletes who rose to their moment in time. Credit should go to the artist, a sculptor who goes by the name Rigo23. Rigo23's most important decision was to leave Smith and Carlos's inventively radical and little discussed symbology intact. On the statue, as in 1968, Smith and Carlos wear beads around their necks to protest lynching, and they are not wearing shoes to protest poverty. Rigo23 made sure to remember that Carlos's Olympic jacket—in a shocking breach of etiquette—was unzipped because, as Carlos said to me, "I was representing shift workers, blue-collar people, and the underdogs. That's why my shirt was open. Those are the people whose contributions to society are so important but don't get recognized."

The most controversial aspect of the statue is that it leaves off Australian silver medalist Peter Norman altogether. This does Norman a disservice, considering that he was not a passive player in 1968 but wore a solidarity patch on his Olympic jacket so the world would know which side he was on. But Rigo23 did this, over the initial objections of John Carlos, so people could climb up on the medal stand with Smith and Carlos and do everything from pose for pictures to lead speak-outs. Norman, who traveled to the unveiling ceremony from Australia, endorsed the design wholeheartedly, understanding that its purpose is less to mummify the past than inspire the future. "I love that idea," said Norman. "Anybody can get up there and stand up for something they believe in. I guess that just about says it all."

Perhaps the main reason the statue is so good, so different, from things like Martin Luther King Jr. shot glasses and Mohandas Gandhi mouse pads, is that it was the inspiration not of the school's board of trustees but of a group of students who pushed and fought for the school to pay proper respect to two forgotten former students who epitomized the defiance of a generation.

And, fittingly, the day of the unveiling was not merely a celebration of art or sculpture but a bittersweet remembrance of what Smith and Carlos endured upon returning to the United

States, stripped of their medals and expelled from the Olympic Village. At the ceremony, Smith recalled,

> The ridicule was great, but it went deeper than us personally. It went to our kids, our citizen brothers, and our parents. My mother died of a heart attack in 1970 as a result of pressure delivered to her from farmers who sent her manure and dead rats in the mail because of me. My brothers in high school were kicked off the football team, my brother in Oregon had his scholarship taken away.

Carlos added, "My family had to endure so much. They finally figured out they could pierce my armor by breaking up my family and they did that. But you cannot regret what you knew, to the very core of your person, was right."

It was also a day to speak explicitly about the challenges of the future and not turning living, breathing struggles into a history that is as inanimate as a hunk of marble. "Will Smith and Carlos only be stone-faced amidst a beautiful plaza?" speaker Professor Ethel Pitts-Walker asked the crowd. "For them to become immortalized, the living must take up their activism and continue their work."

Peter Norman said,

> There is often a misunderstanding of what the raised fists signified. It was about the civil rights movement, equality for man.... The issues are still there today and they'll be there in Beijing [at the 2008 Summer Games] and we've got to make sure that we don't lose sight of that. We've got to make sure that there is a statement made in Beijing, too. It's not our part to be at the forefront of that, we're not the leaders of today, but there are leaders out there with the same thoughts and the same strength.

The last word went to Tommie Smith, proud of the past but with an understanding of the challenges in the future. "I don't feel vindicated," Smith said. "To be vindicated means that I did something wrong. I didn't do anything wrong. I just carried out a responsibility. We felt a need to represent a lot of people who did more than we did but had no platform, people who suffered long before I got to the victory stand.... We're celebrated as heroes by some, but we're still fighting for equality."

When it came time to unveil the statue, the "Star-Spangled Banner" was played as a symbol of how far we've come since 1968. Fittingly, there was a problem: the curtain became snagged on the statues' raised fists. In the wake of Hurricane Katrina, we need our antiracist history and our antiracist heroes now more than ever. We need more fists gumming up the works.

(Norman passed away in October 2006 at the age of 64. The two lead pallbearers at his Australian funeral were Tommie Smith and John Carlos.)

CHAPTER SEVEN

Barry Bonds Gonna Git Your Mama: When Steroids Attack!

Listening to Congress, the media, and the endless yipping of sports radio, it seems that an anabolic specter is haunting America. *USA Today* likened steroids to "the bubonic plague of baseball, a pestilence." Congress held heavily hyped hearings and called steroids in baseball an "emergency public health crisis"—this while 45 million people live without health care. And last year, in a time of war and global conflict, George W. Bush—the Decider in Chief—took time out of the State of the Union address to speak on the evils of steroids. The message was clear. Our children are at risk. Our "national pastime" is at risk. Our sacred baseball records are at risk, preyed upon by evil, freakishly muscled athletes. As World Anti-Doping Agency chair, the unfortunately named Dick Pound, said, "How would you like to take your son to a baseball game and you've got your hot dog and you've got your Coke and you say, 'Son, someday if you fill your body with enough shit, then you can play in your country's national game.'"

Clearly having gotten all the mileage they could out of Janet Jackson's breast, the press has chosen steroids as the new Weapon of Mass Distraction. But in their efforts to hold up steroids as Public Enemy Number One, all the congressional echo chamber accomplishes is the utter distortion of our attitudes toward sports, competition, and medicine. This is not to say that steroids are Flintstone vitamins and should be put in the drinking water. They can result in some dangerous biochemistry. But the pitchforks and torches surrounding the discussion prevent an honest look at what they are, what they aren't, and what role they should play—or not play—in sports.

What's a Steroid?

Let's start with what it's not: it's not the source of all evil in the world. It's not, as baseball commissioner Bud Selig claimed, a "horrible substance that must be eradicated." A steroid is simply synthetically produced testosterone. Scientists have attempted to use testosterone to build muscle going back more than 1,000 years, but the modern era of steroids starts in 1889 when prominent French scientist Charles Edouard Brown-Sequard tried to figure out how to increase the strength and mass of workers in the service of the industrial revolution. Brown-Sequard began to inject himself with a liquid extract derived from the testosterone of dogs and guinea pigs. He claimed that the injections "increased [his] physical strength and intellectual energy, relieved [his] constipation and even lengthened the arc of [his] urine."

Brown-Sequard may sound a likely villain for the next Spider-Man sequel. But his experiments were very much aligned with the dominant ideologies of Western Europe and the United States at a time when bosses were trying to figure out exactly how hard an industrial working class could be pushed before they would die. Working people were literally lab rats, and children, women, and men, young and old, were torn from their homes and put to work for sixteen hours a day, creating a very unstable capitalist system that looked like it wouldn't last the week. Capitalism, of course, survived and gave birth to a number of institutions to preserve its workforce and pass on its "morals" and "values," such as the family, religion, and regimented, professional sports. And it was in sports that Brown-

Sequard's findings found their home.

As the sporting industry exploded in the 1920s, athletic trainers and their charges immediately saw the possibilities of using his research. Even the Big Bambino himself, Babe Ruth, injected himself with extract from a sheep's testicles, hoping for increased power at the plate (and in the bedroom). He attempted this only once, and it made him incredibly ill; the Yankees covered the story by telling the press that the Babe just had one of his famous bellyaches. Even though the Yankees tend to celebrate all things Babe Ruth, they have never, to my knowledge, had "Sheep Testicles Day" at the stadium.

In the 1950s, testosterone was finally produced synthetically and became known as steroids. The first athletes to use steroids were not baseball or even football players, but Olympians. State-sponsored steroid regimens were very much a part of the Cold War in the West as well as the East, as both sides rushed to see whose athletes could be pumped up faster. The scope of East Germany's state-managed doping system wasn't revealed until after the Berlin Wall fell years later, when it was found that more than 10,000 athletes were given drugs, many without their knowledge, some at as young as twelve years of age, leading both to Olympic medals and long-term health problems.

In the 1960s, steroids found their way into NFL locker rooms, with trainers putting them right next to the plates of players at mealtime, or leaving them in lockers. According to Steve Courson's book *False Glory*, the 1970s Pittsburgh Steeler dynasty teams, which won four Super Bowls in six years, passed 'roids out among the linemen like candy. One player said simply, "We knew that if we didn't take the pills we didn't play."

Many NFL players from that era have lived with terrible health problems, and some have died well before their time. Most famously, Lyle Alzado passed away in 1992 of brain cancer that he insisted was linked to his prodigious steroid use. Alzado, as well as sympathetic scientists, asserted that the turn of the century would see "graveyards filled with athletes" that juiced. But this didn't happen. As damaging as they were, steroids haven't proven to be nearly as dangerous as alcohol, tobacco, or the ever-present "legal" painkillers trainers inject into players to get them on the field.

This gets to the central issue about steroids. Like any drug or pill, if abused outside a doctor's care, they can cause all kinds of health problems. They can damage the heart, lungs, and liver. They can also affect the serotonin levels in the brain, leading to the depression and mood swings referred to as "'roid rage," which has been linked tangentially to several suicides. Also, 300,000 high school athletes took steroids last year, a dangerous trend because of the damage steroids can do to those whose bodies are still developing.

But taken under a physician's oversight, steroids can allow people to heal faster, build muscle mass, and train longer than they would be able to otherwise. Steroids have also been a lifesaver for people with HIV/AIDS and MS. According to a recent report from HBO's *Real Sports,* there is no evidence that steroids are unsafe when taken under a doctor's supervision.

Given the above facts, it is no surprise that steroids became especially attractive to Major League Baseball players in the 1990s. Baseball is a grueling marathon of a sport that comes with all kinds of nagging injuries, due to a near nine-month season, complete with winter ball and a 162-game schedule.

The great lie, however, is that major league owners, trainers, and Commissioner Bud Selig were just "shocked" to learn that steroids had found a home in major league clubhouses. The real shock is that the media and Congress have let them get away with this crude fiction. There is a reason steroid testing wasn't in the collective-bargaining agreement until 2003:

the infusion of steroids in baseball—the "juicing of the game," as writer Howard Bryant put it—was as orchestrated by owners as Hat Day and $8 beers. As one player said to me, "It's crazy that punishment is an individual issue but distribution has always been a team issue."

The juicing of the game began in earnest in 1994 when a players' strike mutated into an owners' lockout that led to the cancellation of the World Series. In a century that saw two world wars, a Great Depression, and Reaganomics, this was the first time the World Series had ever been cancelled. The game's popularity sank to historic lows.

DSHEA and the Den of Idiots

The major league owners—called by late Orioles owner Edward Bennett Williams "A Den of Idiots"—consciously decided, "We need dingers. Home runs are how people will return to the ballpark."

While the Den of Idiots were wringing their hands about how to get more home runs, an amazing piece of legislation passed unanimously in the U.S. Congress at the bipartisan behest of President Bill Clinton and Utah senator Orrin Hatch: the Dietary Supplement Health and Education Act (DSHEA).

Despite focus-tested buzzwords like "health" and "education," DSHEA was little more than a criminal giveback to the pharmaceutical industry. DSHEA's purpose was to shift the burden of proof from the health supplement industry to the Food and Drug Administration (FDA). Previously, a manufacturer had to prove a product's safety before marketing it. After DSHEA passed, the overloaded, underfunded FDA had to prove a product to be unsafe. As Dr. Stephen Barrett wrote,

> Most people think that dietary supplements and herbs are closely regulated to ensure that they are safe, effective, and truthfully advertised. Nothing could be further from the truth. Although some aspects of marketing are regulated, the United States Congress

has concluded that "informed" consumers need little government protection. This conclusion was embodied in the Dietary Supplement Health and Education Act of 1994, which severely limits the FDA's ability to regulate these products.

DSHEA's passage spawned the almost overnight creation of the $27 billion supplement industry and turned the locker room of the average team into a GNC store. Because of DSHEA, teams began to import completely legal weight-lifting and dietary "aids." Many of these are now banned substances. Androstenedione—or andro, a highly potent steroid derivative—was legal, available over the counter, and listed as a food supplement. After the 1998 home run race, during which Mark McGwire kept andro in his locker, sales rose 500 percent to $55 million per year. Substances like andro were available in every clubhouse. It started with a few teams, but the pressure to keep up pushed other teams to stock it as well. As former Mets GM Steve Phillips said, "I'm hired to win ball games and if other teams are doing it, I want my players doing it, too." This mentality had deadly consequences. Ephedra, which was completely legal, was linked to the deaths of both Oriole pitcher Steve Bechler and Minnesota Viking offensive lineman Korey Stringer. Now that it has been proven unsafe, it is illegal.

But few were counting the dead because home runs and the media and fan frenzy that accompanied them were making baseball Madison Avenue-hot for the first time since people were doing the Charleston and saying "23 skidoo." Owners milked the new Powerball to the hilt and used cartoons of freakishly muscled players as part of ad campaigns. They also embraced the puckishly sexist Nike slogan: "Chicks Dig the Long Ball."

Increased offense and media buzz meant increased money. In 1995, with the sport on life support, the owners sold their broadcast rights for 565 million bucks, which represented a major loss. In 2001, they sold the playoff rights alone for $2 billion.

Balls were flying over the fence at a record, ungodly pace. It was far more pervasive than the wildly promoted Mark McGwire/Sammy Sosa home run chase in 1998, in which both players broke Roger Maris's record of sixty-one home runs in a season. Consider that between 1876 and 1994 the goal of hitting fifty home runs in the course of a single season had been reached eighteen times. From 1995 to 2002, it was done another eighteen times. Slap hitters were hitting twenty homers. Twenty-home-run guys were up to thirty. As Joe Morgan said, "I would be broadcasting a game and there would be players hitting balls in a way that they had no business hitting them." Morgan was told by his bosses at ESPN not to raise any concerns about this fact.

Morgan's unease about the "cheapening of the home run" was rooted in reality. But it would be wildly ignorant to accept the conventional wisdom put forward by everyone from the sports media to the U.S. Congress to the baseball moralists that steroids are the reason or even most of the reason for the 1990's power boom. It doesn't even come close to telling the whole story. It's an argument born of hysteria.

The owners actually had a multipronged strategy to make Major League Baseball more like beer-league softball—and it was subtle as a blowtorch. As veteran baseball writer Bob Klapisch said, "Somewhere someone decided that baseball needed more runs. It was made at a very fundamental level. And little by little, step by step, this became the new reality. There has been too much to write it off as coincidence." People call this a conspiracy theory, but baseball has a proud history of conspiracies. For six decades, without ever putting the idea to paper, owners kept out African-American players. In the 1980s, they colluded to keep down salaries and deny players the right of free agency, costing players, according to an arbitrator's ruling, millions of dollars. This is what these guys do. They sit in a room and make unaccountable decisions.

Sources of the Boom

The reasons for the home run boom can be seen in every city, and felt in every urban budget, every underfunded school, every shuttered rec center, and every library that closes early. Since 1989, nineteen publicly funded baseball parks have been built.

The new parks are "fan-friendly"—unless your kid happens to go to a school whose shrinking budget paid for these monuments to corporate greed. They are, in any case, long-ball-friendly with shorter fences. It doesn't take George Will to tell us that shorter fences mean more home runs.

Then there are the balls and bats themselves. Countless baseball insiders believe that the ball is now wound tighter than it was twenty years ago. As for the bats, as recently as fifteen years ago, players used untreated ash bats. Now the bats are maple and lacquered. That means the ball goes farther.

Add on the impact of technology: players now go into the clubhouse after every at-bat to look at videotapes and study and correct their swing immediately in a way previous generations could not have dreamed of doing. They even have video iPods with which they can analyze their latest swing as soon as they step down into the dugout.

Next we have the incredible shrinking strike zone. The area where a pitched ball can be called a strike has shrunk, in the words of pitcher Greg Maddux, to "the size of a postage stamp." The owners consciously engineered this trend, and when umpires refused to assent to a microscopic, uniform strike zone, Major League Baseball crushed their union and installed machines to monitor their abilities. The smaller strike zone means that pitchers have to hit very precise spots to get a strike. That means batters can target those areas for upper-cut home run swings. Hall of Fame pitcher Jim Palmer said, "The loss of the high strike has changed the game more than any pill."

Then there is the issue of basic evolution. Smaller stadiums, harder bats, tighter balls are all part of baseball today. But players are also just better than they were eighty, fifty, twenty, even ten years ago. More players from Asia and Latin America like Hideki Matsui and Manny Ramirez mean a broader talent pool. And it is a well-recognized fact that—in every sport from running to swimming—athletes get better over time. The male winner of the 1932 Summer Olympics swimming gold medal in the 100-meter freestyle wouldn't even make the Junior Olympics team today. If Babe Ruth were alive, he would be a fat guy watching baseball on TV. If Ty Cobb were alive, he would be laughed off the field for holding his bat with his hands about six inches apart. It is just a different game.

But an equally big reason that power numbers are up is that the game finally shed its nineteenth-century view of strength conditioning. Baseball is a sport that makes a fetish of nostalgia. The enduring wisdom until the 1990s was that if "Iron Man" McGinnity didn't do it in aught three, it shouldn't be done. For example, it has been the conventional wisdom for most of baseball's history that lifting weights would destroy your swing, causing the muscles to bunch up. The great power hitter Jim Rice, bragged that he never touched a weight during his whole career. Many teams even had a practice of fining or suspending players if they were caught pumping iron. Now weight lifting is a part of every team's regimen as they have realized—to the shock of the old-timers—that being stronger means you can hit the ball farther.

All of these factors are independent of illegal steroids. I made this case last winter on a radio show and a writer for *Sports Illustrated* asked me if I also believed in the Tooth Fairy and Santa Claus. First let me be clear that the data on Ms. Fairy and Mr. Claus are inconclusive at best. But the best proof is that in 2006, the off-season saw intensive testing and far fewer positive results, while home run numbers this year were up. Before he was injured, Albert Pujols was on pace for eighty-four home runs.

Well Then, Why Use Them?

If the increase in home runs is a result of weight lifting, smaller parks, shrinking strike zones, better bats and balls, and basic evolution, a very logical question is raised: Why do so many players take steroids? Here we come to a part of the story never covered in the press: the question of class. Often conflicts between owners and players are portrayed in the press as squabbles between billionaires and millionaires. This leaves out the fact that the billionaires have more often than not carried that bank account for generations while the millionaires didn't exactly come over on the Mayflower. Sports are a lottery ticket out of poverty. The gap between success and failure is razor thin, but the practical difference is astronomical. A minor league player makes on average about $1,200 a month while an even marginal MLB player can make $500,000 a year.

Poverty marks the background of most pro athletes, but in baseball this tendency is particularly extreme. Sammy Sosa, before he was even a teenager, stitched soles in a shoe factory for, as he said, "pennies, just enough to survive." As discussed in chapter three, a rising percentage of players comes from Latin America, with 30 percent of minor leaguers coming from the D.R. alone. Teams fund multimillion-dollar "baseball academies" to develop talent on the cheap. But it bears repeating that, for every star like Pedro Martinez or Miguel Tejada, there are thousands of Dominican players cast aside.

And the Dominican Republic is attractive to major league execs for more reasons than its sunny beaches and never-ending supply of prospects. Steroids are legal in the D.R. Top prospects can find ways to supplement their skill with a no-risk supply. But those not in the top tier often take cheaper animal steroids. Minor leaguer Lino Ortiz took this route, went into shock, and died.

This is billionaires telling people from desperately poor backgrounds to do what they say or have fun in the cane fields. Sure they're free not to juice. They are also free to go back to the ghetto or back to the island.

Steroids and the War on Drugs

Many good people see the exploitation and desperation that factors into steroid use and demand tougher laws. This is, however, a dead end and no answer. Criminalizing steroids, just like criminalizing street drugs, is failed policy that, at the end of the day, condemns more people to addiction and prisons. In 2001, the Pew Research Center released a report stating that three out of four Americans believe the "war on drugs" is an absolute failure. In 1980, the U.S. government spent $1.5 million fighting the "war on drugs." In 2003, they spent $50 billion. This doesn't include the costs of having the largest per capita prison population in the world. And the majority of new prisoners are in for nonviolent drug offenses.

This might lead one to wonder who benefits from the drug trade. Well, according to George W. Bush, that answer is obvious. "It's so important for Americans to know that the traffic in drugs finances the work of terror, sustaining terrorists, that terrorists use drug profits to fund their cells to commit acts of murder." Yes, in Bush's world, drugs help the suiciders.

But in reality the people who benefit are those working in the criminal justice industry, the prison industrial complex, tough-on-crime politicians, and, of course, the drug lords, both inside and outside the CIA, who become filthy rich by exploiting the misery of others.

As disgusting as the war on drugs is, it is even worse when it comes to steroids. Criminalization means there is a multibillion-dollar black-market steroid industry. The *Atlanta Journal-Constitution* recently looked into this issue, writing, "[T]ougher laws and heightened enforcement…have fueled thriving counterfeit operations that pose even more severe health risks." Across America, doctors are continuously reporting treating far more athletes for the side effects of fake steroids than they ever did with the pharmacy standard variety.

Barry Bonds: The Juice and the Noose

There should be a rational discussion in the media, rooted in the medical and scientific community, about the pros and cons of decriminalization, regulation, and education in regard to steroids. Instead we have been treated to hysteria and backlash, some of it as subtly racist as a burning cross.

By not looking at the underlying reasons players juiced in the past, by not honestly examining the difference between use and abuse, we end up with an argument that's overwhelmingly reactionary. This is obvious when we consider the case of Barry Lamar Bonds, aka the root of all anabolic evil.

The attacks on Bonds are off the page. First and foremost, I will say openly that I believe Bonds to be the greatest player of his generation and maybe ever. Throughout the '90s, he averaged a 30/30: thirty-four homers and thirty-six stolen bases. He has eight Gold Gloves and seven MVPs. He is the only player in history with 500 home runs and 500 stolen bases.

But from 2001 to 2004, Bonds literally mastered the game. In this time frame, he set three single-season records for walks and earned the top two records for on-base percentage and the top slugging percentage in history. And in 2001, he hit seventy-three home runs. Remember, steroids don't help with hand/eye coordination and no one ever put a bat on the ball like Barry Bonds. There is a great story of Bonds at the All-Star Game calling out every pitch from the dugout right when it left the pitcher's hand while the other All-Stars just gaped in wonder. Boston Red Sox slugger David Ortiz, who is no slouch himself, said, "When I am home and Bonds comes up, it's the house rule that no one is allowed to talk."

Of course, Bonds also has been the subject of relentless speculation since his training facility BALCO was indicted for the distribution of steroids and human growth hormones. And despite the fact that Bonds has never failed a drug test for steroids (although it was leaked that he tested positive for amphetamines), he has been subjected to a seething hatred in the press that is utterly unprecedented. Nothing is off-limits. I've seen it all: comparing him to O. J. Simpson? Sure. Comparing him to a child molester? Sure. Call for a lynching? These are the words of John Seibel on ESPN radio: "If he did it, hang him. Now I'm not saying hang him. I'm not saying hang him from a tree. I'm not saying strap him to a gurney and inject poison in his veins."

Hear the comments of Rich Melloni, leading antisteroid scientist. Listen to the class contempt and subtle racism in this comment from someone who is supposed to be an anodyne medical expert: "If Barry Bonds and these other athletes don't want the responsibility of being someone others want to emulate, then he should work at Wal-Mart. Otherwise he should stay away from children. He should stay away from MY children."

Or in Houston, a city chock-full of racist hysteria since the advent of the so-called "Katrina crime wave," where Bonds was beaned, the crowd cheered, and sportswriter Dan Wetzel wrote, "It would be pathetic if it wasn't so perfect."

There is no question Bonds is not the cuddliest of star players and is never shy about showing off the massive chip on his shoulder. His battles with the sports media—who he largely thinks of as idiots—are legendary. His conflicts with players are also epic. As one teammate once said, "When Barry says 'fuck you' he actually means it."

He's not cuddly cutesy poo. He has said that he is less interested in passing Henry Aaron's all-time home run record than Ruth's number two total because he wants to wipe from the books anyone who played in the segregated era. He is also

Barry Bonds responds to media attention while stepping onto the field for the first day of spring training, 2007 (AP/Eric Risberg)

someone who has never shied from saying things political like, "[Are] steroids cheating? You want to define cheating in America? When they make a shirt in Korea for $1.50 and sell it here for 500 bucks. And you ask me what cheating means?" This is why the press hates him and why he has developed a fiercely loyal following. Anyone can "play one game at a time," but to call out global sweatshops because you are pissed off at a sportswriter? That's special. My favorite moment during the baseball congressional sham hearings was when they were asked why they didn't subpoena Barry Bonds and they said, "Barry tends to get off subject."

Does all of this mean that Barry Bonds is the object of a racist witch hunt? I have had to publicly argue this issue against some of the finest minds of my generation. (All right: John Rocker and Jose Canseco.) The dominant argument I hear, whether from Mr. Rocker or Mr. Liberal Blogger, is that I am an idiot if I think that the Bonds steroid mania is purely about bigotry run amok. Unfortunately, that is not my argument. To be clear: I don't think that everyone against Bonds is a racist. I don't think every sportswriter who wants Bonds punished is a racist. And I certainly don't believe anyone who believes in harsh penalties for steroid use is a racist. One can hate Barry Bonds and also spend Sundays singing "We Shall Overcome" with the Harlem Boys Choir before reading select passages from *Go Tell It on the Mountain*. But to argue that race has nothing to do with the saga of Barry Bonds is to embrace ignorance frightening in its Rocker-esque grandiosity.

Of course, you can always simply agree with San Francisco Giants owner Peter Magowan, CEO of Safeway Supermarkets and anti-union zealot, who believes that it is a remarkable sign of racial progress that Barry Bonds is flayed before the public. Magowan said, "I don't believe this is a case of racism. In fact, I think this shows how far we've come. If the media brought this up 20 years ago, they would have been considered racists."

Now that's progress. The media can be as racist as they want without being called on it. The fact is that racism smears this entire story like rancid cream cheese on a stale bialy.

First and foremost, there are the death threats. *USA Today* has reported that Bonds is being deluged with letters that threaten both his life and the life of his family. I was a guest on a predominantly African-American radio program out of Cincinnati called *The Nathan Ive Show,* and we were deluged with calls by older African Americans who recalled with chilling clarity the trials of Henry Aaron. When Aaron approached Babe Ruth's home run record, the death threats and slurs came rolling in like a white-power Halley's Comet on a thirty-two-year cycle. As Dr. Harry Edwards, the famed sports sociologist, recently said, "The same animosity and resentment that Hank Aaron suffered through when he broke Babe Ruth's record has been exacerbated because of the cloud of steroid suspicion. This is a visceral response to a black man [passing] Babe Ruth."

Then there is the way the media are covering the issue. There is no question that Bonds has spent his career treating the press the way a baby treats a diaper. But Bonds is not the first athlete to sneer at a reporter or two. In fact, Mark McGwire was a notoriously surly personality until he was presented to us as a grinning Paul Bunyan. It's not who you are, but who the media tells us you are. When it comes to Bonds, the press has called for everything but a big scarlet S for steroids on his chest, all of which has the appearance of a hellacious double standard.

When a prominent ESPN talk show host says, "If [Bonds] did it, hang him," it is little more than a railroad job of a prominent and outspoken African-American superstar on the precipice of being the home run champion. Not all the racial bias is that overt. I was on the CNBC talk show *The Big Idea with Donnie Deutsch,* where I debated the issue of Bonds, and faced off with sports radio host Scott Wetzel, the Reverend Jesse Jackson, and Deutsch himself. After the guests left, Deutsch got the last word. Here is sports media analyst Jonathan Weiler on what transpired:

> Perhaps the most revealing moment of the evening came toward the end of the show. Deutsch counted down five sports personalities who have gone wrong. Number two on Deutsch's list was [white Yankees pitcher] Randy Johnson who Deutsch described as a "jerk." Deutsch said that Randy has always been surly with

the media (a "white version of Bonds") and that while his sullen personality may have been OK when his ERA was [below] 2.00, now that his ERA is over 5.00 his "Barry Bonds personality is catching up to him." Earlier, Deutsch had said that "most of America now roots for excellence" and then, in an apparent non sequitur, asked rhetorically "if Barry Bonds had been a likeable guy all these years…wouldn't we have rooted for him, too." In case you missed it, Deutsch has just asserted, without realizing it, that two surly guys have been subject to two different standards of evaluation. On the one hand, the "white Barry Bonds" and his unpleasant attitude were tolerated as long as he was great. On the other hand, the real Bonds's lack of likeability meant that he was never going to get favorable treatment from the fans *even when he was the epitome of baseball excellence and before there was any whiff of impropriety about his performances.*

The media has laid the groundwork for Major League Baseball to take the extraordinary step of forming a commission to "investigate and root out steroids in the game," led by former senator George Mitchell. But the probe is already being derided as a sham. How seriously would we take an investigation into Iraq's missing weapons of mass destruction if it was headed by Dick Cheney? Would we accept an examination of racial profiling if it was led by John Ashcroft? Of course not. It would be a farce. And so it is with Senator Mitchell in charge. Mitchell sits on the board of the Boston Red Sox. He is also chairman of the Walt Disney Company, the parent company of ESPN, the main national broadcast partner of baseball. In other words, he has an actual material interest in keeping the spotlight off the owners, including what they knew and when they knew it, and keeping it on the players. Particularly Barry Bonds.

According to one writer with a serious pipeline into the commissioner's office, Richard Justice, the investigation is "totally [aimed at Barry Bonds]. He is the number one player going for the most hallowed record…. There may be other names that come out but this is all about Barry Bonds…. Bud wants the perception that he is doing this the right way.... I promise you he will not get the chance to break Hank Aaron's record. I will be willing to bet you. I think Henry Aaron and Bud Selig will be grilling brats in Bud's backyard."

In other words, this is all smoke in our eyes, blurring the fact that this is really about getting Bonds out of the game before he passes Aaron. It doesn't look like Bud is going to be able to accomplish this, but both he and Aaron have sent signals that they won't be at the park if and when Bonds breaks the record.

Are Selig's actions racially motivated? The question is too simplistic. The fact is that Bud is deflecting criticism off the owners by putting the heat on the most prominent player in the game who happens to be Black. Whether this is conjured up in some back room or not is beside the point. MLB owners seem willing to sacrifice Bonds if it keeps Congress and the public off their backs. This is why some prominent baseball people are loudly speaking a word rarely said in the world of sports: race. It is important to listen to what baseball players are saying about this.

All-Star Minnesota Twin Torii Hunter, another of baseball's dwindling African-American superstars, speaking before Bonds passed Ruth's record, called the investigation "stupid." "They can say what they want, but there's no way they would launch an investigation if Barry Bonds was not about to break Babe Ruth's record." Hunter went on to say:

> It's so obvious what's going on. He has never failed a drug test and said he never took steroids, but everybody keeps trying to disgrace him. How come nobody even talks about Mark McGwire anymore? Or [Rafael] Palmeiro [who tested positive for steroids in 2005]? Whenever I go home I hear people say all of the time, "Baseball just doesn't like black people." Here's the greatest hitter in the game, and they're scrutinizing him like crazy. It's killing me because you know it's about race.

Dave Stewart, a former twenty-game winner and front office exec who is now an agent, said to one reporter, "People keep talking about how he's not supposed to keep hitting homers and doing phenomenal things because he's 40-plus. Well, Roger Clemens is 40-plus, too, and nobody ever brings his name up. Why not? Is it because he's white?"

Matt Lawton, who unlike Bonds has tested positive for steroids, said, "If (Bonds) were white, he'd be a poster boy in baseball, not an outcast."

Radio personality Scott Wetzel says that Black players who feel there is a racial double standard are "ignorant." This is part of the problem: an overwhelmingly white sports media establishment calling Black players ignorant if they dare speak about their reality.

None of this means that any critique of Bonds is inherently racist or that there doesn't need to be some way to deal with performance enhancers. It means that the overheated rhetoric needs to cease. It means that if baseball decides it doesn't want steroids in its game and wants to "clean up its own house," it should realize that it is cheap, gutter politics to focus on one person as if that person is the root of all anabolic evil. They should realize that, in the current climate, their actions embolden a racist fringe. If they don't realize it, we sure as hell should.

A couple years ago, Bonds said, "This is something we, as African-American athletes, live with every day. I don't need a headline that says, 'Bonds says there's racism in the game of baseball.' We all know it. It's just that some people don't want to admit it. They're going to play dumb like they don't know what the hell is going on."

That is absolutely right. It's not defenders of Bonds who are putting race on the table, but whether you are a Bonds supporter or not, all antiracists need to take it off.

But because it is still on the table, two Americas now exist on this issue. I have done both mainstream sports radio and Black radio, and the reaction couldn't be more different. Mainstream: "We're not racists. We just hate his guts because he's a cheater!" Black radio: "Do you think Bonds will be shot?" Literally. This is now being further exacerbated by the federal government. The FBI has approached players about wearing a wire and getting Bonds on tape to admit steroid use. They want to imprison Bonds for perjury, tax evasion, anything short of kidnapping the Lindbergh baby. One writer cited an agent saying, "He's our Capone."

Baseball, therefore, which is supposed to be the national pastime, becomes instead another stick to divide us.

So What Do We Do?

The entire steroid mess needs to be reframed so we understand that it is really an indictment of how big-time sports operates in these modern times. Sports is an enormous industry run to make money, and all of sports—from Little League to the major leagues—is subject to this fact. Bosses exploit worker-athletes and squeeze them to produce, just like any other industry—work longer, harder, faster. This is why baseball and the bosses loved Cal Ripken. The guy played 2,632 straight games. This is a neoliberal wet dream. The worker who never gets sick. The pressure to perform has accelerated dramatically in the last few decades with scientific advances. It has led to a mass industry of performance-enhancing techniques, supplements, and drugs.

To produce, athletes have always taken performance-enhancing drugs. As Buck O'Neil, the then ninety-one-year-old Negro League great who passed away in 2006, said, "We didn't use steroids because we didn't have them." Performance enhancement has always been an accepted part of sport that was, in fact, encouraged by bosses. Moreover, in order to survive the new productivity squeeze in sports, athletes turn to other drugs at an increasing rate, from painkillers and vitamin regimens to dietary schemes and supplements.

If OSHA investigated sports, they would find a litany of offenses because sports injures its workers at an amazing rate. It has one of the highest on-the-job injury rates of any industry. Think of the experience of watching games—players taken off the field injured, many for the rest of their lives. Again, to survive, athletes have to medicate themselves. Watching retired athletes is just painful. Go to a NFLPA veterans dinner and you will see people in their forties and fifties walking like broken old men. To be a pro athlete is to rob yourself of middle age. It's a deal with the devil that the poor make to produce for the rich. The minute they can't produce, they're as expendable as a day-old newspaper.

Drug use is, therefore, a result of class in the sports industry, of bosses squeezing their workers to produce. That's why it's stupid to blame professional athletes for leading young athletes to take performance-enhancing drugs. This is as stupid as saying that violence in our society is the result of kids watching violent TV shows. Both violent TV shows and social violence are symptoms of the underlying competitive pressures of a system that forces people to fight with one another over everything from jobs to sneakers. All the moralizing about athlete role models is a diversion from what will continue in sports, however many scapegoats they find.

Understanding it this way shapes what we should demand. We should oppose criminalization and massive testing programs, since all this will produce is ways for athletes to evade programs—like taking masking agents that can be unsafe—while not touching the underlying motives that drive athletes to turn to drugs. It also leaves out all the performance-enhancing drug consumption that is legal and approved—like painkillers.

Instead, we should call for an easing of the labor conditions and pressure that produce the drive toward drug consumption. You would have to change the very reality of athletics, and in the case of baseball, that would mean shorter seasons. A sane discussion of the game, one controlled by the players, would sound like this, "Gee, we are putting all this pressure on our bodies, and the travel is killing us. What do you say we play 140 games instead of 162? Sound good?"

Frankly, I don't think fans would mind a shorter year, either. All pro seasons are too long. In 1999, when the NBA played a fifty-game season due to a strike, a poll of fans said that they actually preferred the shorter season. But the profiteers would never allow that. So instead of making working conditions more manageable, owners put tremendous stress on players to hit home runs or find another line of work. Players feel a deep pressure to not lose their spot because of a nagging injury. A manager favors a player who shows he will "go that extra mile." Juice or fall behind.

We should also stand for less of a gap between minor and major league wages and benefits as part of standardized contracts not dependent solely on reaching incentives. These are demands that should be and should have been championed by the Players Union. This is what the Players Union got wrong. Donald Fehr, who calls himself "an unrepentant '60s radical" and runs one of the most disciplined unions in the United States, correctly called out the hypocrisy of the steroid hysteria. He correctly said he would defend players that wouldn't testify to Congress. He correctly called out the power boom as being a lot more complicated than steroids. He correctly understood that the main reason the owners flip-flopped from buying steroidal substances wholesale to becoming teetotalers was because it allowed them to bash the union. But Fehr never spoke to the reason players feel such insane pressure to perform and what the union could do to ease those pressures. This meant that, for the first time in forty years, the union was divided, as players who weren't juicing but felt the pressure to do so went public and said, "This guy doesn't care about us!" And Fehr was left at the mercy of the owners, with the Players Union weakened as a result.

We need a sane, scientific discussion about the pros and cons of steroids and human growth hormones. Unfortunately, Congress, the media, and the sports establishment have done and will continue to do everything they can to prevent it from happening. So we have to ask ourselves: Where do we collectively want to see sports in relation to performance-enhancing drugs in five years? The way current trends are headed, sane scientific discussion and decriminalization are not in the cards. Instead, expect more political grandstanding, more justice department crackdowns, and more young people using ever-more illicit concoctions in an attempt to acquire an illusory ticket to stardom. Bonds will be retired with aching knees, labeled a cheater, and—perhaps—denied entry into the Baseball Hall of Fame. And, unabated, players will be discovering ways, both creative and dangerous, to beat the test.

CHAPTER EIGHT

The Uses of Sports: How People in Power Exploit the Games

T here is so much inspired joy on the playing field that it's easy to forget how people in power use sports to advance their own narrow agendas. Sports has always held a tremendous sway over the popular imagination. Politicians from the days of Teddy Roosevelt have successfully used the games to manipulate public sentiment. That is not to say sports are some kind of Jonestown Kool-Aid with the power to lead us like lemmings off a cliff. It's merely a tool—a tool both political parties are quite adept at using to their advantage. Our bipartisan emperors drape themselves in sports as a way to connect with the workaday reality of ordinary people. In normal times, they do this for the noble purpose of selling themselves to voters. In these troubled times, they use sports to sell this country's endless war on the Middle East. This was exposed in the ugliest possible way following the death of Pat Tillman.

When former Arizona Cardinals football player turned Army Ranger Pat Tillman died in Afghanistan, people mourned from coast to coast, while the war propaganda machine worked into overdrive. We were told he died a "warrior's death" charging up a hill, urging on his fellow Rangers. His funeral was a nationally televised political extravaganza, with Senator John McCain among others delivering eulogies over his open grave. His commander in chief George W. Bush took time during last fall's

Pat Tillman, photographed in uniform in 2003 (AP)

presidential campaign to address Cardinals fans on the Jumbotron at Sun Devil Stadium. Republican congressman J. D. Hayworth was one of many singing Tillman's praises. "He chose action rather than words. He lived the American dream, and he fought to preserve the American dream and our way of life."

At the time, I wrote a small column stating that Tillman—who refused "hundreds if not thousands" of offers by the Pentagon to shill for the "War on Terror"—would have been repulsed by all the attention. I wrote that to Bush, McCain, and their pro-war ilk, Tillman was proving far more useful dead than alive. He had joined the Rangers for ideals like freedom and justice, but he fought in a war for oil and empire. I wrote that, in death, Tillman was little more than "a pawn in their game."

This observation didn't click with the pro-war/occupation camp, as hate mail and death threats poured in to the sleepy newspaper where I labored. These people insisted that the bipartisan war brigade was celebrating his heroism, not exploiting his death—and by not simply standing and saluting, I was being traitorous.

We now know, of course, that they were duped about Tillman's death. Duped like the country was duped about WMDs. Duped into cheerleading a war that's made the world a more dangerous place and accomplished little more than a new generation of mass graves, containing more than 650,000 Iraqis and—as of January 1, 2007—3,002 U.S. soldiers. Duped into suffering higher gas prices and diminished civil liberties.

I can only wonder if those so protective of Pat Tillman's memory will ever exhibit a fraction of the bravery being shown by Pat's parents, Patrick and Mary. In September of 2005, the divorced couple decided to go public with their fury at a government that lied over the body of their dead son.

Patrick and Mary found out that Pat did not die at the hands of the Taliban while charging up a hill, but was shot by his own troops in an instance of what military bureaucrats call "fratricide." Patrick and Mary found out that Tillman's men realized they had gunned him down "within moments" of his being hit. They know that the soldiers—in an effort to cover up the killing of the All-American "poster boy"—burned Tillman's uniform and body armor.

They learned that over the next ten days, top-ranking Army officials, including the all too appropriately titled "theater commander," Army General John P. Abizaid, hid the truth of Tillman's death, while Pentagon script writers conjured a Hollywood ending. They know that the army waited until weeks after the nationally televised memorial service to even clue them in about "irregularities" surrounding their son's death. They strongly suspect that the concurrent eruption of the Abu Ghraib prison scandal may have played a role in the cover-up, as the Army attempted to avoid a double public relations disaster. "After it happened, all the people in positions of authority went out of their way to script this," Patrick Tillman told the *Washington Post.* "They purposely interfered with the investigation, they covered it up. [T]hey realized that their recruiting efforts were going to go to hell in a hand basket if the truth about his death got out. They blew up their poster boy."

Mary Tillman, a fiercely private person like her ex-husband and son, spoke with a frankness that should put dissembling military planners to shame. "It makes you feel like you're losing your mind in a way," she said. "You imagine things. When you don't know the truth, certain details can be blown out of proportion. The truth may be painful, but it's the truth. You start to contrive all these scenarios that could have taken place because they just kept lying. If you feel you're being lied to, you can never put it to rest." Now the Tillmans, consciously or not, are lending their voice to a growing chorus of military family members determined to speak out against this war. Organizations like Gold Star Mothers for Peace and Military Families Speak Out are made up of people handling their grief by refusing to be political props and instead making the country bear witness to their pain.

"Every day is sort of emotional," Mary Tillman said.

It just keeps slapping me in the face. To find that he was killed in this debacle—everything that could have gone wrong did—it's so much harder to take. We should not have been subjected to all of this. This lie was to cover their image. I think there's a lot more yet that we don't even know, or they wouldn't still be covering their tails. If this is what happens when someone high-profile dies, I can only imagine what happens with everyone else.

One of the ways the Tillmans are fighting back is by revealing a picture of Pat profoundly at odds with the G.I. Joe image created by Pentagon spinmeisters and their media stenographers. As the *San Francisco Chronicle* put it in September 2005, family and friends are now unveiling "a side of Pat Tillman not widely known—a fiercely independent thinker who enlisted, fought and died in service to his country yet was critical of President Bush and opposed the war in Iraq, where he served a tour of duty. He was an avid reader whose interests ranged from history books...to works of leftist Noam Chomsky, a favorite author." Tillman had very unembedded feelings about the Iraq war. His close friend Army Spec. Russell Baer remembered, "I can see it like a movie screen. We were outside of [an Iraqi city] watching as bombs were dropping on the town.... We were talking. And Pat said, 'You know, this war is so fucking illegal.' And we all said, 'Yeah.' That's who he was. He totally was against Bush." With these revelations, Pat Tillman the PR icon joined WMD and Al Qaeda connections on the heap of lies used to sell the Iraq war.

◆ ◆ ◆ ◆

This isn't the only time the Bush administration has used a figure from the world of sports to make themselves less repellent. Bush, a former Yale cheerleader, has always been a world-class jocksniffer, much more comfortable around athletes than reporters; the kind of guy in your junior high locker room who could snap towels with the best of them. There are few people he has cozied up to more than cycling hero Lance Armstrong. Unfortunately, Armstrong has swallowed many of his own beliefs to play presidential bike buddy.

Last summer, Armstrong and Bush took a seventeen-mile

bike ride around Bush's Crawford compound, where they gazed at the landscape that Bush calls "my slice of heaven." Armstrong gushed about Bush's riding prowess afterward, saying to ABC News, "That old boy can go.... I didn't think he would punish himself that much, but he did." By the way, the war and occupation of Iraq "never came up."

This is hard to swallow. Armstrong, also the country's most well-known cancer survivor, took a strong stand against the war right after his amazing seventh consecutive Tour de France victory. With the sweat still pouring down his face he said, "The biggest downside to a war in Iraq is what you could do with that money. What does a war in Iraq cost a week? A billion? Maybe a billion a day? The budget for the National Cancer Institute is four billion. That has to change. Polls say people are much more afraid of cancer than of a plane flying into their house or a bomb or any other form of terrorism."

Armstrong's Texas Toady Two-Step was even more maddening given that Crawford was not exactly neutral vacation space for George W. Bush at the time. In fact, his five-week siesta was gloriously disrupted by the real world. Cindy Sheehan lost her son Casey in the Iraqi carnage, and went to Crawford to make her anguish Bush's problem. She requested an audience with the president, and legions of supporters flocked to her side. Sheehan, with striking moral and political clarity, demanded not only answers, but immediate and total troop withdrawal from Iraq. She garnered international attention at a time when Bush's poll numbers had never been lower. Yet Bush scoffed at the idea of meeting with Cindy, saying, "I need to get on with my life."

Lance Armstrong biked into a political hornet's nest. He had an opportunity to not just talk the talk, but also walk the walk. But Armstrong neither talked nor walked. Maybe it's unrealistic to think that Lance could have suggested a bike detour to Camp

Casey. Perhaps it's a flight of fantasy to imagine that Lance would organize a Critical Mass bike ride to jam the gates of Crawford. But his utter silence, given both what he knew about Iraq and the presence of Camp Casey, spoke volumes.

To understand how Lance Armstrong could float so blithely from "Man of Principle" to "Man of Crawford," we need to understand the sport of cycling and the unique position that Lance occupies within this cloistered world. His privileged status compels him to stand alone, apart from his fellow riders, as sure as it compelled him to ride with Bush and leave Camp Casey in the dust.

The Vicious Cycle

If ever there was a sport that needed a union, it is professional cycling. Succeeding on "the Tour" is literally a matter of life and death. In the past decade, two professional riders have crashed and died while racing, one on Lance's team. Also, during the 2005 Tour, a top Australian amateur, Amy Gillett-Safe, was killed while training in Germany. Team directors and doctors have ultimate control over riders and their health choices, reminiscent of the old NFL days when Novocain substituted for medical care. The one-day spring races, "the Classics," are run over courses designed to be long and brutal—including cobblestones, narrow farm tracks, steep hills—and of course they are commonly raced in the rain. As cycling maven and good friend Jesse Sharkey once told me, "The difficulty of the conditions is part of the allure of the sport, but the travesty is that riders themselves have virtually no say in any of the basic features of the racing world—from the courses to the clothing they wear, and often even what they eat and drink."

Lance is perhaps the sole exception. He is one of the only cyclists who sets his own terms. He is like Michael Jordan on the 1996 Bulls or Eddie Murphy in the 1982 season of *Saturday Night Live*. He is a man apart, the Tour be damned. Armstrong decides what events he will do (very few) and what conditions he will race under (he dropped out of the Paris-Nice race this year when the weather got nasty). In other words, while the overwhelming majority of cyclists barely eke out a living, Armstrong does it his way. He sees no benefit in solidarity and therefore doesn't exercise it. To be fair, all of the above are the basic realities of the sport—Lance didn't invent them. But his position could be used to speak out for a more just system.

Drug testing is a great example of this. In a sport whose currency is physical agony, drugs have been, for many, the breakfast of champions. In 1998, the Festina team doctor was caught with a car full of doping supplies and 400 vials heading into France. Like most drugs in professional sports, doping in cycling has always been a team-sponsored affair. However, when the media and police frenzy erupted, it was the riders who were dragged naked from their hotels, cavity-searched, and jailed. French champion Laurent Jalabert, speaking on behalf of all the riders in the race, said, "We are revolted by what is happening. We are treated like cattle and in consequence today we will no longer ride."

But Lance, in his June 2005 interview with *Playboy,* took the company line: "...all I can say is thank God we're tested."

> When baseball players were charged with using steroids, what was their defense? Nothing. Saying "It's not true." Whereas my defense is hundreds of drug controls, at races and everywhere else. The testers could roll up here right this minute. They knocked on my door in Austin last week. In a way it's the ultimate in Big Brother, having to declare where you are 365 days a year so they can find you and test you. But those tests are my best defense.

This strain of "anti-solidarity" in Armstrong's character was on sad display in his ride with Bush. While they worked up "a healthy sweat," family members of the fallen waited in vain to hear a plausible reason why Casey Sheehan and so many others continue to die. Lance had ample opportunity to ask the same question. He chose silence. Not only with Bush, but also toward those at Camp Casey who thought they had an ally in Lance Armstrong. As his ex, Sheryl Crow, once sang, "Did you see me walking by? Did it ever make you cry?"

It is upsetting that Armstrong was willing to ride with Bush, allowing Dubya to bathe in his superstar glow for the cameras while Sheehan and friends were keeping vigil. But this was nothing compared to the shameless scene presented when Bush, suffering some of the worst poll numbers of his presidency in the months after Hurricane Katrina, had Muhammad Ali brought to the White House. On November 9, 2005, Bush hung a Presidential Medal of Freedom around the bowed head of the former heavyweight boxing champion—and the most famous war resister in U.S. history—Muhammad Ali. Ali was one of a bevy of recipients of the Presidential Medal of Freedom at a White House ceremony. With Karl Rove and Donald Rumsfeld chuckling behind him, Bush paid unctuous homage to Ali.

> Only a few athletes are ever known as the greatest in their sport, or in their time. But when you say "The Greatest of All Time" is in the room, everyone knows who you mean. It's quite a claim to make, but as Muhammad Ali once said, "It's not bragging if you can back it up." And this man backed it up.... The real mystery, I guess, is how he stayed so pretty. [Laughter.] It probably had to do with his beautiful soul. He was a fierce fighter and he's a man of peace.

A video of the ceremony posted on the White House website shows Bush, a chicken-hearted man of empire, using Ali as a prop while rhapsodizing about "peace." To see the once-indomitable Ali, besieged by Parkinson's disease and dementia, eyes filmed over, hands shaking, led around by a self-described "war president" is enraging.

About the only thing Bush and Ali have in common is that they both moved mountains to stay out of Vietnam. The difference, of course, was while Ali sacrificed his title and risked years in federal prison, Bush joined the country club otherwise known as the Texas National Guard, showing up for duty every time he had a dentist appointment. But the Champ still had one last rope-a-dope up his sleeve. As a playful Bush moved in front of Ali, he apparently thought it would be cute to put up his fists in a boxing stance. Ali leaned back and made a circular motion around his temple, as if the president must be crazy to want to tangle with him, even now.

This moment recalled the Ali who was never so beloved, so cuddly, so harmless. This was a fleeting glimpse of the Ali who once was able to say things that would have made John Ashcroft demand a federally funded exorcism. This was the Ali who said, "I ain't no Christian. I can't be when I see all the colored people fighting for forced integration get blown up. They get hit by the stones and chewed by dogs and then these crackers blow up a Negro church." This was the Ali who mocked anyone who told him what a "good example" he'd be if he just "wasn't Muslim."

Back then, Ali leveled criticism at all forms of the criminal enterprise, asking, "Why should they ask me to put on a uniform and go 10,000 miles from home and drop bombs and bullets on brown people in Vietnam while so-called Negro people in Louisville are treated like dogs and denied simple human rights?"

> I have said it once and I will say it again. The real enemy of my people is here. I will not disgrace my religion, my people, or myself by becoming a tool to enslave those who are fighting for their own justice, freedom, and equality.... If I thought the war was going to bring freedom and equality to 22 million of my people, they wouldn't have to draft me, I'd join tomorrow. I have nothing to lose by standing up for my beliefs. So I'll go to jail, so what? We've been in jail for 400 years.

If Ali said things like that today about our current war, it would earn him not a medal but a one-way trip to Gitmo.

Perhaps a far more fitting and true tribute to Ali was on display at an antiwar demonstration, where an older woman of African descent held up a sign that read simply, "No Iraqi ever left me to die on a roof." This was a direct reference to a quote attributed to Ali that "no Vietnamese ever called me 'nigger.'" Both statements, in a few short words, encompass both the anger and internationalism so needed today. These are statements not of pacifism but of the need for struggle to end war. This is the Ali that they can never bury—not even under the pall of devastating illness and a mountain of cheap medals.

◆◆◆◆

But the allies of the radical right do more than use sports and athletes to their political advantage. They are also many of the same people who control the sporting establishment. This was seen in the period preceding USA Basketball's failed attempts at winning the 2006 basketball world championships in Japan. Like Team USA in baseball, USA Basketball has seen its status tumble like Taco Bell futures. In the 2002 world championship, the former Goliaths of the hoops universe stumbled to a sixth-place finish. At the 2004 Olympiad in Greece, they won the bronze medal but suffered more losses than the team had endured in its entire Olympic history.

It's understandable that Jerry Colangelo, managing director of USA Basketball's men's team, and coach Mike Krzyzewski tried to pull out every trick to turn things around. The 2006 team, arguably unlike the 2004 Olympic team, had the talent to win gold, but represented the newest generation of players and was greener than a Minnesota banana. Featuring young superstars like LeBron James, Dwight Howard, and Dwyane Wade, some of their starting lineups ended up being, on average, younger than 23. And they went against seasoned international teams who had been playing with one another since childhood. With such a raw USA squad, Colangelo and Coach K saw the forging of team cohesion and unity as a top priority. But their methods reflected the politics of both men more than an effective strategy for victory. As Colangelo explained to *Chicago Tribune* columnist Sam Smith, "Coach K and I were having dinner last summer and talking about ways to connect this team with America. We talked about engaging ourselves [with the military]: 'Can this become their team? America's team?' It seemed like a natural." The two brought in people like Arizona Republican senator John McCain and celebrated soldier Colonel Robert Brown to speak about how, Smith wrote, "the military, like a basketball team, requires a unified, unselfish approach."

It is not surprising that Coach K loved the military angle. He's a graduate of West Point who led the Army squad for five years. And there is nothing new about coaches using the language of war to inspire a winning team. But how did "engaging with the military" translate in the era of unending war? It meant that Colangelo and Krzyzewski, to tremendous publicity, brought out soldiers maimed and crippled by the war in Iraq to inspire their "troops" in high-tops. This included Captain Scott Smiley, who is now blind after a Mosul suicide car bombing sent shrapnel into his brain, and Sergeant Christian Steele, who had part of his hand blown off. As Smith wrote, "It was a more than subtle message that playing with 'USA' on your jersey means a lot more than trying to win a medal. And it seems to have produced the desired effect of breaking down individual team loyalties and more quickly uniting this American team."

The young team, reportedly, was moved to tears. Not surprising at all. Anyone who has spent time among wounded vets knows how devastating that experience can be. But there is something unnerving about Colangelo and Coach K's style.

Etan Thomas, the power forward/center for the Washington Wizards, saw the military presentation on NBA TV and knew in his gut that it was wrong. He said to me,

> I don't have a problem with the troops talking to the players on their own. But for them [to be] brought in to build a better basketball team just feels wrong. If I was there, my reaction would have been completely different. The fact that Captain Scott Smiley has lost his sight would not have made me feel patriotic pride. It would have made me feel ashamed, angered, and saddened that this soldier was blinded at the service of a war we shouldn't have been in in the first place.

To use a deeply unpopular war—from which, according to a recent Zogby poll, 72 percent of troops want to escape and only 40 percent even support—and its injured for public relations purposes feels more like exploitation than motivation, especially when spearheaded by Jerry Colangelo. Colangelo once owned part of the NBA's Phoenix Suns as well as MLB's Arizona Diamondbacks. Currently, he's chairman and CEO of WNBA's Phoenix Mercury, and he also has aspirations that extend beyond a gold medal in Beijing in 2008. Colangelo has been pouring his money into efforts to strengthen ties between Republican politics and the religious right. He was a deputy chair of the Bush/Cheney 2004 campaign in Arizona, and his deep pockets contributed to what is called the Presidential Prayer Team: a private evangelical group that claims to have signed up more than 1 million people to drop to their knees and pray daily for Bush. During the election summer of 2004, as Max Blumenthal has reported, Colangelo bought ads on 1,200 radio stations urging listeners to pray for the president.

Colangelo has never been shy about using sports to project his politics. On April 5, 2003, he designated the Phoenix Suns' contest against Minnesota "Arizona Right-to-Life Day."

The former Diamondbacks CEO also helped launch a group, along with other baseball executives and ex-players, called Battin' 1.000, a national campaign that uses baseball memorabilia to raise funds for Campus for Life, the largest student antichoice network in the country. Battin' 1.000 stands against all abortions, even in the case of incest or rape. Its motto: "Pro-life—without exception, without compromise, without apology."

Colangelo has a fellow political traveler in Mike Krzyzewski. Coach K is a longtime Republican donor who made waves when he hosted a 2002 fund-raiser for North Carolina senatorial candidate Elizabeth Dole at the university-owned Washington Duke Inn. His group, to the consternation of many non-Republican faculty and students, was called "Blue Devils for Dole."

In addition to their politics, Colangelo and Coach K have something else in common: there is no published evidence that either ever served in combat. They might have gained a different perspective on the meaning of sports and war had they actually suffered the pain, boredom, fear, and death of a live battle.

One injured veteran Colangelo and Krzyzewski didn't bring in was Army Specialist Danielle "D-Smooth" Green, who lost her hand in a grenade attack on a Baghdad police station. She would have been particularly appropriate as a motivator for USA Basketball because in college she was also the starting point guard for Notre Dame. But Green told reporters from her hospital bed in 2004, "They [the Iraqis] just don't want us there.... I personally don't think we should have gone into Iraq. Not the way things have turned out. A lot more people are going to get hurt, and for what?"

Her question still hasn't been answered. Maybe Colangelo hopes that with all the exciting basketball to watch, we just won't get around to asking it again.

But of course, it's not just Bush and their Republican cronies that use sports to deflect attention away from their crimes. In the Democratically dominated city of Detroit, the 2006 Super Bowl was used to cover up a city in tremendous pain. *Washington Post* sportswriter Tony Kornheiser called the

National Football League's two-week-long pre–Super Bowl party binge in Detroit, "a celebration of concentrated wealth." But all this bacchanalia—complete with ice sculptures peeing Grey Goose vodka and two tons of frozen lobster flown directly to the stadium—happened in one of the United States' most impoverished, ravaged cities.

Detroit's power elites in government and the auto industry rolled out the red carpet while many of its people shivered in fraying rags. The contrast between the party atmosphere in the stadium and the abject urban suffering around it was so stark, so shocking, and so utterly revealing that news coverage on the city's plight appeared in the sports pages of the *New York Times* and the *Detroit Free Press,* among others.

Only a Bush speechwriter could fail to notice the gritty backdrop behind the limos that clogged the streets and the escort services that flew in female reinforcements like so much shellfish. Detroit—and there is no soft way to put this—is a city on the edge of the abyss. Its 2005 unemployment rate was 14.1 percent, more than two and a half times the national level. Its population has plummeted since the 1950s from over two million to fewer than 900,000, and more than one-third of its residents live under the poverty line, the highest rate in the nation. In addition, the city has in the past year axed hundreds of municipal employees, cut bus and garbage services, and boarded up nine recreation centers.

As the Associated Press wrote, "Much of the rest of Detroit is a landscape dotted with burned-out buildings, where liquor stores abound but supermarkets are hard to come by, and where drugs, violence and unemployment are everyday realities."

Detroit resident Ryan Anderson wrote me a chilling email, saying,

> The mood is one of Orwellian-flavored siege: dire warnings of a 30-day police speeding ticket bonanza, designed to raise $1 million for the construction of a damn bridge welcoming out-of-town-

ers to the Motor City; the mayor, the governor, and every other notable on the radio urging us all to "show 'em what we got" [read: don't further sully our already bad reputation]; and the homeless being taken to a three-day "Superbowl Party," where they'll get the actual food and shelter they need until the big game's over, after which they'll be kicked back out on the streets. Welcome to the Poorest City in America, sponsored and enabled by lily-white Oakland County.

I also got a letter from Anita Cerf, a teacher in Detroit, saying,

I am appalled by the living conditions of its residents as contrasted with the hype for the Super Bowl and the fancying up of downtown for all the rich out-of-town guests. I live on the East Side, which probably has one of the highest poverty rates in the country, and I teach high school dropouts on the Southwest Side. My students have horrific problems, many of which stem from these economic and social conditions. It's disgusting.

Mitch Albom of the *Detroit Free Press* described the "three-day party" thrown by the Detroit Rescue Mission to cleanse homeless people from the city's landscape: "Lines formed before sunset, dozens of men in dirty sweatshirts, old coats, worn-out shoes. They had to line up in an alley, because, [the shelter's director says], the city doesn't want lines of homeless folks visible from the street. Even at a shelter, they have to go in the back door."

But these days Detroit is dealing with more than normal tough times. Around the time the Super Bowl was played at Ford Field, the Ford family announced that it would eliminate up to 30,000 jobs and close fourteen plants in the next six years. The cuts mean it's the unemployment line, and maybe the Rescue Mission, for about a third of the 87,000 Ford workers who are members of the United Auto Workers (UAW).

For a city that built a stable "middle class" out of union struggle and the auto plants, this is injury added to insult. But have no fear. NORAD, the North American Aerospace Defense

Command, will be flying sorties over Ford Field to protect everyone from terrorist missile attacks. There is no NORAD, however, on the streets of Detroit to protect people from Operation Enduring Class War, otherwise known as the Super Bowl.

Disrobing the Emperors

Just in case the relentless sludge spread across sports by the political class has got you ready to burn your baseball cards and strafe your Stratomatic, I want to end this chapter with the words of Pat Tillman's brother Kevin, a fellow Army Ranger and private person who—through Pat's horrible death—has found his voice:

After Pat's Birthday—November 6, 2006

By Kevin Tillman

It is Pat's birthday on November 6, and elections are the day after. It gets me thinking about a conversation I had with Pat before we joined the military. He spoke about the risks with signing the papers. How once we committed, we were at the mercy of the American leadership and the American people. How we could be thrown in a direction not of our volition. How fighting as a soldier would leave us without a voice...until we get out.

Much has happened since we handed over our voice:

Somehow we were sent to invade a nation because it was a direct threat to the American people, or to the world, or harbored terrorists, or was involved in the September 11 attacks, or received weapons-grade uranium from Niger, or had mobile weapons labs, or WMD, or had a need to be liberated, or we needed to establish a democracy, or stop an insurgency, or stop a civil war we created that can't be called a civil war even though it is. Something like that.

Somehow America has become a country that projects everything that it is not and condemns everything that it is.

Somehow our elected leaders were subverting international law and humanity by setting up secret prisons around the world, secretly kidnapping people, secretly holding them indefinitely, secretly not charging them with anything, secretly torturing them.

Somehow that overt policy of torture became the fault of a few "bad apples" in the military.

Somehow back at home, support for the soldiers meant having a five-year-old kindergartener scribble a picture with crayons and send it overseas, or slapping stickers on cars, or lobbying Congress for an extra pad in a helmet. It's interesting that a soldier on his third or fourth tour should care about a drawing from a five-year-old; or a faded sticker on a car as his friends die around him; or an extra pad in a helmet, as if it will protect him when an IED throws his vehicle 50 feet into the air as his body comes apart and his skin melts to the seat.

Somehow the more soldiers that die, the more legitimate the illegal invasion becomes.

Somehow American leadership, whose only credit is lying to its people and illegally invading a nation, has been allowed to steal the courage, virtue, and honor of its soldiers on the ground.

Somehow those afraid to fight an illegal invasion decades ago are allowed to send soldiers to die for an illegal invasion they started.

Somehow faking character, virtue, and strength is tolerated.

Somehow profiting from tragedy and horror is tolerated.

Somehow the death of tens, if not hundreds, of thousands of people is tolerated.

Somehow subversion of the Bill of Rights and The Constitution is tolerated.

Somehow suspension of Habeas Corpus is supposed to keep this country safe.

Somehow torture is tolerated.

Somehow lying is tolerated.

Somehow reason is being discarded for faith, dogma, and nonsense.

Somehow American leadership managed to create a more dangerous world.

Somehow a narrative is more important than reality.

Somehow America has become a country that projects everything that it is not and condemns everything that it is.

Somehow the most reasonable, trusted, and respected country in the world has become one of the most irrational, belligerent, feared, and distrusted countries in the world.

Somehow being politically informed, diligent, and skeptical has been replaced by apathy through active ignorance.

Somehow the same incompetent, narcissistic, virtueless, vacuous, malicious criminals are still in charge of this country.

Somehow this is tolerated.

Somehow nobody is accountable for this.

In a democracy, the policy of the leaders is the policy of the people. So don't be shocked when our grandkids bury much of this generation as traitors to the nation, to the world and to humanity. Most likely, they will come to know that "somehow" was nurtured by fear, insecurity, and indifference, leaving the country vulnerable to unchecked, unchallenged parasites.

Luckily this country is still a democracy. People still have a voice. People still can take action. It can start after Pat's birthday.

Brother and Friend of Pat Tillman,

Kevin Tillman

CHAPTER NINE

The Way It Was, the Way It Is

I n looking for a way to transform the "Terrordome," sometimes we have to look—as my old professor Peter Rachleff would say—to the past to change the future. When my great grandparents were coming up in the old country, you went to the folks with the most snow on the roof, so to speak, to learn how to go forward. You had to. The old man or woman in the village was the only one who knew what to do if there was a flood, hurricane, or if barricades needed to go up around the shtetl. In the old days, it was the old folk who were "Shtetl fabulous." Our modern world, in grand contrast, rejects age and worships youth. Granted—as we will see in the next chapter—there are a lot of young people who know what's up, but they aren't the ones who get heard. It's Paris, it's Britney, it's those with the least to say who are provided the biggest platforms and loudest microphones. I myself would rather hear from those who have both been part of past struggle and still work to change the future.

I felt this firsthand last year when speaking in Berkeley, California, with sociologist Dr. Harry Edwards. For anyone who studies the history of sports and social movements, Harry Edwards is a defining figure. He is best known as the organizer of the Olympic Project for Human Rights (OPHR), which laid the groundwork for the attempted boycott by African-American athletes at the 1968 Games in Mexico City. Meeting the man was an event unto itself. He comes from a time when how you presented yourself, in dress and even posture, was itself a political statement—and Edwards lives by that. He stands ramrod straight, dressed in jet black from head to toe. Standing next to Edwards, he seems to be anywhere between six feet eight inches and eight feet six inches. The only color that interrupts the blackness is a thick white beard, which he wears without a mustache, giving him the appearance of an Amish Mr. T.

Edwards spoke directly to the idea of using the past as a part of our battle plan to retake the Terrordome. "I think the critical thing to understand coming out of the '60s and the '70s and the '80s and all the struggles that took place was that in every one of those decades the struggle was different," he said.

> The one thing that you find after having been an activist at any serious level is that in struggle, the challenge is dynamic, it's ever-changing, the struggle is therefore perpetual. A lot of people thought Jackie Robinson "integrating baseball" was a final victory; they thought that with Joe Louis being a heavyweight champion it was a final victory; they thought that when the first Black head coach came into NFL, the first Black quarterback, that we were making progress. The reality is that all of those are merely battles in an ongoing perpetual struggle and the only thing that is absolutely guaranteed is that it will be different.

Edwards sees the position of the Black athlete—with dwindling numbers in baseball, boxing, and even basketball, as a harbinger to something frightening.

> The Black athlete is really just a canary in the mine shaft, because what they're really telling us is [about] something happening in the African-American community. They're merely a canary in the mine shafts running up the flag saying we have serious problems of survival in the African-American community. The real issue is not who needs the Black athlete, as Major League Baseball is telling us, as boxing is telling us. The real issue is who needs African-American people? Again, it's indicative of where we are:

follow the Black athletes, and you see where we're all headed as a nation. The only issue is will this generation of young people— and that's who is going to have to do it—have the same kind of courage as past generations had to fight those struggles and to stand up and not so much to push the athlete off as a twentieth-century ignorant gladiator, but to embrace those athletes and spend the time to say, "Hey, young brother, here's the reality, here's the real deal," and it's not important just for you but for Black people in this country.... Because what happens to Black people just [doesn't just] happen to Black people, it just happens to Black people first and worse. Inevitably, Black in America paves the road for [where] the rest of society treads.

Edwards ended with a challenge to his young audience:

You don't have to win the war, but you have an absolute obligation to fight the battles your generation has to fight just as my generation did. The war is perpetual, and you can't have the next generation fight battles that you should have taken but failed to do because the stakes are just that high. And sport is not about fun and games, this is not the toy department of human affairs. Sport is about the most sacred, deeply rooted, most important values, sentiments, and structures in the society, and if you can get to sports and you can get to the athletes, you're way up the road in terms of changing definitions of reality in the society as a whole. We're all in this together.

◆ ◆ ◆ ◆

One person who rivals Edwards for longevity in the world of sports and social justice is Jim Bouton. A former twenty-game winner and All-Star from the New York Yankees, he is best known for the 1970 classic *Ball Four,* the most influential sports book of the twentieth century. *Ball Four* told, with innocence and joy, about the real day-to-day life of a major league baseball player, warts and all. It included stories of Yankees legend Mickey Mantle showing up to the park hung over, and ballplayers, out of curiosity and boredom, having kissing contests with each other on the team bus. Bouton paid a heavy price for writing *Ball Four:* being shunned from the game that he loved. But after *Ball Four,* sports hagiography was never the same.

His latest book, *Foul Ball: My Life and Hard Times Trying to Save an Old Ball Park,* stands proudly in the tradition of the original *Ball Four.* It certainly is not every day you open a "sports book" and see a quote from internationally renowned peace activist Arundhati Roy. But open *Foul Ball* by Jim Bouton and, before you hit page one, her words confront you like a thrown-down glove: "You could, like me, be unfortunate enough to stumble on a silent war. The trouble is that once you see it, you can't unsee it. And once you've seen it, keeping quiet, saying nothing, becomes as political an act as speaking out. There's no innocence."

The book is about how Bouton and friends stood up to one of the great modern heists of our time: the public funding of baseball stadiums. As Bouton writes in the intro,

> The only people, besides team owners, who want new [publicly funded] stadiums are politicians, lawyers, and the media.... Those who don't want new stadiums include just about everyone else—people who (1) prefer spending tax dollars on schools and hospitals, (2) don't own adjacent real estate, (3) know how to add and subtract.... The fiercest competition in sports these days is not between teams or leagues but between governments and their own citizens.

The stadium beast came to Bouton's backyard and he could not "unsee" the havoc that was being caused. *Foul Ball* is the story of Pittsfield, Massachusetts, and Bouton's efforts to save and rebuild historic Wahconah Park, the oldest minor league ballpark in the United States.

Pittsfield is a former GE company town that's fallen on hard times. The mayor, in conjunction with the town newspaper, came up with the idea that an $18 million publicly funded stadium would be the answer to everyone's economic prayers. Bouton started with a simple question: Why build a new McBallpark with public money when we can raise private moneys to restore Wahconah? This simple question opened up a can of worms that reveals in microcosmic form the dirty underbelly of the stadium game: the political kickbacks, the media collusion, and the hand of big business, operating to thwart democracy at its most grassroots level.

By the book's end, Bouton shows that we are a nation of Pittsfields, preyed upon by people with interests antithetical to our own. The modern baseball stadium is merely a monument to those interests: a reminder that democracy is a game only the few are allowed to play. This kind of truth-telling is why, in 1996, Jim Bouton was named in the book *The Sports 100* (published by Macmillan) as one of "The One Hundred Most Important People in American Sports History."

I was fortunate enough to speak on several panels with Bouton—including one in Boston with historian Howard Zinn, where Bouton and Zinn, longtime admirers of each other, met for the first time—and through our interaction, we were able to set up this interview, published here for the first time.

DZ: In the early '60s, you're an All-Star pitcher for the Yankees; in the late '60s, you're writing this incredibly transgressive book, and I just wanted to know if you ever thought about what role the 1960s as an era played in shaping your consciousness and outlook about the world.

JB: Well, I think the '60s affected everybody. Part of what was really good about it was that it just called everything into question—all the assumptions, all the rules, all the ways of doing things, and tossed them all up in the air, and forced everybody to take another look at questioning authority, and you know, it was really a necessary thing to do because we had just sort of inched our way and then leapfrogged into Vietnam without a lot of public discussion about it, taking the word of a handful of leaders....

That was the driving force. That and racism. Blacks were challenging the white status quo, and so there was all that going on. I don't think any of us at the time—certainly not my-self—thought this was going to be some sort of pivotal time in American history. When you're living through history, it just seems like the most natural thing in the world. I don't think it occurred to me that "Gee, all these other people are kicking up a fuss, maybe I should write a book that does the same thing." That thought never occurred to me, but you're part of your en-vironment. I don't know if I would have or could have even thought of writing *Ball Four* during the Eisenhower years. Who knew? Who knows?

Speaking of the '60s, I just interviewed someone who has won-derful memories of you—Dennis Brutus.

Dennis is the greatest man I've ever met. I met Dennis because he was executive secretary of SANROC—the South African Non-Racial Olympic Committee is what SANROC stood for. I was first contacted by a white weight lifter from their group. They contacted me because I had signed a petition in support of the Black South African athletes who were not able to—not allowed to—compete for spots on the South African Olympic team. The country of South Africa was about 80 percent Black and they were being represented by a 100 percent white team, and this petition was appealing to me as a Yankee baseball player and professional athlete in the United States, saying, "Athlete to athlete, is this fair? Not fair? We need fellow athletes to stand up for us and change this injustice." If athletics means anything, it means fairness and it seemed like the simplest thing to do was to sign this petition—a no-brainer! And I just thought I'd be one of hundreds of signatures on it. But I wasn't. It turned out to be about half a dozen, and very few of them were white. They wanted to have this press conference to an-nounce that this group would be going to Mexico City to lobby the American Olympic officials to support a ban of the South African team until they fielded a racially representative team.

Did you meet Avery Brundage there?

No, I didn't meet Avery Brundage. He wouldn't see us. But I almost met him. He saw me coming across a lobby, he recognized me, he knew why I was there, and he scurried the other way. I think he set a new world record for sixty yards across a carpeted lobby. I really thought the American Olympic officials simply weren't aware of the problem, and that once it was called to their attention they would do the right thing. Why would they care who's on the one big team from South Africa? I mean, if they discovered it was an all-white team, and an 80 percent Black country, what's the problem? But they cared because they realized that whole Olympic thing was a club; a men's club of wealthy racists. The whole notion of sports and sportsmanship was a sham. These guys were effectively using the Olympics to travel high on the hog, with international trips, and I'm sure they went very first class, I'm sure they brought their wives and girlfriends. Or both. I'm sure they lived it up, toasting with dictators and potentates.

What was your impression of Dennis Brutus?

Well, Dennis was such a special person. It was such an obvious outrage, and yet here was a man who was very composed, very restrained, a beautiful speaker and writer. Even his penmanship was right out of the 1800s, with this elaborate flowing script. Even just a note from Dennis was really something. He had a sense of calm and reason and was therefore exactly the kind of opponent they must have hated because they couldn't point to him as a screamer, a table-thumper, a rabble-rouser, or any other bullshit, you know. He was more cultured than they were, more refined than they were.

In the 1960s you had interactions with Muhammad Ali. What were your impressions of Ali and what do you think he meant to his time?

I think Muhammad Ali...was one of the great men in history,

and I don't mean sports history—one of the great men in history. He was internationally beloved, for all the right reasons. He took a risk with his career, with his life. He put it all on the line and took a huge risk, paid the price, went to jail, and got his title taken away from him. Here was a guy willing to go to prison for his beliefs. How many of those are there around? Even today we've got absolutely gutless politicians, [who] like this guy Paul Bremer [former viceroy of occupied Iraq] now tells us in his book that he needed more troops at the time. Well, bullshit. Where was he when he should have said it? He's no Muhammad Ali. What a lesson for people, to see this asshole Bremer behaving cowardly, with a history of people like Muhammad Ali who never behaved cowardly. So they're not in the same category of human being as far as I'm concerned. That goes for all of those politicians who were gutless and craven and blind. I read about [JFK defense secretary] Robert McNamara going to go to Vietnam and find out what went wrong. He was what was wrong. Him personally. He doesn't need to go anywhere to discover that. All those lives lost to find an "honorable" way out. It's disgusting to think of those lives lost.

So you write *Ball Four*, and the ownership of Major League Baseball and a lot of players lose their minds when it comes out. What caused the mass panic and insanity? Why do you think your book spurred that?

I don't know. I think for them it was just one more nail in the coffin, just more questioning of authority. The whole edifice was shaking from all the assaults on it and this was just one more instance—gee whiz, even in baseball! Not even baseball can be sacrosanct! That was part of it. I think baseball, football—they've always felt the need to be patriotic, to be on the side of America and might, supporting wars no matter what, and so that conservative bent, to have a break in their ranks: this was a little too much for them. And the truth of it is they hadn't read the damn book. They would have realized if they had read it that the things that they claimed bothered them were just in the context of a larger story. Baseball fans easily absorbed this concept. So many people picked up that book to read it and get angry about it, started reading it, and were saying, "What the hell are they making such a big deal about?" I mean, that was the tone of 99 percent of the letters I received. "I read your book, I kept waiting for this, and waiting for that, and I never saw it. There was nothing in the book that turned me off of the game or the people involved or anything." It was just a love letter. It's just the opposite of what baseball was saying. The commissioner [Bowie Kuhn] said I had "done the game a grave disservice."

There is a quote from David Halberstam about *Ball Four* that it is a book "so deep in the American vein it cannot be called a sports book." How can it be the harmless "love letter" you describe and also have such an impact?

You know, some of the things that were written about *Ball Four* are almost too deep for me. Sometimes when you create a piece of art, you think you're doing this thing over here, and it turns out when you're all done you've done this other thing over there without realizing it. It was only years later when I understood that my closely kept diary became an important piece of journalism because who could imagine it? But that wasn't my intention. I wasn't thinking of writing a revolutionary book or anything like that. We knew that the book was going to raise a fuss and that there were some things in there that had never been said in sports before, but basically we weren't trying to do that.

But the fans liked the book?

Not exactly at first. When the book came out, I was pitching for the Astros, and we were playing the circuit, we were in New

York City to play the Mets. And my mom and dad were going to come from New Jersey to see me; I would only come to town a couple times a summer so we got them tickets to the ball game, and we were going to go to dinner after that ball game at Shea. So anyway the game goes on, and I get called in to the game, I get called in to relieve at Shea Stadium. So when they announced my name—this was right after Dick Young had written three consecutive columns about what a jerk I was. I was a social leper, Judas, and Benedict Arnold, and the book hadn't been out yet, it was just basically excerpts and "Oh, he said all these terrible things," so the fans were reacting to sportswriters' early attacks on me, particularly from Dick Young.

So when I got called into the game, everybody at Shea Stadium booed. It was awful, being a Jersey kid and growing up in the New York area, to be roundly booed by a stadium full of people. It was pretty awful. After the game was over, I went outside and my mom was crying. She said, "Jim, maybe you shouldn't have written that book!" I said, "Mom, the book's not out yet, when it comes out you'd better read it, you'll realize it's not a bad book, this will all blow away, it's only temporary, you've just gotta hang in there a little while longer."

The part of the book baseball executives flogged you for was when you talked about Mickey Mantle, his drinking, and his, at times, prickly personality. I wanted to ask you, on the record, what your memories of Mickey Mantle were, and if you could talk a little about your last contact with him before he passed.

JB: I always had mixed emotions about Mickey. I liked one side of him very much, the teammate side. He was a great teammate, a lot of fun to be around, and great to have in the dugout. He played when he was injured, and he'd break a leg to win a ball game for you. If you were ever in a foxhole, you'd want somebody like Mickey in there with you to just keep going. Unlike Alex Rodriguez, who'd want to get in the other guy's foxhole and hide.

But anyway, Mickey was a great teammate, he was a lot of fun, always joking around, telling jokes, playing practical jokes. So that part, I loved him. But then I would see him being rude to kids, telling them to get the hell out of there, slamming windows down on their pencils. God, I would cringe when he would do that. It wasn't necessary. Just tell the kids you'll do it later or say, "Hey, how you doin'?" sign a couple autographs, and then move on. There's no reason to be nasty about it. And I'd see some sportswriters walk over to him for an interview, and he'd give them a look that would almost crack them in two. I thought he could have handled that a lot better.

He always said he was going to die young. Well, so what? There's a lot of people out there with some disease and they think they might die, it doesn't mean that you can mistreat people. It was a lack of perspective that not just Mickey had but a lot of guys. Take Roger Maris: he's young, he's healthy, he's getting paid a lot of money, and he may or may not break Babe Ruth's home run record. How much fun is that? You can't say, as Maris did in 1961, "I don't care whether I break Babe Ruth's record," and then lose your hair. You either care or you don't care. But in any case, they could never step back and see, "Gee, I'm young, I'm healthy, I've got a great job, I'm making a lot of money, kids look up to me, what else do I want from my life at this stage?" Guys in their twenties just had no perspective. Both of them died too young, which is a damned shame because most older ballplayers realize they did have a good life, and have that perspective they never had when they were younger. I think Roger and Mickey would be the same today.

And you sort of got a taste of that with Mickey Mantle's last contact with you, right?

Yeah, it was—I think it was 1995, Mickey's son Billy passed away. I sent him a note just telling him how badly I felt about Billy, and I had a nice memory of him running around the clubhouse in spring training, a polite little boy. And I also wrote in the note, "I'd like to take this moment to tell you that I hope you're feeling okay about *Ball Four*," that I never wrote it to hurt anybody, and that I always considered it an honor to be his teammate. I just wanted to say that to him. I sent this note to him, just a couple of lines. I never expected to hear back from him, Mickey's not the kind of guy that ever reached out in that way.

Then about ten days later I walked into my office and my secretary is standing by the answering machine, and she said, "I want you to play this one for yourself" and I pressed the Play button, and it was Mickey in his Oklahoma twang. "Hey, Jim, this is Mick. Thank you for your note about Billy, I appreciate it. I'm OK about *Ball Four;* it never bothered me that much. And one more thing—I want you to know that I'm not the reason you don't get invited back for Old Timers' Day. I heard that going around and it's not true. So anyway, thanks again, Bud."

How did it feel when the Jim Bouton ban was lifted and you were eventually able to get back to Old Timers' Day and don the uniform again in 1998?

It was one of those overwhelming days, emotionally. The reason I was back was because my son Michael had written a letter to the *New York Times*—a Father's Day sort of letter to the editor telling the Yankees that Old Timers' Day was always a time for families and that he loved it when I was a player, he loved being part of it, and our family was always a part of Old Timers' Day and we had lost Laurie the year before [Jim's daughter, Laurie Bouton, died in a car accident] and he said, so it's time to invite my dad back; he could use it—he could use all the help he can get right now.

It was just a beautiful letter. And the *New York Times* used it as their Father's Day piece. They got a picture of Mickey and me, and a picture of Laurie and me, and they ran that—what choice did the Yankees have but to invite me back? So they did, and when I went back it was overwhelmingly emotional. I wasn't sure how the players would respond to me, and I wasn't sure how the fans would respond to me. These were Old Timers' Day fans, these were Mickey Mantle fans, I was the guy who wrote those things about The Mick—how would they respond to me? And then there was the reason I was back in the first place—it was because Laurie had died, so I'm there for sympathy reasons, and I was proud of my son Michael for having written such a beautiful letter, so the whole thing was just one emotion after another. Of course, the first response of my teammates was great; they came over and hugged me and the guys were kidding around, it seemed just like old times, like I had just won my twentieth. So it was nice to be back. A couple of guys turned their backs on me, but the rest of the guys were great. And then the fans were marvelous. I was just washed away.

Let's talk about your latest book about stadiums. Why did you start it with that quote by Arundhati Roy?

My wife, Paula, was the editor of the book. She saw that this book was not pulling its punches. I was gonna nail these fuckers. And she knew that. She was concerned about our physical and financial well-being. They could put the screws to us. They could file lawsuits. Rough us up. That's what she was concerned with: she was questioning the wisdom of writing this book, the whole notion. I said, "I have to do this. If I don't do this, I'm not going to be able to sleep at night. I saw this ugliness up close and I can't walk away from it." She said, "Yes, you can, you don't need to do that." Anyway, she was driving the car one day, and she was listening to Alternative Radio...hosted by David Barsamian. On this particular day, there was a speech by Arundhati Roy, and during the course of her talk, she said the quote that's in the front of *Foul Ball*. And Paula was so deeply moved by that she pulled over to the side of the road and listened to the rest of the speech by Arundhati Roy. And she said, "I just heard something on the radio that you have to use in the front of your book—a quote from Arundhati Roy." So we sent away for the transcript, and there it was. She won her over. I couldn't win her over, Arundhati Roy won her over.

Clearly, the intent of the quote is that you see both what happened in Pittsfield and this process of stadium construction on the public dime is what amounts to a silent war.

Yep. We can't walk away from it.

Now, if somebody on the street asked you why you think stadium construction on the public dime is wrong, what would you say? How would you articulate that?

It's such a misapplication of the public's money. I mean, Jesus, you've got towns turning out streetlights, they're closing firehouses, they're cutting back on school supplies, they're having classrooms in stairwells, and we've got a nation full of kids who don't have any health insurance, I mean it's disgraceful. The limited things that our government does for the people with the people's money, to spend even a dime or a penny of it on ballparks is just a crime. It's going to be seen historically as an awful folly, and it's starting to be seen that way now, but historically that will go down as one of the real crimes of American government, national and local, to allow the funneling of people's money directly into the pockets of a handful of very wealthy individuals who could build these stadiums on their own if it made financial sense. If they don't make financial sense, then they shouldn't be building them. If I was a team owner today, asking for public money, I'd be ashamed of myself. Ashamed of myself. But we've gone beyond shame. There's no such thing as shame anymore. People aren't embarrassed to take—to do these awful things.

That gets to my next question. *Foul Ball* brilliantly goes through the mechanics of Pittsfield, Massachusetts, politics: the media,

the political structure, the big businesses. How much of what you dealt with there is particularly a Pittsfield problem and how much of it is a national problem? Particularly the collusion of media, business, and the like.

I really don't know. I'm sure there's a lot of overlap. Pittsfield is a single-newspaper town. Those are going to be less democratic than multinewspaper towns, particularly when the newspaper has an economic stake in some major project in the city. That's never going to get fairly presented or decided upon. I just hope that there are people out there who have a chance to read this book and hold it up in a city council meeting and say, "Read this book. This is what we're doing right here." I think that's been done. It's just that there's no amount of evidence, there's no amount of testimony, there's no amount of arguments that can beat these guys. It has nothing to do with who's got a better idea, what's fair or what's not fair, it has nothing to do with any of that. It's just pure power grabs. You know, you can write a book, but sometimes even that isn't enough. Somebody's got to be moved by it. Somebody else has to get involved. The notion that this could happen in broad daylight in a New England town is still astonishing to me. It's as if nothing happened.

To me, one of the most moving parts of the book was the section after 9/11, when you need to rectify in your mind, "Is it worth fighting for this ballpark, given all that's happened in the world?" and you come to the conclusion that this idea, this principle of fighting where you stand and making a difference in the effort to build a more just world is actually more important to do than ever. Even if Pittsfield is not the center of the universe. Was that the thought process that went through your head?

Yeah, I mean you need to make the fight you can make. You need to clean up your own neighborhood before you can move on to the larger world. I think if somebody from Europe or the Middle East read this book *Foul Ball,* they'd say, "Look at these people here. They're telling us how to win, how to have a democracy? We need to have Americans bring this to our country? They can't even do it right in their own country." I tell people when we're finished bringing democracy to Iraq we might want to consider bringing it home...even in Pittsfield, Massachusetts.

◆ ◆ ◆ ◆

Voices like Edwards and Bouton don't seem to have a place in the twenty-four-hour cycle of the sports media landscape, despite all the history and intelligence they bring to the table. But if there is one athlete from the past who still draws both media attention and the unquestioned awe of today's athletes, it's Jim Brown: NFL Hall of Famer, actor, and activist. In addition to his remarkable athletic career, where he is recognized as both the greatest football player, and arguably the greatest college lacrosse player, to ever take the field, he has done so much more since he walked away from the games. Brown has mediated truces between the toughest gangs in Los Angeles and fought racism from South Central to Soweto. But over the past few years, he was involved in a different kind of fight: the race to save Stan Tookie Williams, who was executed by the state of California on December 13, 2005.

Brown linked arms with a diverse crew of activists from Archbishop Desmond Tutu to hip-hop artist Snoop Dogg demanding that Governor Arnold Schwarzenegger spare Williams's life. Schwarzenegger agreed to a clemency hearing for Williams and told reporters he was "dreading" the decision he had to make.

It's not surprising Williams could inspire such a fierce defense. In 1971, he cofounded the infamous street gang the Crips. In 1981, he was convicted of the murders of Albert Owens, Tsai-Shai Chen Yang, Yen-I Yang, and Yee Chen Lin during two separate robberies. Williams, who maintained his innocence until the end, was convicted in a fashion that would make Bull Connor proud. During a questionable trial, which unfolded against a backdrop of antigang hysteria, the prosecutor likened him to "a Bengal tiger" and his South Central home to a jungle. He was found guilty by a jury from which all Blacks had been removed. In the sentencing phase of his trial, Williams appeared in shackles—a practice that the U.S. Supreme Court has since ruled unconstitutional.

But the unexpected occurred on the way to the death chamber. From the confines of his six-by-ten-foot cell, Williams decided to make a difference. He spent the last twenty years of his life intervening in gang disputes and cowriting with Barbara Becnel a children's book series, *Tookie Speaks Out Against Gang Violence.* "Don't join a gang," he wrote. "You won't find what you're looking for. All you will find is trouble, pain and sadness. I know. I did."

In 2004, Williams helped broker peace agreements between Bloods and Crips in California and in New Jersey, putting a stop to what had been one of the deadliest and most infamous gang wars in the country. Williams went global when Oscar-winner Jamie Foxx portrayed him in the made-for-TV movie *Redemption: The Stan Tookie Williams Story.* In the last phase of the campaign to stop his execution, more than 70,000 people sent emails to the SaveTookie.org website to thank the former gang leader for providing them the inspiration and motivation to walk a straighter path. His supporters have nominated him for the Nobel Peace Prize, and one of his books has won national honors. The *San Francisco Chronicle* published an editorial calling on Schwarzenegger to grant clemency. As Crystal Bybee of the Campaign to End the Death Penalty said, "Stanley Tookie Williams deserves clemency because his powerful message of peace is too precious to silence."

Jim Brown, who founded the organization Amer-I-Can in 1988 to get gangbangers off the express train to San Quentin, intimately knows the value of Williams's work. "To get to real change, you have to have systems in place," he wrote, in an article published in the Nation of Islam's newspaper, *The Final Call,* which also took up Williams's cause. "Then, you put a powerful voice with that system and you get the result. We have worked for years to put a system in place and have now joined forces with the powerful voice of Stanley Williams. Tookie is brilliant and has a fantastic spirit."

But it's this very spirit that the forces of death and reaction in California tried to extinguish when they snuffed out his life.

Just as the politics of racism haunted every aspect of Williams's case, they also defined Schwarzenegger's final decision. And this is exactly the kind of fight Jim Brown craves. "If you think because I'm famous or tough or outspoken that I am not affected by racism, then you don't understand. I am affected by it any time I see a black person who is not receiving an even shake," Brown wrote in his book, *Out of Bounds.* "I don't have to go hungry to feel for the man with an empty belly.... I will fight for my right to be free. I will die for that right. People say, 'Yes the white man has his foot up your ass. Be patient. He must adjust to not having his foot up your ass. Give him another two hundred years. Let him ease it out.' I say no. Take it out. Now."

This approach has earned Brown his share of enemies. "In the eyes of the police I am more than just famous. I'm big, black and arrogant," Brown wrote. "There are cops in Los Angeles who would love to be the guy who sent me to San Quentin for 49,000 years."

But Brown isn't in San Quentin. He is on the outside, ready to rumble for the sake of justice, redemption, and the children who will be hurt because Williams is no longer here to propose an alternative to gang life. As Jim Brown told conservative talk show host John Ziegler on KFI radio in Los Angeles, "When someone like Tookie says, 'This is not the way to do it; I made a mistake in my life,' yes, literally, lives are saved."

In one of his final interviews, Tookie said, "So, as long as I have breath, I will continue to do what I can to proliferate a positive message throughout this country and abroad to youths everywhere, of all colors or gender and geographical area, and I will continue to do what I can to help. I want to be a part of the...solution."

And even in death, Stan has been part of the solution. From the night of the execution, which she witnessed, Becnel has told all supporters that Stan was literally tortured to death during the lethal injection process. Eventually, after much uproar, the state admitted that Stan's death was bungled in every way possible: they collapsed two of his veins, didn't insert a second, back-up IV as protocol required, and administered to him the same amount of drugs they did to tiny, seventy-six-year-old wheelchair-using prisoner Clarence Ray Allen. It took them over 20 minutes to kill him—almost as long as the botched Angel Diaz execution in Florida, the one that precipitated a moratorium on executions there. There is currently a de facto moratorium in California because executions like Stan's—and his was prominent in the hearings on the constitutionality of lethal injection in California—were clearly torture murders. If Stan and his supporters had been silent, Tookie would most likely have been tortured in silence, and the state's machine would still be grinding its prisoners to pulp today.

Sports Talk with Mumia Abu-Jamal

One person who knows the inner workings of death row far too well is Pennsylvania prisoner Mumia Abu-Jamal. There are very few people who can claim to be award-winning journalists, best-selling authors, and respected observers of politics and popular culture, not to mention sought-after college commencement speakers. There are even fewer who can carry those honorifics and be a prisoner on death row. Actually, only one. Abu-Jamal joined the Black Panther Party at age fourteen and became a powerful writer and commentator about multiple issues, but particularly racism and Philadelphia's notorious police department. He earned the nickname "The Voice of the Voiceless" for reporting among the disenfranchised and dispossessed of Philadelphia's mean streets. Abu-Jamal has, of course, been living under the expectation of death since he was sentenced in July 1983 for the murder of police officer Daniel Faulkner, who was shot and killed in 1982.

Abu-Jamal has always maintained his innocence, and organizations such as Amnesty International, Human Rights Watch, the NAACP, and the National Lawyers Guild; the Japanese Diet and the European Parliament; ILWU, AFSCME, SEIU, and the national postal union; the 1.8 million-member-California Labor Federation AFL-CIO; and the city councils of Detroit, San Francisco, and Santa Cruz have all either called for a new trial or demanded his outright release.

Since his imprisonment, Abu-Jamal has continued to develop as a writer and advocate, publishing the books *Live from Death Row* and *Death Blossoms*. Via tape recordings made in his cell, he has given commencement speeches to graduating classes at the University of California at Santa Cruz, Evergreen State College, Antioch College, and Occidental College, and has made frequent commentaries on radio shows. But despite the infinite pages written and endless hours spoken, Abu-Jamal has never given his two cents about the wide world of sports. What does sports history look like from the perspective of someone who became a revolutionary at age fourteen, and gave little thought to a SportsWorld that was seen as a distraction from the struggle? Can today's sports landscape of "40 million dollar slaves" be a site of resistance? How does someone understand the current sports landscape from death row? These are the questions I needed to have answered.

DZ: What are your earliest sports memories?

MAJ: As I thought about it, I first recalled playing football with my brothers (and other neighborhood boys), but it seemed to me that it really wasn't my earliest memory, but my clearest. We played out on the green grass of the projects (back in the days when there was grass, and the projects were new).

As I actually thought about it, other memories came through of my pop taking me to a baseball game; and while I (a rather tall and large child) enjoyed hot dogs and mustard, the game itself held no allure for me. It bored me. And while I loved being with my dad, I found nothing enjoyable about the game.

In the projects, of course, I played neighborhood football, baseball, even basketball, but I confess I wasn't a very good player. When I played basketball, the other guys would call me "hatchet man" because I would come down on them (instead of the ball) when I was losing the play.

I remember coming in the house, and wanting to spend time with my pop, who loved to watch baseball on the tube. I'd watch for ten minutes, and invariably go to sleep. It bored me. Perhaps it was too slow. Because I was such a poor player, there were no "stars" that I looked up to as a kid, unless you count….

Let me guess. Muhammad Ali.

To a young guy growing up in the ghetto, Muhammad Ali was almost a god.

Everybody talked about him, and if ever there was a sports hero to us, it was he. I think Joe Louis was our parents' hero; Muhammad Ali was ours. His impact was powerful, but it went far beyond the realm of sports. He made the idea of the Nation of Islam immensely popular and attractive. My older brother took the name Ali, I'm convinced, largely because of his admiration for Muhammad Ali.

Not only that, he was constantly in the neighborhood, and he would stop and talk, laugh and joke with kids in the area. When he was on the news, on TV, for any reason, people would yell throughout the house, and call friends and neighbors, to make sure we wouldn't miss a word. When it came to his deftness, and unorthodox skills in the ring, again, his influence was outsized. If you got in a fight in the neighborhood, more often than not, your opponent would use a style stolen from Ali: the shuffle, hands low, etc. My older brother copied his style exactly. My younger brother fought Golden Gloves. Before Ali, boxing was seen not as "the sweet science" but a brutal battle for supremacy. Ali made it sweet, and his speed, his uncanny ability to slip (in his earlier career), made it beautiful as well.

Tommy Smith and John Carlos were heroes to us, because, as of '68, Black Power was in the air, and we regarded them as brave, principled athletes, who were also political actors who rocked the world. Also, before Ali, Smith, and Carlos, most Black athletes were rarely heard, and if so, they were seen as "Toms." They seemed like "bougie" Negroes. This may not have been the case (as I've read in your book of Jackie Robinson), but we certainly thought of them that way. We thought of Ali, "That Negro talking that way? About the white man? That Negro crazy! I LOVE him! He say what he wanna say."

Can sports form a site of resistance?

Oh, yeah. It can be. Is it? I don't think so. And I think that's especially so because of the tremendous dough they earn. It's like the old saying, "A rich man is conservative—'cuz he got something to conserve!" One would think, especially in, say, basketball, you would really see the blooming of a resistance site; but, again, I think the crazy money dilutes the tendency.

Why basketball in particular?

Because it, more than any other sport, approximates the hip-hop generation, as it rewards a kind of creativity and improvisation that reflects a hip-hop sensibility. Also, the cornrows, etc. Folks who lived through the '60s recall the drama over Afros and understand how hair can reflect political ideas. But that was then, this is now. Dudes and dudesses won't speak up unless and until a broader, deeper social movement gives them license to do so. Muhammad, for all of his wonderful wildness, was part of a deeper social movement—the Black Movement. It (and other social movements, like the antiwar movement), allowed him to be free, to look beyond his pockets, to his heart, and his soul.

But just like hip-hop (commercially speaking) has been channeled into "safe" avenues of faux-resistance (the difference between early raps about "I'm close to the edge," which dealt with an angry response to poverty and ghettoization, and late stuff about "my Benz, my ice, my bitches," etc., which extols one's property), so too has the commercial sport, which forces cats to don suits while sitting on the bench, or in public, tried to defang the streetness that unsettled massa's Xanax-influenced calm. So, I think that resistance will be bottom-up, instead of top-down.

What are your thoughts on another iconic figure, Jim Brown?

Jim Brown was, and is, the man. He owned the gridiron. And off the gridiron, he owned himself. How many men get to be record-breakin' athlete, actor, and activist in one lifetime? While he never threatened to gain an Oscar for his screenwork, he handled himself quite well, and far more capably then many of his successors (think O. J., etc.) on the screen.

It's his current work that I find the most rewarding, in that he helps young brothas, especially gangbangers in L.A., I think; as a contemporary of Muhammad, he developed a social and collective consciousness that goes way beyond the call. I admire the man.

Why do you think there is so much reactionary refuse in sports?

Sports often mimic the most repressive agencies in the broader life, e.g., the military. Young guys are taught to inflict pain (especially in football, on command). To follow the rules of elders (generals). To go with the program. They are treated like special elites, and after turning pro, paid extraordinarily large fees, which are used to discipline them, by keeping them on the plantation. Because they are so special, so elite, they naturally have to look down upon the sub-elites, hence the racism, sexism, and potential militarisms.

William Rhoden writes in his new book that Black athletes are "40 million dollar slaves." Do you believe that is the case?

I think you can guess where I'm going. Yup, how many of them dudes are free to speak their minds? When is the last time you read, viewed, or heard one do so? (With the possible exception of Charles Barkley.) The money is the trap, and although their cages are golden, they are bound by them nonetheless. They're like beautiful Indian ranis held in plush harems, until they are told to dance for the princes. Be silent. Dance. Entertain me. Make me happy. Oh. Shut up.

I also think it's understandable. For many of them, their greatest fear is a career-stopping injury, or the loss of their contract. For many of them, coming out of poverty, a return to such a state is terrifying. I think that's why almost all athletes are so superstitious. They can't believe their luck. So they dance, in silence. Until they can dance no more.

Let's talk about a contemporary issue. What about public finance of stadiums?

There is something almost obscene about public bucks going

to build what are private corporate holdings, especially in a day and age when schools are crumbling for millions of inner-city kids. It's a kind of legalized super-grand theft. Every time I read, or hear about such a scheme, my mind's eye reflects back to Jonathan Kozol's books, like *Savage Inequalities,* which document poor urban schools, with pools of liquid waste running down the hallways, cracked windows, old, outdated books, and harried teachers, who are too tired, too broken to give a damn. It reminds me that politicians are elected whores, who sell their cities to the highest bidder, while the poor are but scuff on the bottom of their shoes, brushed away, ignored, and damned. I despair when I hear about these things and don't see protests raging about this economic, social injustice.

Are there any athletes today you dig?

Thanks to you and C-SPAN, I admire Etan Thomas, who kicks it raw, in rhyme, or splendid, well-thought-out, impassioned prose. I admire Allen Iverson, for his style, which reflects his ghetto upbringing, and for his sheer will to win. I think he has the biggest heart in the league. I admire Andre Agassi for his social consciousness and his work with kids at his foundation/school.

What of athletes as role models?

In a sense, I've always kind of agreed with [Charles] Barkley, who famously said, "I ain't your role model; your momma and daddy should be your role model." I think Ali was a powerful social and political role model, with perhaps his biggest impact as a booster for the NOI, and his antiwar work. He inspired a generation (at least). But nothing happens in a vacuum. As the U.S. has deindustrialized, and as the prison industrial complex has grown by leaps and bounds, athletes have an outsized impact on young folks who dream of escaping their wretched socioeconomic condition. And whether we wanna admit it or not, athletes are role models—of obedience to authority, to hierarchy; of promotion of groupthink over individual opinion; or a kind of social discipline that pervades society. They are role models, ultimately. The question is, what do they teach us?

Any final thoughts?

Yup, you can't stop me now, Zirin. As someone who grew up, very young, in the Movement (the Black Panther Party), I didn't form a lot of the idolatries that many age-mates did. At fourteen to fifteen, I wasn't fantasizing about being a member of the NBA or the NFL. I was a member of the Black Panther Party, and my thinking was perhaps closest to Chomsky, seeing sports as a diversion from real struggle. But not exactly. I felt Muhammad Ali was doing what all athletes should've been doing, speaking out, boldly, forcefully, for their people's freedom. I also felt that athletes were not only betraying their people, but betraying their genetic inheritance, in the sense that, in precolonial life, people born with extraordinary gifts of strength, or speed, would be taught to use their gifts to protect, or defend the tribe (in precolonial Africa).

Instead, they were paid to play children's games, and did so in virtual silence. So for many years, even after I left the party, I didn't really engage in sports (I mean, mentally). I thought of them as guys (mostly) who sold out, instead of doing what they were born to do. They were born, genetically, to be warriors. Yet, they made millions for billionaires. And a few bucks for themselves, and afterwards, were burnt-out, broken shells, like Joe Louis in his later years. What if they fought, not played, for freedom?

CHAPTER TEN

In Their Own Words

E very generation, the wide world of corporate sports produces an athlete with the moral urgency to step off their pedestal of privilege and focus on greater concerns. A century ago, it was boxer Jack Johnson, flaunting, as W.E.B. DuBois put it, "his unforgivable blackness." In the 1930s, "the Brown Bomber" Joe Louis and track star Jesse Owens took turns spitting in Hitler's eyes, and Mildred "Babe" Didrikson continued to show that a woman could be the equal—if not the superior—of any man. In the 1940s and '50s, Jackie Robinson, Pee Wee Reese, and the Brooklyn Dodgers advanced the cause of civil rights through the transgressive act of the multiracial double play. In the 1960s, Muhammad Ali, Jim Brown, Roberto Clemente, Bill Russell, David Meggyesy, Tommie Smith, and John Carlos showed how mass struggle could be amplified in the world of sports. In the 1970s, Billie Jean King used a wicked forehand— and took to the streets—to demand equal rights for women, and Major League Baseball's Curt Flood showed the labor movement how to go from crumbs to a bigger piece of the pie. In the 1980s, Martina Navratilova came out of the closet and onto center court, girlfriend on her sinewy arm in plain view of all.

The common view is that today's athletes are too selfish, too self-absorbed, too concerned with the rims on their cars to bother themselves with issues like war and injustice. The daily sports pages reinforce this view at every opportunity. But the reality is that a stellar cast of pro players has chafed against silence in recent years, and are sounding off about a host of issues from war, to homophobia, to universal health care. Basketball players such as Steve Nash, Etan Thomas, Sheryl Swoopes, John Amaechi, Josh Howard, Adam Morrison, and Adonal Foyle have all made an effort to be heard. Boxer Felix Trinidad went public for Puerto Rican rights while Oscar de la Hoya showed up in the ring wearing slogans for immigrant rights. Football players like Adalius Thomas have spoken out against the war. Even Ultimate Fighting Champion Jeff Monson, among others fighters, has raised his voice for justice. Rutgers women's basketball coach C. Vivian Stringer told shock jock Don Imus where he could put his sexist, racist comments. And they are just the beginning. Stories circulate of teammates and coaches who share their views but don't want to go public. Even some referees whisper covert statements of support.

Three years ago, the *Nation* magazine writers Peter Dreier and Kelly Candaele asked the question "Where are the Jocks for Justice?" My experience in the SportsWorld is that the "Jocks for Justice" are both everywhere and nowhere. Progressive athletes strain to be heard, but they act as individuals and the media responds with a smothering silence. This does not have to be.

Pro athletes hold claim to a unique and underutilized bully pulpit. Two middle fingers from Atlanta Falcons quarterback Michael Vick have sent sports radio and television into a tizzy. Chicago Bulls center Ben Wallace wants to wear a red headband in defiance of team rules and a raucous debate explodes about something last popularized by Olivia Newton-John. The furor over Barry Bonds's place in history has led to a more honest discussion about racism than anything we get in the mainstream press.

Socially aware athletes could use this platform if they just stopped operating in isolation from one another. If the people I cited called a joint press conference to announce a new organization called—what the hell—Jocks for Justice, it would electrify the cultural landscape. Think I'm exaggerating? Consider the case of Toni Smith. In 2003, the Division III Manhattanville women's hoops captain decided that she was going to turn her back to the flag during the national anthem to protest not only the war abroad but "the injustices and inequities at home." Yipping heads lined up to debate whether Toni had the "right" to express her views. Everyone from ESPN to *20/20* and *60 Minutes* wanted a piece of her story.

Remember, this is Division III women's basketball. Crowds usually rival a well-attended K-Fed concert. If Toni Smith from Manhattanville could, for a brief moment, polarize the SportsWorld, imagine what Steve Nash, backed by an organization, could do.

And yet it hasn't happened, and it's worth asking why. Of the players I have spoken with, two main reasons emerge. The first is pessimism. Like most people in this country, pro athletes don't believe that they have any power to determine the course of this war. The thought is that the media might give them some coverage, but, in the end, nothing would change.

The other roadblock is straight-up fear: fear that taking an unpopular stand would mean a quick ticket out of the SportsWorld along with a total loss of its attendant perks. Most NBA players know the cautionary tales of Craig Hodges and Mahmoud Abdul-Rauf. They took stands against U.S. foreign policy and found themselves drummed out of the league like they were the Bush twins in Buenos Aires. Most athletes came up poor, and it is not a life anyone wants to revisit.

The fear is real but can be conquered. Perhaps the most basic way to help—besides building the kind of movement that allowed Muhammad Ali to emerge in full glory—is to make sure their voices aren't smothered in silence. The pages that follow highlight those athletes who have made a difference—not by visiting hospitals or doing charity work, as admirable as that is—but by engaging in the political battle of ideas.

Etan Thomas: From Baghdad to Death Row

Washington Wizards power forward Etan Thomas plays a gritty, elbows-up style of basketball, but on a microphone he is pure Jordan. In the tradition of Amiri Baraka, his poems are sharp enough to cut concrete and generous enough to nourish the seedlings that sprout in the cracks.

I first heard about Etan's political poetry when a rumor started going around Washington, D.C., that a rather large gentleman with locks was going to U Street coffeehouses reading anti–death penalty, antiracist verse in front of crowds you could fit in a van.

Since then, Etan has risen to every occasion, speaking out at the September 2005 antiwar rally, speaking out against the mistreatment of Katrina refugees, speaking out against the execution of Stan Tookie Williams, and speaking out through a published book of verse fittingly enough called *More Than an Athlete* (Moore Black Press).

On September 24, 2005, Etan took it to the Ali level by delivering a blistering, poetic speech as part of the weekend's antiwar demonstrations in Washington, D.C. His contribution, the full text of which is below, was played in its entirety on *Democracy Now!* and was hailed as "the best of the day" in various nooks and crannies of the blogosphere. It's called "Field Trip."

> Giving all honor, thanks, and praises to God for courage and wisdom, this is a very important rally. I'd like to thank you for allowing me to share my thoughts, feelings, and concerns regarding a tremendous problem that we are currently facing. This problem is universal, transcending race, economic background, religion, and culture, and this problem is none other than the current administration which has set up shop in the White House.
>
> In fact, I'd like to take some of these cats on a field trip. I want

to get big yellow buses with no air conditioner and no seat belts and round up Bill O'Reilly, Pat Buchanan, Trent Lott, Sean Hannity, Dick Cheney, Jeb Bush, Bush Jr. and Bush Sr., John Ashcroft, Giuliani, Ed Gillespie, Katherine Harris, that little bowtied Tucker Carlson, and any other right-wing conservative Republicans I can think of, and take them all on a trip to the 'hood. Not to do no thirty-minute documentary. I mean, I want to drop them off and leave them there, let them become one with the other side of the tracks, get them four mouths to feed and no welfare, have scare tactics run through them like a laxative, criticizing them for needing assistance.

I'd show them working families that make too much to receive welfare but not enough to make ends meet. I'd employ them with jobs with little security, let them know how it feels to be an employee at will, able to be fired at the drop of a hat. I'd take away their opportunities, then try their children as adults, sending their thirteen-year-old babies to life in prison. I'd sell them dreams of hopelessness while spoon-feeding their young with a daily dose of inferior education. I'd tell them no child shall be left behind, then take more money out of their schools, tell them to show and prove themselves on standardized exams testing their knowledge on things that they haven't been taught, and then I'd call them inferior.

I'd soak into their interior notions of endless possibilities. I'd paint pictures of assisted productivity if they only agreed to be all they can be, dress them up with fatigues and boots with promises of pots of gold at the end of rainbows, free education to waste terrain on those who finish their bid. Then I'd close the lid on that barrel of fool's gold by starting a war, sending their children into the midst of a hostile situation, and while they're worried about their babies being murdered and slain in foreign lands, I'd grace them with the pain of being sick and unable to get medicine.

Give them health benefits that barely cover the common cold. John Q. would become their reality as HMOs introduce them to the world of inferior care, filling their lungs with inadequate air, penny pinching at the expense of patients, doctors practicing medicine in an intricate web of rationing and regulations. Patients wander the maze of managed bureaucracy, costs rise and quality quickly deteriorates, but they say that managed care is cheaper. They'll say that free choice in medicine will defeat the overall productivity, and as copayments are steadily rising, I'll make their grandparents have to choose between buying their medicine and paying their rent.

Then I'd feed them hypocritical lines of being pro-life as the only Christian way to be. Then very contradictingly, I'd fight for the spread of the death penalty, as if "thou shall not kill" applies to babies but not to criminals.

Then I'd introduce them to those sworn to protect and serve, creating a curb in their trust in the law. I'd show them the night-sticks and plungers, the pepper spray and stun guns, the mace and magnums that they'd soon become acquainted with, the shakedowns and illegal search and seizures, the planted evidence, being stopped for no reason. Harassment ain't even the half of it. Forty-one shots to two raised hands, cell phones and wallets that are confused with illegal contrabands. I'd introduce them to pigs who love making their guns click like wineglasses. Everlasting targets surrounded by bullets, making them a walking bull's-eye, a living piñata, held at the mercy of police brutality, and then we'll see if they finally weren't aware of the truth, if their eyes weren't finally open like a box of Pandora.

I'd show them how the other side of the tracks carries the weight of the world on our shoulders and how society seems to be holding us down with the force of a boulder. The bird of democracy flew the coop back in Florida. See, for some, and justice comes in packs like wolves in sheep's clothing. T.K.O.'d by the right hooks of life, many are left staggering under the weight of the day, leaning against the ropes of hope. When your dreams have fallen on barren ground, it becomes difficult to keep pushing yourself forward like a train, administering pain like a doctor with a needle, their sequels continue more lethal than injections.

They keep telling us all is equal. I'd tell them that instead of giving tax breaks to the rich, financing corporate mergers, and leading us into unnecessary wars and under-table dealings with Enron and Halliburton, maybe they can work on making society more peaceful. Instead, they take more and more money out of inner-city schools, give up on the idea of rehabilitation, and build more prisons for poor people. With unemployment continuing to rise like a deficit, it's no wonder why so many think that crime pays.

Maybe this trip will make them see the error of their ways. Or maybe next time, we'll just all get out and vote. And as far as their stay in the White House, tell them that numbered are their days.

Etan has also made links with people behind bars by working in prisons and, as mentioned, against the death penalty. Below is a letter to Etan that former death row inmate Stanley Howard wrote upon hearing that Etan was speaking at an event sponsored by the Campaign to End the Death Penalty (CEDP). Stanley, who is a member of the CEDP and always organizing, typed his message to Etan on the back of a fact sheet that explains his case. The letter is republished with permission from both Stanley and Etan. I pass it on so folks can see that athletes don't take political stands for their own amusement or ego, but to be part of something larger than themselves. I also pass it on to demonstrate how a prisoner on death row has as much a capacity to inspire as any jock.

Dear Brother Etan Thomas:

My name is Stanley Howard, and I'm currently incarcerated at the world famous Stateville Correctional Center/Warehouse in Joliet, Illinois.

I'm a 43-year-old Black poor man from Chicago who has spent the last 22 years kidnapped by this unmerciful system—16 of those years were spent trying to stop the State of Illinois from lynching me on Death Row.

I'm no longer suffering on Death Row (fighting yet another wrongful conviction), but my heart is still in the struggle to end the Death Penalty because I can still hear the cries for justice and understanding loud and clear in my ears.

I've recently heard about your upcoming scheduled appearance at a Campaign to End the Death Penalty event, and I just wanted to send these words of thanks to show my sincere appreciation.

I've heard so much about your activism against classism, racism and this unjust system and government, and you'll be surprised to know that you're a great inspiration to many of the guys behind this 30-foot wall. Because, like the title of your book says, you're "More Than an Athlete."

I was on Death Row when it seemed like nobody cared what happened to Death Row prisoners, and worthless politicians were climbing on top of each other to pass laws and rules designed to make it easier to be sent to Death Row; harder to get off; and, faster to execute. They caused 100s to be executed during this time period trying to prove they were not soft on crime.

They were able to kill all these people (some of which had to be innocent, like me), even though we had many well established groups and organizations fighting to abolish the Death Penalty.

Everything began to change with the bold and aggressive grassroots efforts of the CEDP, because they consist of everyday people who are not sitting behind desks pushing paper, but out on the streets organizing, educating, protesting, and agitating the so-called Powers That Be. Everyone on Death Row loves the CEDP, because they changed the face of how this life saving movement is fought—helping to put the Death Penalty under the national spotlight; obtaining a Death Penalty moratorium; highlighting many cases; and, convincing Gov. Ryan to empty out Illinois' Death Row and granting my request for a pardon and three other pardons.

So on behalf of all the Brothers and Sisters still fighting to stop from being lynched on Death Rows around the country, I thank you for joining the struggle and helping to bring this madness to an end.

THEY SAY DEATH ROW—WE SAY HELL NO!!!

Thank You for being More Than an Athlete!!!
Stanley J. Howard
Reg. # N-71620
Stateville Correctional Center
Route 53, P.O. Box 112
Joliet, IL 60434

Sheryl Swoopes: Out of the Closet and Onto the Court

What's the sound of a good story smothered? Ask Sheryl Swoopes. Swoopes is the most prominent women's basketball player of her generation: a five-time All-Star, three-time Olympic gold medalist, and the WNBA's only three-time MVP. In a tribute only corporate America could render, Swoopes is the only female player to have her own basketball shoe: Nike's Air Swoopes.

The thirty-five-year-old Houston Comet veteran just delivered what could be the most significant body blow to homophobia ever weathered by the athletic-industrial complex. She has come out of the closet with pride, defiance, and a palpable sense of joy.

But Swoopes's announcement has been met in the world of sports commentary with what the Associated Press correctly described as "a shrug of indifference." *San Jose Mercury News* columnist John Ryan wrote, "Let's face it: On the list of shocking headlines, 'WNBA player is gay' falls somewhere between 'Romo took steroids' and 'Steinbrenner is angry.'"

The muted response to Swoopes's revelation flows from the sexist treatment of women's athletics on sports pages, where the WNBA faces regular derision and the accomplishments of even elite female athletes—from Mia Hamm to Serena Williams—are downplayed or ignored.

And the Swoopes story hasn't been ignored so much as re-framed to perpetuate the double standard. Sports pundits have shifted the conversation toward how "easy" it is for Swoopes to come out compared to a male athlete. Jim Rome, who no one is about to confuse with Harvey Milk, said on his sports yak-fest *Rome Is Burning* that Swoopes "is in a fringe professional sports league and is anything but a household name in this country. [Male athletes] have a lot more to lose because they have a lot more at stake. Bigger league. Bigger profile. Bigger dollars. Bigger backlash. Bigger ball. Bigger everything."

Ummm...paging Dr. Freud.

Bill Plaschke, a columnist for the *Los Angeles Times,* said on ESPN's *Around the Horn,* "Sadly, I don't think it's going to make much of an impact because, for whatever reason in this country, lesbians are viewed differently than gay men. There's not the stigma against lesbianism that there is against gays and men. Especially in athletics."

And this is just a sampling.

Sheryl Swoopes releasing her sweet shot in 2005 (AP/Tina Fineberg)

Swoopes responded to this line of argument perfectly, saying, "I don't see [an active male athlete coming out] anytime soon. But you know what? I didn't really see this happening, either—at least not now—and it did."

It should probably go without saying that looking to *Around the Horn* or Jim Rome for a serious discussion on sports and sexuality is like reading Ann Coulter for a history of Islam. But tragically, many writers and voices that should be celebrating this moment are choosing to be little more than fun-house reflections of the mainstream sports blather, concentrating on what Swoopes is not: a man.

The most painful expression of this came from someone described on ESPN.com as a "Closeted Division I-A sports administrator." He said, "I and every other gay guy in sports live every day with the fact that it's OK to be a lesbian in sports but not a gay guy. It hurts like hell and is life-altering and causes you to live with fear.… We gotta be in the closet and they don't."

The fact that a whopping two other WNBA players have come out argues against the "OK-ness" of being a lesbian in sports; it is not as if female athletes are magically turning women's sports into a rainbow paradise. And this man's anger seems misplaced. He seems to be angrier at out lesbians than he is at the sexist, homophobic sports culture that is keeping him in the closet. In any case, I am not denying that there is tremendous homophobia in men's sports. But the moment belongs to Swoopes. Especially because, in addition to being the most prominent team athlete to ever come out, Swoopes happens to be African American. As she said, "You have Ellen DeGeneres and Rosie O'Donnell, but you don't have your well-known gay African American who's come out." If you don't think this took guts, see the sick, homophobic rants against gays and lesbians—against Black lesbians in particular—by the Reverend Walter Fauntroy and D.C. Reverend Willie Wilson. You can also ask Keith Boykin of the National Black Justice Coalition, a prominent civil and gay rights organization, who was denied the opportunity to speak at the Millions More March in October.

For African-American women athletes, especially in the WNBA, the closet can be a cavernous, lonely chamber of depression. Many come from small southern towns and communities where homophobia is as thick as the humidity. They then go to college programs where learning to stay in the closet can be as much a part of the coaching drills as layup lines and the three-person weave. Swoopes's courageous stance has the potential to begin to move that weight in the other direction. It also has the potential to reach out to young African-American lesbians made to feel like the twenty-first-century version of Ralph Ellison's Invisible Man. As Selena Roberts wrote in the *New York Times,* "There is no diminishing the importance of each female athlete who publicly declares she wants to love freely in a homophobic culture, to live truthfully in a society divided on gay rights. Somewhere, a girl may feel less alone and less of an outcast because someone like Swoopes—an African-American woman—has further diluted the taboo."

John Amaechi Doesn't Care What You Think About His "Gayness"

"I'm going up to my room for some of my own fresh Earl Grey. I can't stand the hotel's. I'm a bit of a tea snob." Never before have I interviewed a pro athlete who referred to himself as a "tea snob." But then, John Amaechi is hardly the typical ex-jock, and his newly achieved status as "the first former NBA player to be openly gay" has little to do with it. Amaechi, raised in Britain, sounds more like Laurence Olivier than Lawrence Bird. He writes poetry. He has opinions beyond "playing one game at a time." He is a principled man of the left, passionate about challenging the war in Iraq, the NRA, racism, and, now that he is out of the closet, homophobia.

Traveling the country to promote his autobiography, *Man in the Middle*, Amaechi has generated attention both on the Hill and in the streets. The weekend of our interview, he was in Washington, D.C., meeting with both HRCs: the Human Rights Campaign and Hillary Rodham Clinton. He also spoke at a local bookstore, which packed in 200 people and left a line around the block.

But there's one group not rejoicing or even reacting to Amaechi's news, and that's the NBA. They have been, as Amaechi put it, "resoundingly silent." No former pro teammates—only his former Orlando Magic coach Doc Rivers—have made contact with the man they once affectionately called "Meech."

Despite the lack of support from his former teammates and employers, Amaechi takes issue with the idea that sports are somehow more homophobic than society as a whole. "I think it's convenient for people to say, 'Look at these stupid people here. They play a game and they get paid lots of money and look at how ignorant they all are.' Because it takes attention away from how entrenched homophobia is. Have you walked through a high school corridor lately? Good lord! I mean if you're a gay person in high school, you literally feel like a pimple. Or even somebody that's perceived to be gay or lesbian. And not only that. There are still plenty of gay people who can't come out at work because they can still be fired. In thirty-three states you can be fired for being gay. That to me is a crime! There are job security issues for gay people in most areas of life. The examples are numerous. Take the military. You can die for your country, but you can't talk about your partner. And in the NBA, if you're like me and you've worked you ass off to get in the NBA for six years, then yes. I was worried that I would lose my job. It's a legitimate fear."

Amaechi's current journey will involve fighting homophobia at every level of society, not just in the world of sports. This view has given him perspective on the ranting of former NBA player Tim Hardaway, who said—over the radio and in reference to Amaechi—"I hate gay people."

"Hardaway said ignorant things," says Amaechi, savoring his Earl Grey. "And yet, Ann Coulter did the same thing [essentially calling John Edwards a "faggot" at a summit of powerful conservatives]. And quite frankly, I'm tired of her. It actually makes me feel viscerally far more angry to hear someone in her position do that. Make no mistake, Tim Hardaway's voice is massive and booming. I've gotten hundreds of letters and emails from young people who have changed the way they behave, quit their schools, not gone to their jobs, or feared for their safety because of how his words have emboldened people in their environment. So the collateral damage, in terms of the fallout, has been massive. But this woman does it for an audience of people who represent power. Real power. She's the person responsible for the thirty-three states of discrimination. Her words are directly responsible for inflicting pain on young people, people at schools and colleges, in their places of work, their places of faith. She's contributing directly to an atmosphere that makes life less comfortable, less safe, less fulfilling. When you do that, and you do it on purpose—that's evil. And she knows, and she still does it."

This isn't the first time Amaechi has taken on the right. He campaigned against the NRA while a player in Orlando and Utah. "I got a lot of death threats with that one." Then there's the war, which he vocally criticized when it wasn't easy, as a player back in 2003. It was a road trip with the Utah Jazz that pushed him to speak out.

"We were on a trip to Phoenix and we arrived in the arena. Once we got there, it was just shocking! There was this little man running around, blustering, 'Hurry up. We're gonna start the game a few minutes early; if we're lucky the war won't start till half-time.' I was thinking 'Are you kidding me? What you're talking about is hundreds of thousands of people dying. It doesn't matter whether it will be American people or British people or Iraqi people. Just hundreds of thousands of people are going to die, and you're trying to time it up with a basketball game!' What was even more frightening than that was when the war did start at half-time. We all were ushered into locker rooms and we watched the president's announcement, and people were cheering, then through the loudspeakers in the locker room and out on the floor it was 'God Bless America,' and 'Born in the USA,' which is actually an antiwar song! But what people were saying at that time, and the look in their eyes, the baying for blood—it was unbelievable!"

Like his opposition to the war, Amaechi's coming out is likely to create a bit of chaos, and he speaks eloquently about the personal as well as the political ramifications of his action. We discuss Sheryl Swoopes, and whether it is "easier" for women to come out than men. "There is a difference in perception. The perception is that when a woman comes out it reinforces a stereotype. When a man comes out it goes against a very deeply ingrained stereotype. So in that way, people perceive it to be easier. People forget that coming out is not about what people see, it's about what the individual feels. So whether it's hard or easy can't be determined by looking. This process could be magnificently easy for them, but it's not for other people to tell. It's not hard or easy because there's chaos around me, it's hard or easy because of how that chaos affects how I feel."

He is very realistic about the prospect of an NBA player following Swoopes's lead and coming out while active. He is also realistic about the difference one person could make. "We're asking the people with the most to lose financially, emotionally, psychologically, to fall on their swords in the hope that that will change the world. Now, my contention on this, having spoken to Judy Shepherd [mother of Matthew Shepherd, murdered for being gay] just yesterday, adoring her, and really feeling a

John Amaechi sits in peace in February 2007 (AP/Seth Wenig)

great deal of grief over her story, is that if the image of a young boy without his shoes being strapped to a fence and left to die doesn't end homophobia, then a gay Shaq won't either.

"To me, a young boy, semi-naked, no shoes, strapped to a fence in the middle of nowhere—how can you look at that image and then say the f-word? How can you look at that image and then allow people around you to use antigay slurs? When you know it's that kind of atmosphere that leads to that. That's what the Ann Coulters, the Tim Hardaways, the guys like the guy from Philly [76er Shavlik Randolph] that said 'Don't bring your gayness on me,' that's what these people need to understand. Their words don't just leave their mouths and drop to the floor like fruit. Their words leave their mouths and bounce around the world like bullets."

He has some advice for superstar LeBron James, who said he "couldn't trust" a teammate in the closet. "Get a passport is my first answer to him. Get a passport, see the world, experience something beyond your own little bubble. Next, don't give people classic double binds. You can't trust somebody if they don't come out to you, but at the same time you won't say if they come out to you that you'll embrace them. You're the most powerful basketball player in the world right now. So first, before you start making these bold assertions about what is going on inside somebody, make a bold assertion about how you'll treat them."

Now that he's out of the closet, Amaechi is looking forward to raising his political voice. One issue that he wants to opine about is the Don't Ask Don't Tell policy in the U.S. military. "It's absurd in the extreme. It's insulting, it's divisive, and it's ridiculous. That's just one of those things that you look at from the beginning and say, 'That's just dumb.' Why? Because in every conflict that the United States is engaged in now and all the ones it's planning for the next eighteen months, you're going to be standing shoulder to shoulder with militaries that don't follow that policy. The Israeli army doesn't follow that policy. The British army certainly doesn't follow that policy. So, if you can stand shoulder to shoulder with them, then you can stand shoulder to shoulder with them. And once again it is somewhat of a stereotype, but it does appear that a great many of the translators appear to be gay. So you're going to send people to Iraq, and you're going to rely on the fact that the Iraqi guy is going to tell you all the information you need to know, and not have a translator because that person is gay? No, I'm sorry. If I were an American citizen and certainly an American soldier, I'd be the first person to say 'I'd rather shower with a gay guy than get my legs blown off.'"

I ask him if he is frustrated with the positions of the two parties on GLBT issues. "I don't think it's as easy as that. I mean, it's not as easy as all Republicans hate gay people and all Democrats love gay people. That we know clearly. Barney Frank doesn't represent all Democrats. George Bush doesn't represent all Republicans. The problem is that to the world George Bush does represent all Americans. Most of my friends believe that that's how all Americans are; kind of stupid with not much of a worldview. That's the problem. They think Americans are either him or Jon Stewart.

"In terms of how the Republicans are handling the gay issue, in my mind, you don't have the luxury, if you're Dick Cheney, of saying 'I love my daughter, I want her to prosper, and yet I'm going to be part of an administration that actively discriminates against my daughter.' You don't get the luxury. Again, it sounds cruel, but I believe to be principled you have to pick. Your policies say you hate gay people, your daughter is gay. Do you hate your daughter? If the answer is yes, stay where you are. If the answer is no, step away and announce it. I like it when people declare their position. You're engaged then. When it's in the ether, no one knows what's going on."

Expect more from Amaechi in the future: "I've always been a political activist. But in terms of GLBT issues and diversity issues in general, yeah. I'm certainly going to step up now. But I've not been afraid to step up before. One of the major problems we have is that people need to stand up, be counted, and say that it is unacceptable that in my high school kids get assaulted with the word 'gay' meaning stupid or bad or wrong or dumb. Unacceptable that the f-word is being used on a regular basis in workplaces. Unacceptable that coaches talk about 'throwing like a girl.' Unacceptable that coaches and teachers and bosses allow that kind of rhetoric to go on unchallenged. Unacceptable."

Here comes the challenge.

Jeff Monson: Ultimate Fighter for Peace

Make no mistake, Jeff Monson can whoop your ass. Part Hulk Hogan and part Bruce Lee, big, bald, and frightening to behold, Monson is one of the top dogs in the universe of the Ultimate Fighting Championship. The UFC is perhaps the fastest-growing entity in sports. For the uninitiated, the UFC is a series of one-on-one battles in Mixed Martial Arts, where the goal is the physical annihilation of your opponent. Once derided as "human cockfighting," the UFC has broken into the mainstream, with highly rated broadcasts on Fox Sports Net and the horrifically sexist and homophobic Spike TV.

But in the world of Ultimate Fighting, Monson is a man apart. An expert in the art of dispensing pain, he also describes himself as "antiwar," "anticapitalist," and a man who "abhors violence." Amidst a sport where people have nicknames like "The Beast," Monson is known as "The Anarchist." It practically reads like a headline in the *Onion*, like hearing Trent Lott has joined Three 6 Mafia, but Monson embraces being a singular radical presence for an unlikely audience. As he said to me, "Fighting has given me a platform. If I'm Jeff Monson the schoolteacher or Jeff Monson the psychologist, not that many people are going to listen. But if I'm Jeff Monson the UFC fighter, then more people are at least going to hear what I have to say. Not necessarily agree, but hear me."

The young, rowdy fans of UFC don't seem at first glance to be Monson's crowd but, to everyone's surprise, they've been very open to "The Anarchist." "I can't tell you how much support I get at the arena, man," he says.

> It just kind of blows my mind the crowd reaction when I come out. I also get a lot emails from people who go to the arena and say I was an inspiration and appreciate that I speak what I feel. It's exciting and I guess, in a way, unexpected given some of the controversy surrounding the things I've said. I learned that [the audience is comprised of] real, regular people that are open to what I have to say.

And what Monson has to say is not for the faint of heart and won't get him invited to the White House Christmas party.

First and foremost, he makes no bones about being against the war and occupation in Iraq. "The death toll is over 160,000 and most of them are civilians. You know this is for oil. We're not doing this in Darfur, where there's genocide going on. We're doing this in Iraq. We thought it was going to be a cakewalk. We just didn't expect that the people would have this much resistance. People do not like being oppressed. If the choice is standing with oppressor or oppressed, I know what side I'm on."

Monson's antiwar convictions are further strengthened by his interaction with soldiers he meets through his martial arts dojo.

> You know a lot of the people that come to my school are from Fort Lewis, and they're soldiers who are on their way to Iraq. I have no problem teaching them, especially if it's going to keep them alive. I tell these guys when they go, "Man, just keep your head down and friggin' come back." I don't want them shooting people, but definitely don't want them getting killed, either. And if doing some takedown is going to keep them from getting shot, that's more than I could hope for. As a whole, I don't know if I would advocate teaching a method of combat for the purpose of subjecting another people but when it comes down to it, it's the guns that kill the people not jujitsu.

But his critique—one that he is open about with fans and fellow Ultimate Fighters alike—extends beyond the war. He believes in the complete transformation of our economic system. In his own words: "I believe that everyone's born equal, and that everyone should have equality and the same opportunities as everyone else. But the current global capitalist system doesn't allow that. Instead we have people working for less than they're worth so bosses can profit off of their labor. To me, that is evil. It's a class war between the haves and the have-nots and it has to end."

Monson is more than an armchair—or arm-bar—proselytizer. He's an activist who marches for what he believes in. "I speak out and I organize. It's cost me a lot of sponsorship money. I've had the Secret Service come to my house and come to my gym. But there are people that sacrifice a heck of a lot more than I do and it's worth it. I want to be part of the change, not just be this person that is saying 'do this, do that.'"

It sounds good. Yet clearly there must be a contradiction between Monson's sport and his beliefs. There are few sports more cutthroat than the UFC. It takes a spartan mentality, an ability to hurt others without hesitation, and a fanatical competitive drive. Monson confronts these contradictions head-on. "I'm not against competition," he says. "Competition is what drives me. But I'm not in economic competition with someone. This isn't an economic thing for me, it's what I love to do. To me it's a different kind of competition. I'm trying to win but at the same time, I'm not exploiting anybody. The competition in sports and the economic competition in capitalism are completely different. They should be different words."

That may be true of competition, but what about the UFC's celebration of violence? Monson says simply, "I know I could never hurt someone." It's an incredible statement: an Ultimate Fighter speaking about how he could never hurt someone. But

Monson doesn't flinch.

> You know, Ultimate Fighting has nothing to do with the real
> world. To me it's a sport. It's an art form. It's mental. It's two peo-
> ple, both well-trained, who've met the criteria to get to that level,
> to fight in that big of a show. And the guy in there's trying to
> knock me out or submit me and I'm trying to knock him out or
> submit him. It's a violent sport, definitely. But football's a violent
> sport. Scuba diving is dangerous. There's danger involved in
> everything. If we really want to end violence, let's start with the
> real world. We should put in place a system where greed is not re-
> warded, where no one starves or dies in wars for oil, where every-
> one has opportunity, access to free medicine, free schooling.
> Then you won't have violence.

To Monson, the UFC is not part of the problem, feeding
and profiting from a culture of violence. If anything, in his
mind, it's part of the solution, a way to reach a forgotten audience with his message—and redefine how we understand our
messengers.

The Slave Side of Sunday

For most sports fans, heaven would be to play in the National
Football League. We see money, fame, and no expectations of
social responsibility beyond showing up on Sunday ready to
play. In the mind of the fantasy sports fan, it means a big
house, a garage full of cars, and the promise of sexual gratifica-
tion. The last thing any fan would believe—or want to believe—is that racism is endemic to the culture of the NFL.

That's the contention of NFL veteran Anthony Prior, whose
new book, *The Slave Side of Sunday*, invokes an explosive
metaphor to describe life in the NFL. Prior played six NFL seasons with the New York Jets, the Oakland Raiders, and the
Minnesota Vikings, and developed a reputation as a corner-
back with blinding speed, if not blinding stats.

Prior contends that the NFL is rife with a racism that is
both deeply institutionalized and largely unchallenged. "I was

frustrated by not seeing the truth in print," Prior told me in a recent interview. "And I believe that if you want to see it, you should write it."

Prior is a self-published author. In addition to *The Slave Side of Sunday*, his publishing house, Stone Hold Books, produced *Faith on 40 Yards: Behind the Silver & Gold of the N.F.L.* in 2003. The starting point for his new book is the much-derided 2003 statement by Tampa Bay All-Pro defensive tackle Warren Sapp that the NFL acts as a "slave master" to its players. Sapp was pilloried for his comments, but Prior argues that Sapp speaks the truth.

Prior knows that, like Sapp, he will receive criticism for his statements. And on the face of it, his argument does seem ridiculous, if not offensive: How can people who make mega-salaries and play before adoring crowds be likened to slaves? Prior's response is that the answer lies in the lack of control NFL players are allowed to have in their daily lives and in the mega-industry they have helped create. He sees this lack of control being intimately tied with the fact that 65 percent of players are African American, yet only 18 percent of coaches, 6 percent of general managers are Black, and no owners are anything other than white.

"Black players have created a billion-dollar market but have no voice in the industry, no power. That sounds an awful lot like slavery to me," he says.

> On plantations, slaves were respected for their physical skills but were given no respect as thinking beings. On the football field, we are treated as what appears like gods, but in fact this is just the "show and tell" of the management for their spectators. In reality, what is transpiring is that black athletes are being treated with disrespect and degradation. As soon as we take off that uniform, behind the dressing room doors, we are less than human. We are bought and sold. Traded and drafted, like our ancestors, and the public views this as a sport, ironically the same attitude as people had in the slavery era.

Prior names no names, but he contends that coaches and other authority figures in the game use racism to bully African-American players in an effort to instill obedience. "I've heard coaches call players 'boy,' 'porch monkeys,' 'sambos,'" he says.

> The intimidation is immense.... I've seen players benched because a coach saw them with a white woman, or overheard a criticism of his incompetence, or because a player didn't go to Bible study. I've been in film sessions where coaches would try to get a rise out of players by calling them "boy" or "Jemima," and players are so conditioned to not jeopardize their place, they just take it. It's my understanding that management by intimidation is illegal, so why do we allow this to occur? I believe that due to the nature of the race of players who are being intimidated, people tend to overlook this. That is why I wrote this book. People must understand that this is not just intimidation, this is pure racism.

Prior says southern-born athletes are particularly vulnerable, calling coaches "boss" or even "master." He told me a story of one coach making the mistake of talking to a player from the West Coast the same way he talked to one from the South. That coach was quickly reminded of who he was talking to when the player said, according to Prior, "I am a man and you will respect me as a man." Words to live by.

Another institution that raises Prior's ire is Athletes in Action, an evangelical Christian group that is a presence in high school and college athletics and even in professional sports. Before the big game on Super Bowl Sunday in 2006, Athletes in Action sponsored an NFL-sanctioned prayer breakfast in Detroit.

"I call [them] Hypocrites in Action. Almost every time, the minister is white, and the subject matter is right off the plantation," Prior says. He tells a story of going to a Bible study and asking, "What's the subject matter?" and being told, "Living in Obedience." On some teams, prayer becomes compulsory. As Prior says, "This is a wrongfully instilled practice. I wouldn't have issue with this if the tools given were truly in good nature for the progression of mankind, not the regression of players."

Neither the NFL nor Athletes in Action returned calls for comment on Prior's allegations. Prior says he has written his book as a way to advance the idea that African-American players can organize themselves to fight racism beyond the playing field. "As individuals we must create a collective. NFL's Black players have a tremendous strength. This is a power we are scared to exercise yet dream to live." He believes that a workplace action on the eve of the Super Bowl could bring real change. Certainly, the thought of football players holding the multibillion-dollar spectacle hostage and making demands on the NFL ownership to give more back to the impoverished communities that produce their All-Pros is a daring notion. The question is whether Prior and those who agree with him would risk the fruits of Super Bowl glory for the greater good of those who will never see an NFL contract.

The NBA Draft: Prom Night Gets Political

The NBA draft is supposed to be prom night for basketball nerds. It's a place to gawk at pro prospects adorned in garish double-breasted suits that would shame Max Julien. It's the time to watch the diminutive David Stern shake hands with a cavalcade of young men who could rest a drink on his head.

No one views draft night as a place to get a handle on the current political climate in the United States. One would have to be dropping acid to think that anything involving "Screamin'" Stephen A. Smith, Dick Vitale, and Dan Patrick could provide any kind of political insight. Well, call me Timothy Leary and bring on the White Rabbit because the 2006 draft was more politically interesting than anything said in the last year by Tim Russert and his bloated cronies.

Draft night ceased to be spectacle as usual when Adam Morrison from Gonzaga, the NCAA's leading scorer in 2006, was picked third by the expansion Charlotte Bobcats. We learned in the post-draft interview that Morrison, who gets so intense he weeps openly on the court, also cried when Rage Against the Machine broke up. As ESPN's Stuart Scott needled him, Morrison defended his right to cry in plain language: a nice counter to the macho laws of Jockocracy. But Morrison is more than a chronic weeper who sports a bizarre caterpillar mustache and a pageboy haircut out of Degrassi Junior High. He is also someone who has said that his heroes, in addition to Rage, are "Malcolm X, Karl Marx, and Che Guevara." Why Che? As he told *USA Today,* "Just the adversity he dealt with in life, what he did for small countries of the world as a whole. Standing up for lower people, instead of the top tier. That takes a lot of guts on the world level to do that. So that's what's drawn me to him."

Morrison was also a Nader voter in 2004, and someone who is known for getting in raucous debates on the team bus on everything from the logic of capitalism to the merits of national health care. "I've been told that's what you are supposed to do in college," he has said. "It's the last time in your life, pretty much, when you get to question authority.... You're going to be answering to somebody else for the rest of your life." When Gonzaga coach Mark Few advised players to attend church, Morrison stood up and wrote on Few's dry-erase board, "Religion is the opiate of the masses." Let's hope Morrison realizes that this kind of questioning is something he doesn't have to forgo just because he is in the NBA.

But the political march did not stop with Morrison. The number four pick from LSU, Tyrus Thomas, also made an impression. Thomas only played in college for one year, but made a big splash in the NCAA tournament. Through the draft coverage, we found out that his family initially feared they wouldn't be able to watch him in the NCAA because they didn't have the money to get there; in the end, they were aided by a collection at their church. We also learned that Thomas sports a tattoo that reads "No struggle, no progress." As ESPN's Stuart Scott commented, "He's old school! He's down with Frederick Douglass! Boo yah!" (Or words to that effect.)

Stuart Scott also got more than he bargained for with the sixth pick, Brandon Roy. We learned that the University of Washington guard worked sweeping on the docks of Seattle as a janitor in high school, studying for his SATs while pushing his broom. Roy, working nights, did so poorly on the tests he had to retake them. On the second go-around, he scored so highly the testing czars red-flagged him and Roy had to take them a third time under close scrutiny. That time he did even better. Roy told Stuart Scott he learned a lot from the janitors on the docks, mainly that life is hard and basketball could be his way out.

The other dimension revealed by the draft was one that rarely makes it onto television: the reality of poverty in the United States. There was Randy Foye, the stocky Villanova All-American talking about how his mother gave birth to him when she was just fourteen and his father died in a motorcycle accident when he was a baby. Foye was put up for adoption and eventually raised by his grandparents. A graphic at the bottom of the screen simply read, "People Foye Would Most Like to Meet: 'My Parents.'" Then there was Marcus Williams, the talented Connecticut point guard from South Central, L.A., who was caught stealing a laptop computer in college. His mother borrowed money to move across the country and live with him to make sure he stayed out of trouble and didn't blow his big chance.

But not all the political banter was inside the Garden. Draft day also featured a demonstration of several dozen Knick fans demanding that the NBA remove control of the New York Knicks from CEO James Dolan and GM Isiah Thomas. Organized by the website selltheknicks.com, the march was a cry of frustration against a hideous team led by idiots. "I never thought I'd be in a protest march against the Knicks," said Bill Morris to the *New York Post*. "It's a crime it has come to this with the history of this franchise."

James Dolan, a child of wealth who was described by one writer as "having the intelligence of a man-hole cover," recently fired Hall of Fame coach Larry Brown after one season, a 23–59 record, and the league's largest payroll. The Knicks now owe a staggering $410 million in contracts, and are paying three fired coaches not to coach.

The marchers had a sense of humility and perspective that this was perhaps not the most critical issue facing humanity. As Dave Hornung said, "It's not for world peace, which I guess would be better." But for people who oppose corporate corruption, rampant greed, and consumer fraud (Dolan claims to be building a "basketball team"), the Knicks are as good a target as any. Maybe next year the demonstrators will return, led by a certain rookie with a funky mustache and a fellow first-year player showing his love for Frederick Douglass. Or better yet, maybe they all will go to Washington, D.C., with fellow NBA rebels Nash, Thomas, and Foyle with the aim of telling the jock-sniffers of Congress that they stand with Mr. Nash's famous phrase: "No War. Shoot for Peace." Stranger things can happen: like an NBA draft that morphs into compelling political television.

Imus, Sports, and the End of Silence

Shlock jock Don Imus never dreamed one more barnacle of bigotry would sink the ship of his career. But the radio talk show host found himself in the unusual position of having to face the music. That's what happens when you think it's all fun and games to call Rutgers women basketball players "nappy-headed hos." That's what happens when people dare to fight back.

Imus likened his comments to a slip of the tongue—a "crime of passion" as he put it—but his history tells a tale of premeditation. "The I-Man" has an ugly record of using his program as a platform for prejudice. He called African-American journalist Gwen Ifill a "cleaning lady," *New York Times* sports reporter Bill Rhoden a "quota hire," and tennis player Amelie Mauresmo a "big lesbo." He told *60 Minutes* that he hired producer

Bernard McGuirk for "nigger jokes." His cohost Sid Rosenberg described tennis player Venus Williams as an "animal" and referred to Palestinians as "stinking animals," saying, "They ought to drop the bomb right there, kill 'em all right now." Imus built the latter stage of his career on Islamaphobia, braying for war and frequently calling Arabs "ragheads."

Of course Imus is not alone. The confederate confines of talk radio are drenched in degradation. There is Rush Limbaugh who calls Barack Obama and Halle Berry "Halfrican-Americans." There is Michael Savage who says the Voting Rights Act put "a chad in every crackhouse." There are Glen Beck and Michelle Malkin who agitate for the internment of Arabs and Muslims. They are the Shady Bunch—and none deserve a public platform. But the question lingers: why did Imus feel the wrath? Why did he reap the whirlwind?

One reason is that Imus was always different. He was never a Republican Party hack. Members of the media elite, like Tim Russert and Chris Matthews, and Democratic Party power brokers, like Barack Obama and John Kerry, were frequent guests on his show. They lent legitimacy and protection to Imus that has allowed him to be mainstream in a different kind of way than the Limbaughs and Savages. What this whole episode has exposed is the way that the media and the Democratic Party can play all too comfortably on this kind of playing field.

But the outrage stems from the pent-up rage people feel about the way this kind of bigotry continually goes unchallenged. Hurricane Katrina destroyed a majority Black city that continues to die from naked neglect. Women face a constant barrage of sexism in our "Girls Gone Wild" culture and if you challenge it, then you must be a humorless prig. Imus's words touched all of those buttons and unleashed a fury that for many felt more than just.

As Michael Wilbon wrote, "There's nothing rare about Imus's vile attacks. This is what he does as a matter of course.

Imus and his studio cohorts have painted black people as convicts and muggers and worst of all, apes. Not only do they find it funny, they expect everybody else will as well."

Wilbon is absolutely correct. Yet it took Rutgers Coach C. Vivian Stringer and her team to remind the media that Imus's comments weren't just racist but sexist. As she said, "I would ask you, who among you would have heard those comments and not have been personally offended? Are women 'hos'? Think about that. Would you want your daughter called that?... It's not about the Rutgers women's basketball team, it's about women.... It's not about us as black people or as nappy-headed. It's about us as people—black, white, purple, or green."

It didn't surprise anyone in the world of women's hoops that Stringer stood so tall. For more than three decades she has been building her reputation as one of the most accomplished coaches in basketball history. Stringer is the only coach in NCAA history to have led three different schools to the Final Four. One of those schools, the historically Black college Cheyney University, provided one of the most improbable Cinderella stories in NCAA history. Her lifetime record over 35 years is an unbelievable 750–251. This is also the 35th anniversary of Title IX. Title IX was supposed to level playing fields between men and women. In many respects, as discussed earlier, the results have been remarkable. But for women—especially African-American women—sports remain a place of denigration, not celebration. Swimsuit issues, cheerleaders, and beer commercial sexism define women in the testosterone-addled SportsWorld. There is an arsenal of homophobia and mockery sprayed at those who dare sweat, compete, and play hard. Every woman who has played sports and every man with a female athlete in the family felt Imus's words in a way that cut deeply.

But why did this comment, in a career of ugly statements, finally break the camel's back? I think the answer partly lies in how we are taught to understand sports. Remember that Rush

Limbaugh felt the biggest backlash of his career when he said that the media over-hyped Philadelphia Eagles football star Donovan McNabb because of their "social concern" to see a successful African-American quarterback. After thousands of angry calls and emails, Rush was bounced from ESPN. Both Imus and Rush built careers on this kind of bile but when they cross-pollinated their bigotry with sports, a new level of anger exploded. We are relentlessly sold the idea that our games are safe space from this kind of political swill. We are also told that sports are a "field of dreams," a true meritocracy where hard work always meets rewards. But when the playing field is shown to be unlevel, it stings. This sporting reality can wake people up and reveal the hidden inequities in our society that otherwise go unnoticed. When a Rutgers team defies the odds and makes the NCAA finals, and gets called "nappy-headed hos" for their trouble, it presses an all-too-raw nerve.

Imus reaped the whirlwind because Coach Stringer and the Rutgers team refused—like so many of Imus's targets—to be silent. As team captain Essence Carson said, "I know we're at a young age, but we definitely understand what is right and what should get done…. We're happy—we're glad to finally have the opportunity to stand up for what we know is right…. We can speak up for women, not just African-American women, but all women." The lesson in their refusal to be silent should not be lost.

But the bull's-eye reason Imus was canned like a tuna is because the political climate in this country in recent years has shifted. All the "red-state, blue-state" blather is so much bunk. Bush now has an approval rating of 29 percent, slightly lower than Nixon's corpse. His popularity among African Americans in one recent poll was 2 percent—which means beyond Condi Rice and her family, the cupboard is bare. (This is getting embarrassing. Even Soul Brother Number 1 Bob Dole got 12 percent of the Black vote in 1996.) But this goes beyond personalities.

On issue after issue, consciousness in the United States has shifted left, as revealed by a recent Pew Research Center poll. Two thirds of the country disapproves of Bush's handling of Iraq. Fifty-nine percent of people support a path to citizenship for undocumented workers. Seventy-three percent of people agree with the statement that the rich are getting richer and the poor, poorer. According to a Gallup poll, 75 percent of people believe it is the responsibility of government to make sure everyone has health care. This shift in consciousness comes out of people's lived experiences. Income inequality has exploded. The top 1 percent of Americans are now getting the largest share of national income since 1928. The wage gap has nearly doubled since 1980, the dawn of the conservative era.

Even Republican stenographers, like *New York Times* columnist David Brooks, wrote about the 2008 presidential race: "It's clear that this election will mark the end of conservative dominance. This election is a period, not a comma in political history."

If you don't think there has in fact been a shift, ask somebody. Ask someone with some extra time on his hands. Ask Don Imus.

Coach Stringer spoke beautifully about how to understand the response to Imus. Speaking at warp speed to MSNBC's Keith Olbermann, she said,

> We've become so desensitized that we've allowed a lot of things to pass, and we've not been happy.... Too often politicians, leaders, and religious leaders speak for us, and we sit back and don't realize the power in numbers, and when to say enough is enough.... We see [injustice] all the time. A kid that steals something with a plastic cap pistol, and spends ten years in jail, and yet you see, the white-collar workers, you know, thieves that steal millions of dollars [get off]. And I do think that if people stood up, politicians [wouldn't] wait for a poll but [would be] strong enough to make a decision and stand.... You know I happen to be the daughter of a coal miner. My father lost both his legs in a mine. He worked hard each and every day. He only stayed out of the mine six

months until he got prosthetics. I know what it is to work hard and this has been a lifelong pursuit and passion. I've coached for thirty-six years...as a person of conscience, I have seen so much that I would like to see changed, with everything. I would gladly exchange winning a national championship if we, as young ladies, would stand and allow the country to somehow be empowered and that we take back our country.

If you want to understand why Imus is out of work, read Coach Stringer's words again. The fact is that so many of us are sick and tired of being sick and tired. We are sick of the casual racism. We are tired of the smirking, drive-by sexism. We are done with people who make their living by selling the idea that some people are less human than others. We are fed up with the politics of division and hate. We are the majority in this country, but are often entirely without voice. And we can thank C. Vivian Stringer for taking action to change that.

◆ ◆ ◆ ◆

Finally, this chapter wouldn't be complete without a mention of some hands-on grassroots sports organizing: a summer program in El Paso, Texas, that calls itself Basketball in the Barrio. I have visited many basketball camps that serve kids without a lot of money and thought that Basketball in the Barrio would be more of the same. But I knew this camp was different on the first day when top-ranked boxer Juan "Hispanic Causing Panic" Lazcano addressed the campers. The lightweight contender returned to his El Paso, Texas, neighborhood to encourage a room of young children to "follow your dreams." Lazcano was sharp as a tack and surefooted as a saint on Sunday. But a simple question stunned him like a stiff right cross. "Why do you box?"

It was asked by a nine-year-old boy named Mateo and could only have come out of a place like Basketball in the Barrio. Now in its tenth year, the camp is an annual living demonstration of how sports can develop the best angels in our nature. It's also the story of how a shoestring basketball camp can be a bulwark for change.

At the cost of one dollar per person, Basketball in the Barrio opens its doors to the youth of the Segundo Barrio in El Paso. But like the root of a Texas cedar, basketball is only the foundation. The camp also exposes kids to flamenco dancing, muralists, mariachi, and even ballet. These are all aspects of what is called "border culture"—or culture of the "fronterizo." Border culture is the dynamic mix of the United States and Mexico that merges in El Paso and its neighbor city, Juarez, Mexico. In much of Texas, border culture is looked upon with racist derision, something to sneer at, to shun, and to treat as if unclean. Basketball in the Barrio teaches kids to revel in it, like the dry heat of the desert sun.

This is the guiding philosophy of the camp's director Rus Bradburd. Rus is not someone who, upon first glance, resembles a *fronterizo*. He's also a living example of why books shouldn't be judged by their covers. Rus was an assistant men's basketball coach for the University of Texas El Paso (UTEP) from 1983 to 1991, under legendary head coach Don Haskins. It was there that he came to the conclusion that Basketball in the Barrio needed to happen.

"I couldn't stand that most of the kids in El Paso couldn't afford to go the basketball camps in El Paso," says Bradburd, over the surrounding shouts and steady thumping of one hundred basketballs, as dozens of kids performed drills all around him.

All over the country, big-time college coaches, who are already overpaid, are making a fortune off of kids with these deluxe basketball camps. I wanted a camp that was not only accessible, but where we could play a role in talking about border culture and cultural traditions, where these kids could see that their culture is nothing to be embarrassed about but something they could wear as a point of pride.

The kids at the camp span the gamut from expert dribblers, somehow pounding the ball with electric speed through their spindly legs, to those who look like they might trip over the foul line. But all treat the game, and one another, with tender respect.

Amber Avila, age ten, has been attending the camp for three years. She is typical of the children here in that she loves basketball but also holds it in a perspective that would shame many adult sportswriters and armchair strategists alike. When asked what position she plays, Amber says nonchalantly, "Oh, I can play the one, two, or the three." (Basketball lingo for point guard, shooting guard, or small forward.) She says proudly that her dream is to play in the WNBA, but she likes the fact that the camp offers more, because, in her words, "not everyone's dream is to play basketball and we kids need to reach for our dreams." She also enjoys camp because "the boys aren't rude."

One of those polite boys, Chris Travieso, ten, also loves Basketball in the Barrio because, "I can learn about my history and play basketball at the same time. Also, it's a great place to make friends and learn new things."

Amber, Chris, and all the young people embrace the border culture with the same gusto they take to the court. Perhaps the most stunning sight of this year's camp was when a former dancer in the Mexican National Ballet made her presentation. Many of the children had never seen ballet in their lives and some of the coaches feared how a ballet lesson for 120 elementary-age children would go over. But the kids took to it like the parched take to ice water. When this brave, flinty ballerina asked for volunteers, much of the camp, including many of the boys, stormed the court to take instructions on how to stand on their toes and plié.

This entire experience is shaped by a unique collection of instructors who descend upon El Paso from around the country. Doug Harris, a documentary filmmaker and former NBA draftee who travels to the camp from the Bay Area, calls his annual trip to El Paso "a pilgrimage." The word fits because the adults arrive with a sacred, shared commitment to the idea that sports can be a force for social change.

Another coach, Debbie Weinreis, makes her journey from St. Paul, Minnesota. After playing college ball in nearby New Mexico, Weinreis was a pro for fifteen years in Europe. She says that she returns because, "In many camps I've been a part of, there is just too much pressure on the bottom line. Most of these kids will not go pro, but they do have to go on in life. We want them to see that there are options." She also likes teaching in an environment where boys and girls aren't separated but work together. "This camp does a great job of making it a place where girls, who from ages six to ten are more physically advanced anyway, can star."

Many of the coaches work with an organization called Athletes United for Peace. This movement spirit shapes the camp as a bulwark for change. El Paso is a military town that will see an influx of 15,000 troops in the next year. Basketball in the Barrio, in the face of the billion-dollar weaponry the kids witness every day, tries to offer another perspective.

As Bradburd says, "It's a camp that tries to teach peace and tolerance. This is not a flag-waving camp. The kids get enough of that on TV and in school. It's fine that this camp can be one place that doesn't push patriotism down their throats.... [Besides,] how are we supposed to teach kids not to hit each other, to not be bullies, when it's our foreign policy?"

And in El Paso, foreign policy colludes with domestic like few other places in the country. The border has become militarized with hysteria over "illegal" immigration, as well as fears that Al Qaeda will attack from the south. The specter of a "Juan bin Laden" has intensified an atmosphere of mistrust and racism.

A Coors Light billboard in El Paso says it all, with the slogan "Always Cool, Aquí or There." In other words, get it through your heads: you are either "Here" or "There"—but Coors can cross the border even if you cannot.

The beauty of border culture is something unimaginable to the corporations that have stripped El Paso of jobs and made Juarez the home base for their maquiladoras. This makes those around Basketball in the Barrio all the more determined to help people remember and carry on the tradition of the fronterizo. Coach Steve Yellen, a former UTEP player and member of Athletes United for Peace, says, "We want these kids to have pride in their community, pride in their culture, and pride in themselves."

This consistent call for "pride" is not just a well-worn homily, but something all the instructors recognize as a necessary component for survival in El Paso. This is a city, in the words of Javier Diaz, that is "excluded, disconnected, and disrespected" throughout Texas. Diaz, a seventy-five-year-old retired guidance counselor in El Paso public schools, speaks while watching the kids do a dribbling drill called "the impossible catch." "We are an island in the state," he says.

> El Paso is a proud blue-collar town, but we are promoted as being little more than low wages, cheap labor, and not worth giving a damn about. We have a political elite in Texas that wants to just strangle common people like us that live in Segundo Barrio. That's why Basketball in the Barrio is so important. It teaches not just sports but self-respect. It can keep alive border culture, which to me means taking the best of Anglo and Mexican culture and combining them to educate our young about art, beauty, and tolerance. To be a "fronterizo" is to be a whole person.

It's because the camp is forging whole people that young Mateo asked Juan Lazcano that simple question: "Why do you box?" It's a question that defines the worldview of Basketball in the Barrio: Why box when you can learn, when you can play, when you can struggle, and when you can dance?

Marching In:
Tearing Down the Terrordome

New Orleans still suffers in silence. These days, it feels like a city being strangled in slow motion, a city whose current condition makes a lie of every political platitude preached over the past year. Much of the city remains shuttered: hospitals, schools, restaurants; much of the city except for—you guessed it—the Superdome. This came at a price of 185 million bucks, $94 million of which came from FEMA. Never mind that the Dome's adjoining mall and hotel are, as of this writing, still gutted or that the city hasn't seen that kind of money spent on the low-income housing, health care, or any of the cleanup so dearly needed. Never mind, most shamefully, that even the damn levees have yet to be fixed. We are being sold the idea that the road back for the Big Easy begins in the Dome. This was the theme last September when the Dome was reopened for the Saints' first home game in over a year. As one ESPN talking head solemnly told us, "The most daunting task is to scrub away memories of the Superdome as a cesspool of human misery."

Now we are asked to believe the memories are being "scrubbed away." But the reality of refugee apartheid is hardly a memory. The game was held hostage to the awkward fact that the folks starring in ESPN's video montages of last year's "cesspool" were almost entirely black and the football fans in the stands were overwhelmingly white.

But recognizing this would contradict the infomercial for the new Big Easy that was designed to appeal to the typical family, which finds gumbo too spicy and thinks soul is something consumed with tartar sauce. This message found its way into every aspect of ESPN's coverage. In the city that gave us the Marsalis family, the Neville brothers, and Dr. John, the pregame entertainment was an incoherent duet featuring those icons of corporate rock, Green Day and U2, complete with the Irish-born ego formally known as Bono shouting, "I am an American!" The two artists on hand who best represented New Orleans's authentic musical tradition, Irma Thomas and Allen Toussaint, were left to perform the national anthem, a melody so ponderous it could exorcise the soul from Aretha Franklin.

The message behind the return of the Saints was tied together by the Godfather of No-Soul himself, former president George H. W. Bush, who declared that "the pessimists who said New Orleans wouldn't come back are wrong, and the optimists who dug in are doing great!"

Bush the Elder was then asked what he believed to be the great enduring lesson of the Katrina catastrophe. Anyone who hoped to hear "Don't hire a feckless fraternity buddy to run FEMA" was left disappointed. Instead we got: "The great lesson is the American spirit! And never give up on it! It's back and it's coming back more!"

The selling of McOrleans continued, despite the fact that one announcer called the area outside the tourist zone "a graveyard of a community that no longer exists."

But even in the most devastated parts of the city, that graveyard stubbornly throbs with life. As Josh Peter, writing from the Lower Ninth Ward for Yahoo! Sports reported, "A group of 30 people gathered to watch the game next to a FEMA trailer. There were residents struggling to rebuild their homes and volunteers there to help them, sharing red beans and rice. It was a congregation cheering as if it were inside the Superdome instead of inside a garage.... 'We're still here,' Deborah Massey snapped at the TV announcer. 'They can't get rid of us.'"

There was reason for anger that Monday night. There was also reason to cheer. The mood in the stadium was electric and emotional, cathartic and wistful. I could feel Saints fans carrying their team to a 23–3 victory over the favored opponents, the Atlanta Falcons. I laughed and cheered upon seeing a big banner that read "Joe Horn for President"—both a caustic protest and a show of respect for the Saints wide receiver, who proudly says he wants to be "a voice for those who aren't heard." I felt a lump in my throat upon seeing the "Save Our Saints" sign, a reminder that, for all the money spent on the Dome, Saints owner Tom Benson still threatens to move the team to more affluent shores. I shared the crowd's almost giddy love of quicksilver rookie Reggie Bush. And yes, it was nice to actually see a Bush raise up the spirit of New Orleans for once.

It's easy to understand why ESPN announcer and Gulf Coast native Robin Roberts said, "Tonight is about baby steps forward. People are so hungry for a little slice of their normal life." It's also easy to understand why a city that depends so crucially on the tourist dollar would crave positive coverage. But the big answer for the Big Easy does not lie in becoming a gumbo-flavored Disneyland where service-economy dollars are directed to minimum-wage jobs. The city needs a massive federal works project that puts the people of New Orleans to work rebuilding their own city.

New Orleans is crying out for grand acts of daring and leadership. Nothing grand is coming from Washington, D.C., and it is cruel to promote the belief that the drowned city will experience rebirth in a football stadium. The answer begins not with

Bono performs at the Superdome, 2006 (AP/Andrew Cohoon)

"scrubbing away memories of the Superdome" but in amplifying those memories so they fuel a movement to bring back not only the city but every last resident who wants to return. Support for this view came from folks all over the country in the wake of that game. *USA Today* published many of their letters. Here is a sampling:

Ravi Mangla of Fairport, New York:

Using the New Orleans Saints' home game at the Superdome as a metaphor for a city returning to normalcy after a horrific disaster is such arrant dreck. I found myself frustrated Monday, hearing reports describing how "inspiring" and "uplifting" it was for New Orleans' citizens to finally get their team back. What would be more inspiring and uplifting, in my opinion, would be seeing all the people of New Orleans finally getting their homes back.

Mark Washington of Omaha, Nebraska:

As an African-American, I was disturbed about things I saw on TV: Thousands of mostly white faces in the stands being sere-naded by white rock musicians. It wasn't exactly a vision of a re-turning New Orleans…. I highly doubt that the vast majority of former New Orleans residents, who happen to be African-Ameri-cans, would have selected U2 or Green Day as their preferred en-tertainment.

Jack Wood of Fort Wayne, Indiana:

Federal funding contributed hugely to the $185 million it cost to renovate the Superdome in New Orleans? Where are our priori-ties? With garbage still clogging the streets and people still home-less, what could that money have done to correct those conditions? This appears to be just another example of badly placed priorities by Americans. We should all be ashamed to put a football game ahead of human suffering.

Mark Van Patten of Bowling Green, Kentucky:

The restored Superdome is an ugly concrete monument plopped down between interstate highway loops. It reflects the difference in the classes in New Orleans…. When it was convenient, the poor were inhumanely herded there to await rescue. Now, the Su-perdome is ready for business, but the poor will not be welcome because they don't have the money for admission or they have been relocated to another city.

Ira Lacher of Des Moines, Iowa:

How many of the thousands of displaced New Orleanians could have rebuilt their homes with the $185 million that was squan-dered on restoring the Superdome for the use of overpaid profes-sional athletes?

This cavalcade of good sense was met with derision from much of the media. Chris Rose, columnist for the *New Orleans Times-Picayune,* catalogued and slammed these folks for expressing their concerns, writing, "Why are people from other places spending so much effort to tell us that, as a community, we are wrong, misguided, amoral and racist? Why are they making things up?" He also praised ESPN for its "sensitive handling of the tricky 'New Orleans is back/New Orleans is definitely not back' message."

But worst of all, Rose accepts the basic framework expressed in the coverage that this "trickle down" model of "rebuild the Superdome and it will lift every boat" is anything but a sham. It didn't work when the Dome was built thirty years ago and, in the context of a damaged city, fostering these illusions is criminal. But people aren't buying it, which is why the letters are so important. It shows that a sector of our Sports-World has opened its eyes and slammed its door on what the Chris Roses of this world are selling. If sports are going to be reclaimed from the corporate pirates ravaging our cities, it ain't the Saints who need to go marching in. It's the rest of us.

A politics of athletic protest that both looks to its proud history and amplifies the voices of our twenty-first-century athletic rebels will provide us the tools to tear down the Terrordome—tear down the Terrordome and move toward a more just and sane future, both for the SportsWorld and that pesky RealWorld it inhabits.

About Haymarket Books

Haymarket Books is a nonprofit, progressive book distributor and publisher, a project of the Center for Economic Research and Social Change. We believe that activists need to take ideas, history, and politics into the many struggles for social justice today. Learning the lessons of past victories, as well as defeats, can arm a new generation of fighters for a better world. As Karl Marx said, "The philosophers have merely interpreted the world; the point however is to change it."

We take inspiration and courage from our namesakes, the Haymarket Martyrs, who gave their lives fighting for a better world. Their 1886 struggle for the eight-hour day, which gave us May Day, the international workers' holiday, reminds workers around the world that ordinary people can organize and struggle for their own liberation. These struggles continue today across the globe—struggles against oppression, exploitation, hunger, and poverty.

It was August Spies, one of the Martyrs who was targeted for being an immigrant and an anarchist, who predicted the battles being fought to this day. "If you think that by hanging us you can stamp out the labor movement," Spies told the judge, "then hang us. Here you will tread upon a spark, but here, and there, and behind you, and in front of you, and everywhere, the flames will blaze up. It is a subterranean fire. You cannot put it out. The ground is on fire upon which you stand."

We could not suceed in our publishing efforts without the generous financial support of our readers. Many people contribute to our project through the Haymarket Sustainers program, where donors receive free books in return for their monetary support. If you would like to be a part of this program, please contact us at info@haymarketbooks.org.

Order these titles and more online at www.haymarketbooks.org or call 773-583-7884.

Also from Haymarket Books

What's My Name, Fool? Sports and Resistance in the United States

Dave Zirin • *What's My Name, Fool?* offers a no-holds-barred look at the business of sports today. In humorous and accessible language, Zirin shows how sports express the worst, as well as the most creative and exciting, features of American society. ISBN 1-931859-20-5.

The Communist Manifesto: A Road Map to History's Most Important Political Document

Karl Marx and Frederick Engels, edited by Phil Gasper • This beautifully organized and presented edition of The Communist Manifesto is fully annotated, with clear historical references and explication, additional related texts, and a glossary that will bring the text to life. ISBN 1931859256.

No One Is Illegal: Fighting Racism and State Violence on the U.S./Mexico Border

Justin Akers Chacón and Mike Davis • Countering the chorus of anti-immigrant voices, Davis and Akers Chacón expose the racism of anti-immigration vigilantes and put a human face on the immigrants who risk their lives to cross the border to work in the United States. ISBN 1931859353.

Subterranean Fire: A History of Working-Class Radicalism in the United States

Sharon Smith • Workers in the United States have a rich tradition of fighting back and achieving gains previously thought unthinkable, but that history remains largely hidden. In *Subterranean Fire*, Sharon Smith brings that history to light and reveals its lessons for today. ISBN 193185923X.

Soldiers in Revolt: GI Resistance During the Vietnam War

David Cortright with a new introduction by Howard Zinn • "An exhaustive account of rebellion in all the armed forces, not only in Vietnam but throughout the world."—*New York Review of Books*. ISBN 1931859272.

Also from Haymarket Books

Friendlly Fire: The Remarkable Story of a Journalist Kidnapped in Iraq, Rescued by an Italian Secret Service Agent, and Shot by U.S. Forces

Giuliana Sgrena • The Italian journalist, whose personal story was featured on *60 Minutes*, describes the real story of her capture and shooting in 2004. Sgrena also gives invaluable insight into the reality of life in occupied Iraq, exposing U.S. war crimes there. ISBN 1-931859-396.

The Meaning of Marxism

Paul D'Amato • A lively and accessible introduction to the ideas of Karl Marx, with historical and contemporary examples. ISBN 978-1931859-295.

A Little Piece of Ground

Elizabeth Laird • A story of occupied Palestine through the eyes of a twelve-year-old boy. ISBN 978-1-931859-38-7.

The Dispossessed: Chronicles of the *Desterrados* of Colombia

Alfredo Molano • Here in their own words are the stories of the Desterrados, or "dispossessed"—the thousands of Colombians displaced by years of war and state-backed terrorism, funded in part through U.S. aid to the Colombian government. With a preface by Aviva Chomsky.

Vive la Revolution: A Stand-up History of the French Revolution

Mark Steel • An actually interesting, unapologetically sympathetic, and extremely funny history of the French Revolution. ISBN 193185937X.

Poetry and Protest: A Dennis Brutus Reader

Aisha Karim and Lee Sustar, editors • A vital original collection of the interviews, poetry, and essays of the much-loved anti-apartheid leader. ISBN 1-931859-22-1.

In Praise of Barbarians: Essays Against Empire

Mike Davis • No writer in the United States today brings together analysis and history as comprehensively and elegantly as Mike Davis. In these contemporary, interventionist essays, Davis goes beyond critique to offer real solutions and concrete possibilities for change. ISBN 1-931859-42-6.

Sin Patrón: Stories from Argentina's Worker-Run Factories

The lavaca collective, with a foreword by Naomi Klein and Avi Lewis • The inside story of Argentina's remarkable movement to create factories run democratically by workers themselves. ISBN 978-1931859-431.

Black Liberation and Socialism

Ahmed Shawki • A sharp and insightful analysis of movements against racism, with essential lessons for today's struggles. ISBN 1-931859-26-4.

Independent Politics: The Green Party Strategy Debate

Howie Hawkins, editor • Leading indpendent and Green Party activists ask: Can we break the two-party stranglehold on U.S. politics? ISBN 1-931859-30-2.

The German Revolution 1917–1923

Pierre Broué • A magisterial, definitive account of the upheavals in Germany in the wake of the Russian revolution. ISBN 1-931859-32-9.

Literature and Revolution

Leon Trotsky, William Keach, editor • A new, annotated edition of Leon Trotsky's classic study of the relationship of politics and art. ISBN 1-931859-16-7.

The Bending Cross: A Biography of Eugene Victor Debs

Ray Ginger, with a new introduction by Mike Davis • The classic biography of Eugene Debs, one of the most important thinkers and activists in the United States.

About Dave Zirin

Dave Zirin is a columnist for *SLAM* magazine and a regular contributor to the *Nation*. His first book *What's My Name, Fool? Sports and Resistance in the United States* (Haymarket Books) has entered its second printing. He is also the author of *The Muhammad Ali Handbook* (MQ Publications) and the forthcoming *People's History of Sports* (New Press). His writing has appeared in the *Los Angeles Times*, *New York Newsday*, CBSNews.com, *College Sporting News*, the *International Socialist Review*, Commondreams.com, and the *Source* among other publications. He is a frequent guest on numerous radio and televsion programs, inclcuding ESPN's *Outside the Lines* and NPR's *Talk of the Nation*. His website is www.edgeofsports.com. He lives in the Washington, D.C., area.

About Chuck D

As leader and cofounder of legendary rap group Public Enemy, Chuck D redefined rap music and hip-hop culture. Called "one of the most politically and socially conscious artists of any generation" by Spike Lee, he is the author of *Fight the Power* and hosts a weekly radio show on Air America, *On the Real*, with Gia'na Garel. He is a regular commentator on issues of music, culture, and current events for many media outlets.